UNLEARNING CHRISTIAN NATIONALISM

HOW I ESCAPED (AND YOU CAN TOO)

TODD EUBANKS

Cover Design by
OLAYEMI BOLAJI

CABOODLE
Media Ltd. Co.

COPYRIGHT

CONTENTS

1

THE UNRAVELING OF FAITH
AND THE POWER OF WORDS

Goddammit! There, I said it. I wrote it. And, just wait, I'll say it again. Growing up in rural Oklahoma, in the heart of the Bible Belt, that word was more than just profanity. It was the verbal equivalent of a one-way ticket to hell. Goddammit was the ultimate transgression, a sin so grievous it made lying, stealing, and coveting your neighbor's ass, neighbor's wife, or even your neighbor's wife's ass look like minor infractions.

I remember the first time I said it. I was eight years old, sitting cross-legged on the floor of our living room, fingers frantically mashing buttons as I guided Mario through yet another perilous level. My Nintendo Entertainment System staring at me at eye level, its sleek gray body a portal to worlds of adventure. And then it happened, I died. Not just a temporary setback, mind you. In those days, death in a video game meant real consequences. No save points, no continues. Just a red "GAME OVER."

Frustration boiled over, and before I could stop myself, it slipped out: "Goddammit!"

The moment felt like a scene from "A Christmas Story,"

when Ralphie lets loose "the queen-mother of dirty words" after dropping the lug nuts. Except in my world, "goddammit" was the king-father of all dirty words. The nuclear option of profanity.

I froze, suddenly aware of my mother's presence in the room. Her voice cut through the air: "Where did you hear that word?" In that moment, I would've gladly taken my chances with the linoleum floor splitting open beneath me, straight into the gaping mouth of hell, rather than face the wrath of my mother. Satan himself couldn't have summoned a terror as potent as the look on her face.

Quick as a fox, I blurted out, "I heard it on TV." The lie came easily, even as I knew the truth, I'd heard it from my brother. But there was no need to drag him into it. Besides, TV was a convenient scapegoat in our household, already blamed for everything from declining moral values to my fear of the dark.

The reason "goddammit" was considered such a grave offense in our household, and indeed in much of the Christian community I grew up in, was rooted in the Ten Commandments. Specifically, the third one: "You shall not take the name of the Lord your God in vain." This commandment was drilled into us from an early age, right alongside "don't run with scissors" and "clean your plate because children are starving in Africa."

But as I stood there, waiting for the consequences of my outburst, something unexpected happened. The world didn't end. God didn't strike me down with a bolt of lightning. And that's when the questions started creeping in.

The incident left me puzzled. I knew "goddammit" was considered a bad word, but was it really that serious? It seemed odd that a simple phrase could carry so much weight in the grand scheme of things. In my young mind, warped by fire-and-brimstone sermons and endless warnings about the perils of taking the Lord's name in vain, I genuinely wondered: Could someone go to heaven if they said goddammit? Was uttering that word really enough to negate a lifetime of faith?

Little did I know then that this moment would become a thread I'd keep pulling at, gradually unraveling a tapestry of assumed truths about faith, language, and power. It wasn't just about the word itself, it was about how we use language to control, to shame, or to create hierarchies of sin that often miss the point entirely.

It's amazing how a simple word could carry so much weight, instill so much fear, and cause so much confusion. But as I would later learn, this fixation on language, even down to the proper capitalization of "God" in writing, was hardly the tip of the iceberg when it came to misunderstanding what it truly means to honor or dishonor the divine.

The questions multiplied like rabbits. If an all-powerful, all-knowing God was so offended by this particular word, why? Would the creator of galaxies and superclusters really be wounded by what essentially amounts to a verbal stubbed toe?

These weren't just theological puzzles to solve. They were the first cracks in a foundation of certainty that would eventually crumble, giving way to something deeper, truer, and far more challenging than the simple rules-based religion of my childhood.

This journey of questioning, of unraveling long-held beliefs, is really a process of unlearning. Unlearning the easy answers, the comfortable certainties, the unexamined assumptions that have shaped our faith for far too long.

It didn't add up. And it made me wonder: what else didn't add up? This question haunted me, lurking in the shadows of every sermon, every Sunday school lesson, and every declaration of faith. It was like a loose thread on a sweater, the more I pulled, the more it unraveled. And with each tug, the fabric of my carefully constructed beliefs began to fray at the edges.

I found myself standing at the entrance of a rabbit hole, peering into its depths with a mixture of fear and curiosity. What other unquestioned beliefs were hiding down there? What other "truths" might crumble under scrutiny? For years, I just put a rock over it. But eventually, the rabbits started slipping out.

Take, for instance, the popular interpretation of Jesus' words about the eye of the needle. He said, "...For it is easier for a camel to go through the eye of a needle, than for a rich person to enter the kingdom of God!" (Luke 18:25). How many times have you heard pastors explain that Jesus was referring to a small gate in Jerusalem that a camel had to kneel to pass through? It's a comforting thought, isn't it? Makes the whole 'rich man entering the kingdom of heaven' thing seem a bit more possible.

There's just one problem: it's not true. There's no historical evidence for such a gate. And Jesus wasn't offering a loophole. He was making a provocative statement about the impossibility of entering the Kingdom of Heaven through our own efforts. "The things that are impossible with people are possible with God" He said.

By softening Jesus' words, the radical edge of His message is dulled. We've turned a message of God's infinite power into a feel-good story about our own power. And in doing so, we've used the divine name to comfort ourselves rather than acknowledge the awe-inspiring power of God and the boundless, transformative grace He offers. We've minimized the infinite to fit our finite understanding, robbing ourselves and others of the chance to experience the true magnitude of God's love.

But a few bad sermons isn't a big deal, right? As I peeled

back the layers of my assumptions and unquestioned beliefs, I found that the rabbit hole went much, much deeper.

The questions multiply, breeding like rabbits. Each answer only spawned more questions, and soon I found myself suffocating in a sea of uncertainty while the shoreline of my childhood beliefs receded into the distance, just like my hairline.

But here's the thing about doubt - it's not comfortable, but it's not necessarily bad either. It's the pebble in your shoe that forces you to stop and reassess your journey. It's the splinter that makes you examine your own skin more closely.

So here I am, at forty years old, beginning to unlearn the lessons of "goddammit" from my youth. Not as an act of rebellion, but as a starting point. A jumping-off point into the deeper waters of faith, love, and what those truly mean. This realization sets the stage for a journey I never expected to take - a journey of questioning long-held beliefs, challenging ingrained assumptions, and rediscovering the essence of faith beyond cultural conditioning.

You know what keeps me up at night? It's not the fear of slipping a goddammit when I stub my toe. No, what really haunts me is this gnawing realization that we've somehow managed to create a Christianity without Christ at its center.

For generations, we've had a roadmap. A neat, tidy package of beliefs and behaviors that defined what it meant to be a "good Christian." Go to church on Sundays. Vote Republican. Don't say "goddammit." Simple, right?

Wrong.

That roadmap led us straight into a spiritual dead end. A place where our faith became more about cultural identity than Christ-like transformation. Where our politics trumped our principles. Where our fear drowned out our love.

I remember sitting in church, my teenage frame awkwardly folded into a chair that seemed designed for discomfort, watching another PowerPoint presentation fade onto the screen. Like every Sunday, I had my bulletin ready to dutifully write down the points, each one conveniently starting with the right letter.

"Today we'll learn about F.A.I.T.H," the pastor announced, turning to the screen. "F is for Following God's law. A is for Attending church. I is for Inviting others. T is for Tithing faithfully. And H is for Helping!" But for the first time, I found myself not swept along. The thought came uninvited: Are we really going to reduce faith to an acronym? And why do all these points serve to maintain the institution rather than to teach us about faith?

It was like being colorblind all your life and suddenly seeing a rainbow. Overwhelming, beautiful, but also unsettling. Because here's the thing about certainty - it's soft. It's safe. It's a warm Snuggie with sleeves on a cold night, and I had been wrapped in that so-called blanket for my entire life.

But doubt? Doubt is the alarm clock that blares the same song every morning, like you're stuck in some twisted version of Groundhog Day or forced to listen to Baby Shark one more time on a roadtrip. It's the never-ending loop that makes you question if you'll ever move forward, no matter how many times you try to change the tune.

And this is where the wheels really start to fall off because once you start to doubt, you can't stop. It spreads like a virus, infecting every aspect of your beliefs. If "goddammit" wasn't the unforgivable sin I'd been taught it was, what else had I been wrong about?

The questions came fast and furious:

- If we're saved by grace, why are we so obsessed with following and enforcing rules?
- If Jesus hung out with sinners and outcasts, why are we so focused on building walls and defining who's in and who's out?
- If we're called to be peacemakers, why do we seem so eager to wage culture wars?
- If our citizenship is in heaven, why are we so fixated on politics?

And here's where it gets interesting and where my journey really began. Because as uncomfortable as these questions were, as much as they shook the foundations of everything I thought I knew, they also felt... right. Like I was finally scratching an itch that had been just out of reach my entire life.

And it reminds me of Pastor Dr. Phil Sallee, who led New Beginnings Church in Bixby, Oklahoma for about 20 years. I had the privilege of sitting under his teaching for eight years, and his approach to tackling difficult questions has stuck with me ever since.

Dr. Phil had a unique way of navigating uncertainty, though he never explicitly taught it or even seemed to realize he was doing it. It was something I noticed over time, a pattern in his approach that struck me as profoundly effective.

When faced with a complex issue or a seemingly unsolvable problem, he'd often start by identifying what we *don't* want. It's a simple yet profound approach. Instead of immediately trying to find the *right* answer, he would begin by eliminating the *wrong* ones. I understood why he did this, even if he never articulated it himself: sometimes, it's easier to recognize what doesn't align with God's will than to immediately grasp what does.

He'd say, "In the end, Jesus is Lord. Everything else is small stuff. Don't sweat the small stuff." Then he'd guide us through a process of elimination, helping us identify the outcomes or solutions that clearly didn't align with Christ's teachings or character.

This method isn't about finding quick fixes or easy answers. It's about creating a framework for thinking, a starting point for our journey. By identifying what we *don't* want, what *doesn't* align with the heart of God, we can begin to chart a course towards what we *do* want, even if we can't see the final destination.

So, in the spirit of Dr. Phil's approach, let's start by identifying what we believe doesn't align with God's will and biblical teachings:

- We don't believe God intends His name to be used as a weapon of control rather than a source of love
- We don't believe Christ's kingdom advances through political power rather than sacrificial service
- We don't believe God's truth requires specific political affiliations
- We don't believe Jesus calls us to seek cultural dominance rather than humble service
- We don't believe worship should prioritize performance over transformation
- We don't believe Christianity should be unrecognizable compared to Christ's teachings
- We don't believe scripture was given as a weapon
- We don't believe institutional preservation should override prophetic truth
- We don't believe God calls us to confuse patriotism with godliness

- We don't believe churches should be known more
  for opposition than love
- We don't believe faith requires rejecting observable
  truth or denying reality
- We don't believe God values our certainty over our
  honest seeking
- We don't believe Christ wants us to exclude the
  very people He would embrace

By identifying what we believe *doesn't* align with God's heart, we begin to see the outlines of what *does*. We start to glimpse a faith that's more authentic, more Christ-like, and more aligned with the Kingdom of God as revealed in scripture.

The words we choose to sanctify and the ones we choose to condemn tell us more about ourselves than about God. Our language becomes a mirror, reflecting back our fears, our prejudices, and our desperate need for control. In the end, maybe it's not about the words at all.

I've sat back and watched as the faith I'd been raised in became increasingly entangled with politics, with cultural identity, and with a particular vision of American life that seemed far removed from the revolutionary teachings of a first-century Jewish carpenter. The cross and the flag became so intertwined that it was hard to tell where one ended and the other began.

And I couldn't help but wonder:

Is this what Jesus had in mind?

Memory has a way of preserving certain moments with perfect clarity while blurring others into obscurity. One such memory takes me back to a very late night, driving a late 70's

GMC motorhome down a dark highway from Northern Texas. The beast of a machine, twenty-three feet of brown automotive nostalgia complete with a curved windshield and orange velvet interior, represented more than just a vehicle - it was a tangible link to my past, to my grandfather who had passed away just a year before.

It was just like the one he had owned. Let me tell you, this wasn't just any RV - it was a piece of my childhood, a symbol of freedom and adventure built with metal and memories. My grandfather, who was like a father to me, had passed away in 2018, and when I found one of these rare beauties for sale, I couldn't resist. Even the barn dust from twenty years of storage and its tired engine begging for attention couldn't dim my enthusiasm.

So, it's nighttime, and I'm piloting this hideous brown time machine down the interstate. The headlights cut through the darkness, illuminating a path forward while my mind wanders backward through time. I pull up to a tollbooth, and this young guy working there says, "Dude, that's so groovy!" Suddenly, I'm the coolest guy on the planet, king of the road in my vintage chariot.

I felt invincible, noticing people at gas stations turning their heads, pointing, and staring. "Yeah," I thought, "feast your eyes on this vintage beauty!" Pride swelled in my chest with each passing mile and each admiring glance.

Then, as I'm cruising down the highway, a truck pulls up next to me and starts honking. The driver's yelling something out of his window. I can't quite make it out, but I'm sure he's complimenting my sweet ride. I honk back - toot toot! - and give him a thumbs up. "Yeah!"

But he keeps yelling. Curious, I roll down my window to hear what he has to say.

 Your sewer hose is dragging!!!

Yep, you heard that right. All those stares? The pointing? The honking? It wasn't because I was cruising in a cool vintage RV. It was because I was leaving a trail of shit behind me, literally pulling a Dave Matthews Band down the interstate (and if you don't know that reference, you definitely should Google it).

I was so caught up in my pride, so sure of how awesome I looked, that I completely missed the fact that I was dragging poop behind me like some sort of mobile septic disaster. Pride has a way of blinding us to our own mess, doesn't it?

And you know what? I think that's a pretty good picture of where we find ourselves with our faith sometimes. We're so proud of our beliefs, so sure we've got it all figured out, that we completely miss the mess we're dragging behind us. We're turning heads alright, but not for the reasons we think.

Maybe it's time we stop honking our own horns and start listening to the voices trying to tell us we're leaving a radioactive trail in our wake. Because sometimes, the most important messages come from unexpected sources, and they're rarely the ones we want to hear.

Don't get me wrong - much of what I was taught came from a place of love, or at least what my community understood love to be. But sometimes love gets twisted, wrapped so tightly in rules and restrictions that it starts to look more like fear. Sometimes what we think is protecting people is actually suffocating them.

The questions that started with a childish "goddammit" have led me down paths I never expected to travel. They've forced me to confront the comfortable lies we tell ourselves, the ways we use religion as a shield against the messy, beautiful complexity of real faith. Each questioned assumption has been like pulling a thread from an intricately woven tapestry - necessary, terrifying, and irreversible.

I've watched as the certainties of my childhood have dissolved like morning fog in the heat of lived experience. The neat categories of sin and salvation, the clear boundaries between sacred and secular, the confident declarations of God's will - all of them have blurred and shifted, revealing something both more frightening and more beautiful than I could have imagined.

These days, I find myself inhabiting the spaces between certainties. The gray areas that once terrified me have become holy ground, where doubt and faith dance together in an endless waltz. The questions that once felt like threats to my faith have become doorways to a deeper, more authentic relationship with God.

We've created a version of Christianity that's more focused on controlling behavior than transforming hearts. We've turned the radical, boundary-breaking message of Christ into a checklist of dos and don'ts. We've replaced the wild, untamed Spirit of God with a domesticated deity who conveniently agrees with all our cultural preferences.

And worst of all? We've done it all in God's name.

This book isn't just about my journey of unlearning. It's about all of us, about the ways we've allowed our faith to be co-opted by cultural Christianity, about how we've traded the revolutionary love of Christ for a comfortable religion that demands nothing and changes nothing. It's about the hard, necessary work of stripping away the accumulated layers of cultural conditioning to rediscover what it truly means to follow Jesus.

The path ahead isn't easy. Unlearning rarely is. It requires us to question everything we thought we knew, to hold our beliefs with open hands rather than clenched fists. It demands a willingness to sit with uncertainty, to embrace the possibility that we might be wrong about things we've failed to examine more closely.

But here's the truth that keeps pulling me forward: The faith that emerges from this process of unlearning - is far more authentic than the one I started with. It's a faith that can handle doubt, that welcomes questions, and finds God in the mysteries as much as in the answers.

So let's begin this journey together. Let's dare to ask the hard questions, to challenge our assumptions, to unlearn the comfortable certainties that have kept us from experiencing the full, wild, transformative power of God's love. Because maybe, just maybe, what we need isn't more rules about what words we can't say, but a deeper understanding of what it truly means to honor the divine.

The journey of unlearning awaits.

2

GOD AND COUNTRY

THE EMERGENCE OF CHRISTIAN NATIONALISM

W hen did the cross become a weapon? I remember one of the first moments it occurred to me. There it was, on the screen: a sea of flags at another rally. American flags flew proud and familiar, symbols of patriotism and freedom. But mixed in, just as prominent, were Confederate flags, their stars and bars a stark reminder of a past we supposedly left behind. And beside those? Nazi flags, symbols of genocidal fascism flying proudly on American soil in an American crowd.

But wait, there, tucked in the middle like a dirty little secret, were Christian flags, goddammit! My stomach churned. My mind reeled. What the hell was going on? How could symbols of patriotism, racism, genocidal fascism, and the Christian faith all fly together like alliances in war?

Welcome, folks, to the world of Christian Nationalism. Where God and country blend into a toxic cocktail that'd make Jesus himself reach for the Pepto-Bismol. That was the scene of the "Unite the Right" rally in Charlottesville, Virginia, on August 11, 2017.

That image of flags haunted me, a visual echo of something deeper taking root in American Christianity. The cross, once a symbol of sacrificial love, now flying alongside emblems of oppression and genocide. It was like witnessing a faith I'd known since childhood transform into something unrecognizable, something that made my soul recoil.

Those flags in Charlottesville weren't an anomaly - they were revealing something ancient and insidious about how faith becomes a weapon. Each symbol carried its own dark history: the Nazi flag, borrowed from a regime that twisted Christianity to justify genocide; the Confederate flag, wielded by those who used scripture to defend slavery; and there, between them, the Christian flag itself, no longer a symbol of grace but a battle standard for cultural warfare. The sight of them together felt like watching centuries of history collapse into a single moment, a visual echo of how faith and power have danced their deadly waltz through time.

In the pages that follow, we'll explore this merging of cross and crown, this transformation of sacred symbols into instruments of control. From the blood-soaked fields of Civil War America to the church-blessed horrors of Nazi Germany, we'll trace how Christianity has been coopted by movements that turned love into law and grace into governance. More importantly, we'll examine how these same patterns persist today, hiding in plain sight in our own churches, our own communities, and in our own hearts.

So buckle up, buttercup. We're about to embark on a journey that might just change how you see your faith, your country, and yourself. Are you ready to have your understanding of God and country turned upside down? Because once you see it, you can't unsee it.

Let's break it down: At its core, Christian Nationalism is

the belief that America is, or should be, a Christian nation. But here's the thing: Most people who hold these beliefs don't call themselves Christian nationalists. The term feels derogatory to them, a label slapped on by critics. As recent as 2021, Franklin Graham said in an interview with The New Yorker's Eliza Griswold, "Christian Nationalism doesn't exist... [It's] just another name to throw at Christians... The left is very good at calling people names." [2.1]

But whether they embrace the label or not, the ideology is real, and it's reshaping American Christianity in ways that would make the apostles roll over in their graves. It's the idea that American identity and Christian identity are inextricably linked. It's the conviction that our laws, our culture, and our very way of life should be dictated by a particular interpretation of Christian values. It's the belief that America has a special covenant with God, that we're somehow more blessed, more favored than other nations. It's the idea that political power is a means of advancing God's kingdom on earth. But here's where it gets tricky: Christian Nationalism isn't just about loving God and country. It's about fusing them together in a way that distorts both.

Now, you might be thinking, "But that's not me! I don't believe those things!" And maybe you don't, at least not consciously. Or maybe you do, and you have a justification for them. But Christian Nationalism is often so ingrained in our culture, so woven into the fabric of American Christianity, that we don't even recognize it. It's like that old analogy about fish not knowing they're in water. We're swimming in an ocean of Christian Nationalist ideas, and we don't even realize we're wet.

Let me show you what I mean. Here are some common statements that might indicate Christian Nationalist leanings:

- "America was founded as a Christian nation."
- "We need to take our country back."
- "True patriots support Christian values."
- "America was founded on Christian principles"
- "Our laws should be based on biblical law."
- "Christians are under attack in this country."

And these ideas show up everywhere in our daily lives. The Pledge of Allegiance rings out in Sunday School classrooms, VBS, and church events. "God Bless America" peppers our prayers and speeches. Our churches host special services for Memorial Day and Veterans Day, treating military service as a form of Christian ministry. We've created political tests for faith - can't be a "real Christian" if you vote for that party, right?

These ideas are so normalized that they often go unchallenged. They're the water we swim in. And that's what makes them so dangerous. Because when we accept these ideas without question, we're not just embracing a political ideology. We're distorting the very essence of our faith. We're turning the universal message of God's love into a nationalistic rallying cry. We're replacing the kingdom of God with the kingdom of America.

Make no mistake, Christian Nationalism is a problem. It's not just a harmless expression of patriotism or faith. It's a distortion of both that has real-world consequences. It turns the faith into a political weapon, the Bible into a policy manual, and Jesus into a mascot for a particular vision of America. It creates an us-vs-them mentality that divides rather than unites. It replaces the radical, inclusive love of Christ with a narrow, mean-spirited, exclusionary vision of who belongs and who doesn't.

Let's dive into the belly of the beast. It's time to talk about the twisted theology that fuels Christian Nationalism and this isn't your grandmother's Sunday School lesson.

Remember that old hymn, "Onward, Christian Soldiers"? Well, it seems like some of us took that metaphor a bit too literally. We've traded in the armor of God for the armor of the state, crafting a theology that would crucify the early church martyrs.

At the heart of Christian Nationalism lies a theology of power - an intoxicating brew of religious fervor and political ambition. It's the belief that to advance God's kingdom, we need our hands firmly gripped on the levers of government, our voices dominating the cultural conversation, our values carved into the stone tablets of law. On the surface, it sparkles with righteousness - fighting the good fight, standing up for what's right, being a voice for Christian values in a broken world. But beneath that gleaming veneer lies a theology that's wandered so far from Jesus' teachings, it's practically stumbled into a different religion entirely.

Let's break down this theological house of cards:

First, there's the "Christian Nation" myth - the granddaddy of Christian nationalist theology. Like a family heirloom passed down through generations, we've polished this belief until it shines: America was founded as a Christian nation, we have a special covenant with God, we're somehow His favorite child in the family of nations. Never mind that many of the Founding Fathers were deists, not Christians. Never mind that the Constitution doesn't mention God or Christianity. Never mind that Jesus said His kingdom is not of this world. We've convinced ourselves that America is God's chosen nation, His shining city on a hill. And if that means ignoring history, twisting scripture, and turning a blind eye to our nation's sins? Well, that's a small price to pay for being God's favorite, right?

Then there's the Crusader mentality. Somewhere along the line, we decided that the best way to spread the gospel was through cultural and political domination. We're not just sharing the good news; we're on a mission to conquer the land for Christ. It's like we read about Jesus washing His disciples' feet and thought, "Nah, let's go with the Crusades instead." We've traded the towel and basin for a sword and shield, forgetting that Jesus specifically told Peter to put his sword away.

Perhaps most insidious is how we've superimposed our national success onto God's favor - as if America's prosperity somehow proves divine preference. We point to our nation's wealth and power as evidence of God's blessing, forgetting Jesus' own words in Matthew 5:44-45:

> But I say to you, love your enemies and pray for those who persecute you, so that you may prove yourselves to be sons of your Father who is in heaven; for He causes His sun to rise on *the* evil and *the* good, and sends rain on *the* righteous and *the* unrighteous.

What if our national prosperity isn't a sign of special divine favor at all, but simply rain falling where rain falls? What if we've mistaken circumstantial blessing for cosmic endorsement? This convenient theology allows us to equate national success with divine approval, turning material prosperity into a kind of spiritual currency.

And here's where it gets really ugly - the "ends justify the means" mentality. In our quest to "save" America, we've decided that any means are justified. Supporting leaders whose actions are antithetical to Christian values? Check. Demonizing and marginalizing those who disagree with us? Check. Using fear and hatred as political tools? Double check. We've convinced ourselves that as long as we're fighting for the "right" side, God will overlook the methods. It's like we've taken "Be wise as serpents" and forgot all about the "innocent as doves" part.

In our fervor to create a "Christian" nation, we've made an idol out of national identity. We've fused our faith so tightly with our patriotism that we can no longer separate the two. We've created a god in America's image, a deity who cares more about national borders than human hearts, who's more concerned with political victory than with justice and mercy.

This isn't just theological drift - it's a full-scale shipwreck. Because here's the truth: The Kingdom of God isn't advanced through political power or cultural domination. It's not about controlling others or forcing our values on society. It's about love. It's about service. It's about self-sacrifice. It's about pointing people to seek God for themselves. It's about a kingdom where the last are first, where the poor are blessed, where enemies are loved, and where true power is found in weakness.

But what happens when we turn the cross into a campaign slogan?

I remember sitting in my childhood church, watching as the American flag took its place beside the altar, equal in height to the Christian flag. Even then, something felt off - like we were trying to serve two masters while pretending they wanted the same things.

First off, let's talk about what Christian Nationalism is doing to our witness. Remember Jesus' words in John 13:35, "By this all people will know that you are My disciples, if you have love for one another"? Well, it seems we've rewritten that to say, "By this everyone will know that you are my disciples, if you win elections and impose your will on others."

The irony cuts deep when I think about that old hymn we used to sing: "They'll Know We Are Christians By Our Love." These days, they know us by our political affiliations, our cultural wars, our endless crusades against whatever boogeyman Fox News has conjured up this week. We've become known more for what we're against than what we're for, more for our judgment than our mercy, more for our political power plays than our sacrificial love.

And let me tell you, the watching world has noticed. We're pushing people away from Christ faster than you can say "Make America Great Again." Each time we merge faith with political power, we're not just losing credibility - we're actively creating barriers between people and the God we claim to serve.

But there's more. Because Christian Nationalism isn't just damaging our witness - it's corroding the very foundations of our democracy. When we start believing that our nation should be run according to our interpretation of biblical law, we're not just ignoring the Constitution. We're spitting in the face of the religious freedom our forefathers fought for.

Think about it: We're creating a system where some citizens are more equal than others based on their religious beliefs. Where policy is determined not by what's best for all, but by what aligns with a particular theological viewpoint. It's a short step from there to theocracy, folks. And last I checked, theocracies aren't exactly known for their stellar human rights records.

But perhaps the most insidious impact of Christian Nationalism is what it's doing to our own souls. It's turning us into the very thing Jesus spoke against. We've become the Pharisees, so convinced of our own righteousness that we can't see how far we've strayed from the heart of God. We've traded in love for power, mercy for judgment, service for domination.

I see it in my own heart sometimes - that seductive whisper that says winning is more important than loving, that the ends justify the means, that God's kingdom somehow needs our political muscle to advance. It's a lie as old as the desert tempta- tion: "Again, the devil took Him along to a very high mountain and showed Him all the kingdoms of the world and their glory; and he said to Him, 'All these things I will give You, if You fall down and worship me'" (Matthew 4:8-9).

The implications ripple out like waves from a stone thrown into still water. Each compromise, each fusion of faith with political power, creates new distortions:

- In our communities, where different faiths are seen as threats rather than neighbors
- In our churches, where the measure of true belonging increasingly depends on how well one's politics align with their faith
- In our social circles, where fellowship becomes conditional on shared political views
- In our families, where political disagreements become grounds for division
- In our own hearts, where the simple command to love gets buried under layers of ideology and partisan loyalty

Let me tell you something: The Kingdom of God doesn't need America to thrive. It doesn't need political power or cultural relevance. It needs people willing to love sacrificially, to serve selflessly, to stand with the marginalized and oppressed.

The stakes couldn't be higher. This isn't just about politics. It's not just about America. It's about whether we're going to actually follow Jesus or just use His name to push our own agenda. It's about whether we're going to be known for our love or for our lobbying.

The world is watching. And more importantly, so is He.

Everything we've talked about? This isn't just theoretical for me. Those shadows of Christian Nationalism - I've lived in them, breathed them, worn them like a second skin. The journey from there to here leaves traces, like rings in a tree marking seasons of growth and struggle.

By the time I was twenty, I was a poster child for Christian Nationalism. I dove headfirst into conservative politics, wrapping myself in the flag and the cross, using them as shields against a world that felt increasingly chaotic and threatening. They became my armor, my identity, my truth - or so I thought.

And you know what? I became the worst kind of hypocrite. On the surface, I was the model Christian conservative. But beneath that veneer? I was a mess of contradictions. I was racist, looking down on people of color while claiming to follow a Middle Eastern savior. I was a bigot, spewing hatred towards the LGBTQ+ community while secretly having my own opposite-sex and same-sex relationships. I was a liar and a cheater, presenting a false image of righteousness while ignoring the ways that I claimed to hold dear.

The worst part? I used my faith and my politics as a club, bashing others for the very sins I was committing. I created an aura around myself that repelled anyone different, anyone who might have challenged my worldview or shown me a better way. My pride was off the charts. I thought I had all the answers. I thought I was on God's side, fighting the good fight. In reality, I was pushing away the very people Jesus would have embraced.

It's not easy admitting all this. But if we're going to talk about the dangers of Christian Nationalism, I need to be honest with you about my own journey through it. Because here's the truth: I'm not unique. My story isn't an outlier. It's a pattern I've seen repeated over and over in Christian conservative circles. We wrap ourselves in certainty because we're afraid. We cling to power because we feel powerless. We create enemies because it's easier than loving our neighbors.

But God didn't leave me there. He put people in my path who challenged my assumptions, who lived out a faith that looked more like Jesus and less like a political platform. It wasn't sudden. It was a long, ugly process of unlearning and relearning. Of facing my own hypocrisy and asking for forgiveness. Of realizing that I needed God's grace more than anyone.

And you know what? That process isn't over. I'm still learning, still unlearning. Each day brings new opportunities to choose between the comfortable lies of Christian Nationalism and the challenging truths of actually following Jesus.

So here we are, standing at a crossroads. And I'm asking you to join me in making a choice. Are we going to keep playing church, or are we going to start being the Body of Christ? Are we going to keep singing "God Bless America," or are we going to start being a blessing to all nations? Are we going to keep trying to change laws, or are we going to focus on changing hearts – starting with our own?

These aren't easy choices. They're not meant to be. They're meant to challenge us, to shake us out of our complacency, to force us to confront the ways we've distorted our faith. The path ahead isn't clear or comfortable, but it's necessary. Because in the chapters that follow, we're going to dig even deeper into what it means to truly follow Christ in a world that constantly tempts us to settle for less.

The choice is yours. But remember - once you see the truth about Christian Nationalism, you can't unsee it. And that knowledge comes with responsibility. The question is: What will you do with it?

3

THE REAL THIRD COMMANDMENT
BEYOND 'GODDAMMIT'

T hree. It's a number that seems to follow us, doesn't it? Third time's the charm. Three strikes and you're out. Beginning, middle, end. And here we are, in the third chapter, diving deep into the Third Commandment. There's a beautiful symmetry to it, a divine irony possibly. Because this commandment, the one we've so often reduced to a simple prohibition against casual profanity, might just be the key to understanding everything that's gone wrong with how we practice our faith, how we engage with politics, and how we interact with the world around us.

We've missed the point for so long.

I remember sitting in Sunday School, young and impressionable, being told that the Third Commandment was all about not saying "Oh my God" or using the Lord's name as a curse word. It seemed so simple then. Don't say bad words, and you're good.

But as I've grown older, I've seen the darker side of how

faith can be weaponized. I think about my sister-in-law, finding herself in a marriage where her husband demanded she be a "godly wife" by a warped definition, all while treating her in ways that were far from godly. I watched as the Bible became a tool of oppression in his hands, driving a wedge not only between them but worse, between her and God.

But it's not just in personal relationships, either. I've watched Christianity become a political battering ram. I've seen the name of God invoked to justify things that make my stomach churn. And I've realized we've been reading this commandment all wrong.

> It's time we took another look. It's time we understood what it really means to take the Lord's name in vain.

Let's start at the beginning, shall we? Exodus 20:7, the Third Commandment: "You shall not take the name of the Lord your God in vain, for the Lord will not leave him unpunished who takes His name in vain."

Simple enough, right? Don't use God's name carelessly or profanely. Don't throw it around like a casual expletive. That's what I was taught, what most of us were taught. And yes, there's value in treating the names of God with respect. But what if we've been missing the forest for the trees? What if this commandment is about something far deeper, far more profound than just watching our language?

For years, this concept had been gnawing at me. The first commandment tells us to have no other gods. The second, to make no idols. And then the third... don't say a specific word? It didn't add up. As I've grown, it's made even less sense.

Then it hit me. I came across a statement Donald Trump had made in July 2015. He said,

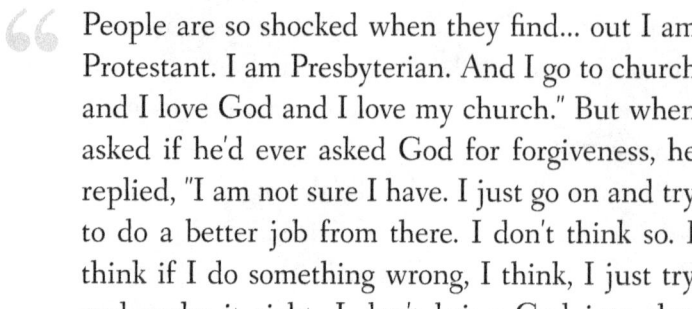

People are so shocked when they find... out I am Protestant. I am Presbyterian. And I go to church and I love God and I love my church." But when asked if he'd ever asked God for forgiveness, he replied, "I am not sure I have. I just go on and try to do a better job from there. I don't think so. I think if I do something wrong, I think, I just try and make it right. I don't bring God into that picture. I don't.

— 3.1

In that moment, it was like scales fell from my eyes. Here was a man claiming to be Protestant while openly admitting he had never asked God for forgiveness - the most fundamental aspect of Christian faith, the very starting point of a relationship with God. In Christianity, acknowledging our need for forgiveness and accepting Christ's salvation is quite literally step one. It's Christianity 101. Yet here he was, invoking God's name while simultaneously revealing that his faith was empty, hollow, and carrying no real weight in his life. And suddenly, I understood what the Third Commandment was really about.

You know those moments when something clicks, when a truth you've been circling suddenly comes into sharp focus? This was one of those moments. Everything I thought I knew about the Third Commandment shifted. It wasn't just about casual profanity or religious disrespect - it was about this. This hollow claiming of God's name. This empty performance of faith. This using of Christianity as a prop while missing its entire essence. I sat there, staring at Trump's interview transcript, and for the first time, I truly understood what the third commandment was talking about.

See, here's the thing: The Bible wasn't written in English.

That "in vain" we've been fixating on? It's a translation of the Hebrew word שָׁוְא (shav'). And shav' is a whole lot more complex than our simplistic understanding of vanity.

The Hebrew word Shav' appears 52 times in the Bible. And you know what? It's never just about casual words, not once. Instead, it's used to describe things that are false, empty, or worthless. It's used in contexts of lies, of false worship, of actions that are fruitless.

In other words, taking the Lord's name in shav' isn't about saying "Oh my God" when you stub your toe. The concept runs far deeper. Throughout scripture, shav' appears in contexts that go well beyond casual speech. When the prophet Jeremiah confronts false prophets who claim to speak for God, he describes their words as shav' - empty, worthless claims that misuse God's authority (Jeremiah 23:16). When Isaiah condemns empty religious rituals, he calls them offerings of shav' - actions that claim God's backing but lack true substance (Isaiah 1:13).

These biblical examples reveal something profound: shav', in the context of the Third Commandment, is about any way we might use God's name - His authority, His backing - in ways that are false, empty, or worthless. It's about claiming divine sanction for our own purposes, about using God's name as a tool rather than treating it with the reverence it deserves.

This understanding forces us to confront an uncomfortable truth: shav' isn't just about the words we speak. It's about how we represent God in the world. And here's where it gets personal - when we present ourselves as Christians, when we invoke that identity without substance and authenticity, we're engaging in a form of shav'. We're using God's name - because that's what "Christian" means, "little Christ" - in ways that are empty and false.

It's about using Christianity as a shell or a hollow façade.

I've seen this with my own eyes right here in Little Rock. When the largest church in our city hosted a political prayer breakfast for Sarah Huckabee Sanders' inauguration, they charged $100,000 for four reserved seats. [3.2] Let that sink in. A hundred thousand dollars to pray in God's house. That's shav' on such a massive scale, it would make a Texas megachurch's parking lot look small.

I remember sitting in my living room, staring at the news in disbelief. A church - a place meant to welcome all, just as Christ welcomed all - putting a price tag on prayer with a political candidate. The same Jesus who drove merchants from the temple would surely have something to say about turning prayer into a political fundraiser.

This isn't isolated. I watch fellow believers nod approvingly when political candidates use scripture to justify policies that harm the vulnerable. I've seen Christians enthusiastically support measures that separate families, deny healthcare to the needy, push away the very strangers we're commanded to welcome, or defend a politician's immoral behavior because they use the language of Christianity.

We need to ask ourselves: When we invoke our Christian identity - whether in our social media profiles, our business practices, or our political activism - are we truly reflecting God's character? Is this filled with the love, grace, and justice of Christ? Or is it empty, false, and self-serving? Because if it's the latter, well... we might not be saying "goddammit," but we're breaking that Third Commandment just the same.

And that realization? It changes everything.

Let's dive deeper into this Hebrew word - שָׁוְא (shav'). It's not just an ancient term gathering dust in old scrolls. No, this word is alive, pulsing with meaning that's as relevant today as it was thousands of years ago.

Shav' shows up 52 times. Fifty! That's not a typo. And every single time, it's packing a punch that goes way beyond "don't curse using God's name."

So what does it mean?

Shav' is like a Swiss Army knife of negative concepts. It's falseness, emptiness, worthlessness all rolled into one. It's the hollow echo of a promise unkept, the worthless chaff left after the wheat's been harvested, the lie that leaves a bitter taste in your mouth.

While the nuances of shav' are rich and varied, different Bible translations tend to emphasize certain aspects of its meaning. Here's a list of how a few of the major Bible translations translate the word: useless, lies, vain, false, vanity, empty, worthless, futility, and deceptive. For references on every instance where shav' is mentioned, please refer to the appendix.

Let me break it down:

First, there's falseness. Shav' is about lies, about deception. It's saying one thing and meaning another. Sound familiar? It should. We see it every day in politics, in business, even in our churches.

 'These people honor me with their lips, but their hearts are far from me. They worship me in vain; their teachings are merely human rules.'

— MATTHEW 15:8-9, NIV

Then there's emptiness. Shav' is about things that look good on the outside but are hollow within. It's the whitewashed tomb Jesus talked about - all shiny and clean on the outside, full of dead men's bones on the inside. It's the pray-in-public-for-show but never-in-private kind of faith.

> If I speak in the tongues of men or of angels, but do not have love, I am only a resounding gong or a clanging cymbal.
>
> — 1 CORINTHIANS 13:1

And let's not forget worthlessness. Shav' is about actions that ultimately amount to nothing. It's the spiritual equivalent of rearranging deck chairs on the Titanic. It looks like you're doing something, but in the end, it's all sound and fury, signifying nothing. The Psalmist captured this perfectly:

> Unless the Lord builds the house, they labor in vain (shav') who build it; Unless the Lord guards the city, the watchman stays awake in vain (shav')
>
> — PSALM 127:1

Even our most impressive efforts are worthless if they're disconnected from God's purposes. But here's where it gets really interesting. Shav' isn't just used in the context of speech. It's used to describe false worship, idolatry, and futile actions.

Remember the golden calf? That was shav' in action - people claiming to worship God while really just satisfying their own desires. And we've perfected that art. We've got golden calves in every church these days - they just look like American flags and political candidates now. We've traded the golden statue for red, white, and blue banners and campaign posters, but it's the same old shav'.

Look, we're experts at making our shav' look respectable. We dress it up in suits and ties, wrap it in patriotic bunting, and call it "Christian values." But here's the truth - when we take those "Christian values" and use them to champion policies that push people to the margins - people we've labeled as "sinners" - that's shav'. When we claim to follow a God who commands us to welcome the stranger while supporting policies that crush the vulnerable? That's shav'. When we worship a Savior who ate with outcasts while creating systems that turn outcasts away? Pure shav'.

This kind of shav' isn't just breaking a commandment. It's corrupting the very essence of what it means to follow Christ. We've taken the most revolutionary message in human history - a message of love so radical it got its messenger crucified - and turned it into a cultural identity that demands nothing and changes nothing.

We've traded the living water of authentic faith for the stagnant cesspool of cultural Christianity. Instead of allowing our faith to reshape us into the image of Christ, we've reshaped Christianity into our own image.

These patterns of shav' have become so woven into the fabric of our faith that they can be hard to spot at first. But like a loose thread that reveals a garment's flaws, once you start tugging at it, the whole tapestry begins to unravel.

Because once you start seeing shav', you can't unsee it. And it's everywhere.

Think about it - why would God make misusing His name one of the Big Ten? Right up there with murder and adultery? It seems almost out of place, doesn't it? But here's what I've come to understand: This commandment wasn't just about protecting God's reputation. It was a warning about how His name could be weaponized.

When God gave this commandment, He wasn't just worried about casual profanity. He was looking ahead, seeing how people would use His name as a tool of power, a weapon of control, a way to claim divine authority for human agendas. The Third Commandment was a protective barrier, a divine guardrail meant to prevent many of the atrocities we have seen through history and exactly what we're seeing today.

History has shown us what happens when this guardrail gets ignored. Time and again, people have taken God's name - His authority, His backing, His divine seal of approval - and turned it into a weapon. They've used it to justify everything from minor manipulations to mass genocide. The warning against shav' wasn't just about individual piety; it was about preventing the corruption of faith itself.

Think of it like a vaccine. God knew that using His name for empty purposes - for shav' - was like a virus that could infect not just individuals but entire religious systems. The Third Commandment was meant to inoculate us against this disease. But like any vaccine, it only works if we use it.

The transformation from warning to weapon doesn't happen overnight. It starts small - a little shav' here, a touch of empty religion there. But like a cancer, it grows. It spreads. It metastasizes until entire religious systems become built on the empty use of God's name.

This is what makes shav' so dangerous. It's not just about breaking a rule. It's about breaking faith itself. It's about turning what should be a life-giving stream into a poisoned well. And once that well is poisoned, everyone who drinks from it gets sick.

God saw this coming. He knew how tempting it would be to use His name for our own purposes, to claim divine backing for human agendas. That's why He put this warning right up front, in the fundamental laws of faith. But somewhere along the way, we stopped seeing it as a warning. We reduced it to a simple rule about swearing, missing the much deeper protection it was meant to provide.

And that's exactly how shav' works - it doesn't announce itself with fanfare. It creeps in quietly, disguising itself as righteousness, wrapping itself in religious language until it becomes almost impossible to distinguish from authentic faith.

We're not just dealing with individual acts of empty religion anymore. We're facing entire systems built on shav', structures of faith that have turned God's name from a blessing into a bludgeon. And untangling this mess? Well, that's going to require us to look at some pretty dark corners of both our past and our present.

But before we dive into those depths, we need to understand how individual acts of shav' can grow into something much bigger and much more dangerous. Because what we're dealing with today isn't just about personal misuse of God's name - it's about entire systems built on empty faith.

You know how a single termite isn't much of a problem? But give them time, let them multiply, and suddenly you've got a house that's being eaten alive from the inside out. That's what we're dealing with when it comes to shav'. What starts as individual acts of empty religion can grow into entire systems that hollow out our faith from within.

This is where it gets scary. Because we're not just talking

about personal hypocrisy anymore. We're talking about institutionalized emptiness. When enough people engage in shav', when enough leaders claim God's backing for their own agendas, when Christians prioritize power over authenticity - it creates a feedback loop. A system that perpetuates itself, that rewards empty religion and punishes genuine faith.

In these systems, shav' isn't a bug - it's a feature. The empty use of God's name becomes normalized, expected, even celebrated. It becomes woven into the very fabric of religious life until it's almost impossible to separate authentic faith from hollow performance.

And the most dangerous part? These systems of shav' don't look evil. They often look righteous. They come dressed in their Sunday best, wrapped in religious language, bearing all the outward marks of genuine faith. They can quote scripture and use Christian language. But underneath? It's all empty calories. Spiritual junk food that fills you up but provides no real nourishment.

And here's where it gets personal: Once these systems are in place, they start shaping us. They train us to value appearance over substance, to prefer comfortable lies over uncomfortable truths, to choose power over humility. They teach us to use God's name without really honoring His character.

The result? A form of Christianity that's more focused on preserving its own power than transforming lives. A faith that's more interested in winning political seats than winning hearts. A religion that knows how to talk about Jesus but has forgotten how to walk like Him.

And nowhere do we see this system of shav' more clearly, more devastatingly, than in the rise of Christian Nationalism.

If there's one thing that embodies the essence of shav' in our modern context, it's this toxic fusion of faith and patriotism. Christian Nationalism isn't just a political stance. It's not merely a strong sense of patriotism combined with Christian beliefs. No, it's something far more dangerous. And let me tell you, it's shav' through and through.

When we claim that America is a "Christian nation," what are we really saying? Are we acknowledging the complex, often problematic history of Christianity in this country? Are we recognizing the diverse tapestry of faiths and beliefs that have always been part of America? Or are we using Christianity as a tool to exclude, to create an "us vs. them" mentality?

I remember watching rallies where flags bearing crosses flew alongside American flags and Nazi flags, where "God Bless America" was chanted like a war cry. And I couldn't help but think: Is this what Jesus meant when He said His kingdom was not of this world?

Christian Nationalism uses the language of faith to pursue political power. It takes the name of Christ and slaps it onto a particular vision of America, one that often stands in stark contrast to the teachings of Jesus Himself.

But here's the devastating truth: Christian Nationalism doesn't just harm those outside the faith - it corrodes the very heart of Christianity. This corrosion is perhaps the most damaging effect, second only to the tangible harm inflicted on the very people God calls us to love.

Christian Nationalism takes the life-changing, soul-transforming message of the Gospel and reduces it to a mere political platform. It twists the radical, boundary-breaking love of Christ - a love that shattered social, ethnic, and economic barriers - into a narrow, exclusionary ideology.

This distortion doesn't just misrepresent Christianity; it

actively undermines its core essence. It replaces the universal, sacrificial love that Christ embodied with a tribal, self-serving mentality. In doing so, it not only fails to attract people to the true message of Christ, but it actively repels them, creating a stumbling block for those who might otherwise be drawn to the genuine love and grace of God.

The damage runs deep, corrupting our understanding of what it means to follow Christ and tainting the witness of the Church in the world. It's a betrayal of the very foundations of our faith, and its consequences ripple far beyond the political sphere, touching the spiritual lives of both believers and non-believers alike.

When we talk about the dangers of Christian Nationalism, we're not treading new ground. Jesus himself confronted a similar issue in his time. Consider His words in Matthew 23:37-39:

> Jerusalem, Jerusalem, you who kill the prophets and stone those sent to you, how often I have longed to gather your children together, as a hen gathers her chicks under her wings, and you were not willing. Look, your house is left to you desolate. For I tell you, you will not see me again until you say, 'Blessed is he who comes in the name of the Lord.'

These aren't just words of frustration. They're a lament over the blindness that religious nationalism can create. The Jewish people of Jesus' time were so caught up in their identity as God's chosen nation that they missed God's messenger standing right in front of them.

Sound familiar? It should. Because we're doing the same thing today.

Just as the Jews of Jesus' time clung to their national and religious identity, many American Christians today wrap themselves in the flag and call it faith. We're so focused on being a "Christian nation" that we're missing the very heart of Christ's teachings.

We fight tooth and nail for the Ten Commandments to be displayed in courthouses and Bible's to be put in classrooms, but engage in shav' by using God's name to justify our own agendas rather than embodying His love and justice.

This blindness isn't just ironic. It's tragic. Because just like the religious leaders of Jesus' time, we're in danger of missing God's work in our midst. We're so busy trying to maintain our Christian nation that we're forgetting what it actually means to follow Christ.

Jesus wept over Jerusalem because he saw this blindness. He recognized how their religious nationalism had become a barrier to true faith. And I can't help but wonder: Is he weeping over us today?

Are we, in our zeal to "keep America Christian," actually pushing ourselves further from the heart of God? Are we, like Jerusalem, refusing to be gathered under His wings because we're too proud of our own religious identity?

The truth is far more profound and challenging: God isn't an American, nor is He confined to any earthly nation. Jesus wasn't just apolitical - He was often explicitly anti-political, actively resisting attempts to draw Him into partisan conflicts or nationalistic movements.

Remember when the crowds tried to make Him king by force? He withdrew to a mountain by himself (John 6:15). When asked about paying taxes to Caesar, He deftly avoided the political trap, saying "Give to Caesar what is Caesar's, and to God what is God's" (Matthew 22:21). Even at His trial, Jesus declared, "My kingdom is not of this realm" (John 18:36).

Christ consistently pointed to a reality that transcends our earthly divisions and political machinations. The Kingdom of Heaven, He proclaimed, isn't aligned with any nation, party, or political ideology. It exists on a completely different plane, challenging and often contradicting our worldly power structures.

This calls us to reevaluate our allegiances, to question whether we're truly following Christ or merely using His name to sanctify our own political agendas. It demands that we look beyond the narrow confines of nationalism and partisanship to embrace a faith that's as boundless and radical as Christ Himself.

When we buy into Christian Nationalism, we're not exalting God. We're not even really exalting America. We're exalting ourselves, our own tribe, our own narrow vision of what this country should be.

And in doing so, we're taking the Lord's name in vain in the most profound way possible. We're turning the God of the universe into a mascot for our political team. We're reducing the revolutionary message of Christ to a bumper sticker slogan.

We're aligning ourselves more with the very idolatry and false gods that the first two Commandments warn against than with the true worship of the living God.

So what do we do about all this? How do we resist the allure of Christian Nationalism? How do we reclaim a faith that's true to Christ's teachings, that's full of substance rather than shav'?

Well folks, we're about to wade into some deep waters here. We're going to peel back the layers of Christian Nationalism like an onion that's been sitting in the sun too long - and it's gonna make us cry. We're going to trace its dark history through time, expose its insidious influence in our churches and communities, and confront some ugly truths.

We're going to see how this ideology has twisted our faith, corrupted our witness, and left a trail of broken people in its wake. We'll examine how it's affected everything from how we vote to how we love our neighbors (or don't).

But before we dive into those murky waters, we need to talk about something even more fundamental. Something that's been missing from our faith for far too long. Something Jesus wouldn't shut up about, but we've somehow managed to forget.

Jesus said in Matthew 22:36-40 that the greatest commandment was to love God, and the second was to love your neighbor as yourself. He said all the Law and the Prophets hang on these two commands. Not some of it. All of it.

So how in God's name did we end up with a faith that's more known for what it's against than what it's for?

What we're witnessing isn't just a failure to love - it's what Romans 1:31 describes as "unmerciful." Paul lists this characteristic alongside other signs of a depraved mind like "without understanding" and "unfeeling," and it's pitiful how accurately it describes much of American Christianity today.

I see it in the callous responses to human suffering: The shrugs when children were caged at the border. The dismissal of refugees seeking asylum. The quick judgment that people in poverty "deserve" their situation. The cold calculation that some people's healthcare needs are simply too expensive to address. Even during the height of the COVID-19 pandemic, I watched fellow Christians argue that protecting vulnerable people wasn't worth the inconvenience to their daily lives.

This lack of mercy reveals something profound about our spiritual condition. Throughout scripture, mercy is presented as a core attribute of God and a fundamental expectation for His people:

> He has shown you, O mortal, what is good. And what does the Lord require of you? To act justly and to love mercy and to walk humbly with your God.

— MICAH 6:8

> Be merciful, just as your Father is merciful.

— LUKE 6:36

Yet somehow, we've created a version of Christianity that can recite scripture, attend church, and proclaim love while showing no mercy to those in need. This isn't just a political stance or a difference of opinion - it's a spiritual malformation that cuts to the very heart of what it means to follow Christ.

The kind of love that Jesus talked about. The kind that loves enemies, that turns the other cheek, that goes the extra mile. The kind that touches lepers, that eats with sinners, that washes the feet of the one who will betray you.

That love? Where is it?

Instead, we have this anemic, sanitized version of love that looks suspiciously like voting the right way. Faith without love isn't just incomplete. It's shav'. It's empty. It's false. It's worthless.

You can have all the right theology, all the correct doctrine, all the perfect church attendance. But if you don't have love, you're just a noisy gong or a clanging cymbal (1 Corinthians 13:1-2). You're taking the Lord's name in vain every time you claim to be Christian.

So here's what I propose: The Personal Impact Test. It's simple, really. Ask yourself this: Does my faith change how I treat others? Does it make me more loving, more compassionate, more willing to sacrifice for those in need?

Or does it just make me feel superior? Does it just give me a tribe to belong to, an identity to cling to? Because if your faith isn't making you more loving, it's not faith at all. It's shav'.

I've had to face this hard truth myself. I've had to confront the times when my Christianity was more about being right than doing right. When it was more about judgment than mercy, more about exclusion than embrace. And let me tell you, it's not a comfortable realization. It's like looking in the mirror and seeing a stranger.

We need this discomfort. We need this soul-searching. Because until we confront the love deficit in our faith, we're going to keep taking the Lord's name in vain. We're going to keep using Christianity as a shield, a weapon, a political tool, instead of living it out as the radical, transformative love that Jesus preached.

So I challenge you - and myself - to take the Personal Impact Test. To honestly evaluate whether your faith is changing how you treat others. Whether it's making you more loving, more compassionate, more Christlike.

The love deficit in our faith is real. It's pervasive. It's destroying our witness and corrupting our souls.

If we're honest with ourselves, we've drifted so far from the original message that I sometimes wonder if we're even reading the same words of Jesus as the early Christians. The implications of this drift, this emptying of our faith through shav', reach far beyond our church walls into every aspect of how we live out (or fail to live out) our faith in the modern world.

So where does this leave us? Knee-deep in a pile of shav', that's where. We've created a Christianity that Jesus might not recognize. A faith that's more about cultural identity than spiritual transformation. A religion that's comfortable with power but uncomfortable with sacrifice.

It's time for a reckoning.

We need to strip away the layers of cultural Christianity, peel back the veneer of religiosity, and get to the heart of what it means to follow Christ in the modern world.

This process of unlearning isn't about rejecting our faith, but about stripping away the distortions that have accumulated over time, allowing us to see our faith anew.

It's not about abandoning our faith. It's about rediscovering it. The implications are profound. It might mean rethinking our political allegiances. Reimagining our role in society. Redefining what it means to be a Christian in America. It's not going to be easy. It might cost us status, our sense of identity and belonging, or even relationships.

It's time to decide: Are we content with this shav', or are we ready for something real?

The implications of shav' aren't just theoretical - they're written in blood across the pages of history. Because here's the terrifying truth: When we use God's name for empty purposes, when we twist faith into a tool of power, people get hurt. Real people. And nowhere is this more evident than in the dark legacy of Christian Nationalism.

As we'll see, this isn't a new problem. The marriage of faith and nationalism has left a trail of devastation that stretches back centuries. From the blood-soaked fields of the Crusades to the shadow of the Third Reich, from the justification of slavery to the modern-day atrocities ahead - when we wrap the cross in the flag, the results are devastating.

The question isn't just whether we're content with all this shav'. The question is whether we're willing to face the brutal truth about where it leads.

4

THE DARK HISTORY OF CHRISTIAN NATIONALISM IN AMERICA

THE TANGLED ROOTS

L et me take you back to the founding of America, to those early days when Christianity shaped our nation's character. When our forefathers first arrived on these shores, they established communities built on Christ's teachings of peace and radical love. They saw the Native peoples as equals deserving of fair treatment and honest dealing. Every land purchase was negotiated with respect, every treaty honored as sacred.

These early Christians brought something revolutionary to the New World - a faith that transformed how people lived together. They created settlements where all religions were welcome, where no one was forced to practice any faith against their conscience. Women spoke freely in their gatherings, their voices valued equally with men's. They refused to bow to hierarchies of class or status, treating every person as worthy of the same respect.

When others sought to profit from the evil of slavery, they stood firmly against it. They were among the first to condemn human bondage as incompatible with God's will, many refusing to own slaves even when it cost them economically. Their communities became havens where all people could live in dignity, regardless of race or status.

In times of conflict, they chose peace over violence, even when it meant suffering themselves. They wouldn't serve in militias or take up arms, believing that Christ's command to love our enemies meant exactly that. They lived simply, rejected empty rituals, and sought to demonstrate their faith through actions rather than words. But here's what your history books won't tell you:

These Christians were hunted. Persecuted. Imprisoned. Exiled. And Killed.

Their crime? Following Jesus too literally. Looking too much like Christ and not enough like empire.

They were called Quakers. And while we love to talk about America's Christian heritage, we don't mean their Christianity. We mean the Christianity of their persecutors. The ones who hanged them in Boston Common. The ones who seized their property and exiled them from their homes. The ones who found their authentic faith too threatening to tolerate.

The Quakers showed us another way was possible. They weren't perfect, of course. Some individuals struggled with the allure of wealth and power. Others failed to fully live up to their ideals of equality. And like any religious movement, they had their share of internal conflicts and contradictions.

But their core beliefs and practices - their commitment to peace, their recognition of human equality, their rejection of empty ritual and hierarchy - these stood in contrast to the domineering Christianity that would come to shape much of American history. And for that witness, imperfect though it was, they faced brutal persecution.

When people claim America was founded as a Christian nation, they're right - but those people were imprisoned, tortured, exiled, or killed. And the Christianity that shaped America wasn't the one that looked like Jesus. It was the one that looked like power. The faith that survived wasn't the one that loved enemies and welcomed strangers. It was the one that hung the gentle followers of Christ and called it God's will.

The Quakers showed us another way was possible. And for that, they had to be destroyed. Because authentic faith is always a threat to religious nationalism. It exposes the emptiness at its core. It reveals the sham behind the sacred claims.

Remember this the next time someone talks about America's Christian heritage: There was a Christianity that actually followed Christ. But that's not the Christianity that survived.

The Christianity that won would take many forms through American history, each more distant from Christ's teachings than the last. By the 1920s, it had evolved into something the Quakers could scarcely have imagined.

On a warm summer evening in 1925, the skies over Washington D.C. glowed with an eerie light. Thirty thousand white-robed figures marched down Pennsylvania Avenue, their faces hidden behind pointed hoods. Crosses blazed, not as symbols of salvation, but as fiery warnings. American flags waved alongside banners proclaiming "100% Americanism."

This wasn't some fringe gathering. This was the Second Ku Klux Klan at the height of its power, boasting millions of members nationwide. And in their twisted ideology, they saw no contradiction between their white supremacist views, their claim to Christian values, and their assertion of American patriotic fervor.

While we might want to dismiss the Klan as a lunatic fringe, the truth is far more uncomfortable. The Second Klan didn't operate in the shadows. It was mainstream. It was popular. It drew support from politicians, preachers, and ordinary citizens alike.

William Vance Trollinger writing for *The Journal of American History* said:

> While the first Klan focused its hatred on the newly freed slaves and their Republican supporters, the second Klan offered white Protestant Americans an expanded list of social scapegoats including Catholics, Jews, and immigrants. While the original KKK was confined to the South, the new version was truly national, with perhaps 4 million members at its peak. For a few years from coast to coast America was ablaze with crosses.
>
> — 4.1

But the rise of the Second Klan in the 1920s wasn't only a result of racism. It was a grotesque manifestation of a deeper and darker ideology: Christian Nationalism. Here, in broad daylight, was the unholy marriage of national pride and protestant identity.

And, the ideas it championed? The fusion of Christian identity with American nationalism. And that didn't die with the Klan's decline. It evolved. It adapted. It put on a suit and tie, traded the hood for a lapel pin, and walked right into our churches and capitols.

Today, we might not see burning crosses or white-robed marchers very often. But the ideology still persist in more subtle, socially acceptable forms. It's in the politician who claims God's endorsement for a policy of exclusion. It's in the preacher who equates patriotism with godliness. It's in the voter who believes that being a "real American" means simultaneously being Christian.

This isn't just about history. It's about now. It's about how we've allowed a warped fusion of faith and nationalism to corrupt both our democracy and our spirituality.

As we dive into this dark history, we're going to confront some uncomfortable truths. We'll trace the tangled roots of Christian Nationalism from colonial times to the present day. We'll examine how it's been used to justify everything from slavery to segregation, from Native American displacement to modern-day xenophobia.

This isn't intended to demonize Christianity as a whole or dismiss the positive roles faith has played in American history. It's about understanding how the merger of religious and national identity has often led us astray from the very principles both claim to uphold.

By understanding this history, we can begin to disentangle the unholy alliances that have formed between faith and power, between Christianity and nationalism. Only then can we hope to forge a path forward that honors both our diverse national identity and the true teachings of Christ.

The story that unfolds in the following pages isn't pretty. It's going to challenge us. It might make us angry, or sad, or deeply uncomfortable. Good. We need to be uncomfortable. Because until we confront this history head-on, we're doomed to repeat it.

It's time to unravel the tangled roots of Christian Nationalism in America.

The roots of Christian Nationalism in America run deep, tangling their way through our history all the way back to the colonial era. It's a story that begins long before the Second Klan marched down Pennsylvania Avenue, before the Civil War tore the nation apart, even before the ink dried on the Constitution.

Let's talk about the Puritans.

Now, I grew up hearing about these folks like they were the patron saints of American Christianity. "City upon a hill," and all that jazz. But here's the thing: while the Puritans might have been seeking religious freedom, they weren't exactly champions of it.

These were people who believed they had a divine mandate to create a godly society. Sounds noble, right? Except their version of a "godly society" looked suspiciously like a theocracy where only their particular brand of Christianity was welcome.

Does the name Roger Williams ring a bell? He's the guy that founded Rhode Island. He got kicked out of Massachusetts for suggesting that maybe, just maybe, the government shouldn't be in the business of enforcing religious beliefs. The Puritans weren't having any of that "separation of church and state" nonsense.

And here's where the seeds of Christian Nationalism start to sprout. The Puritans didn't just want to practice their faith freely. They wanted to create a Christian nation. Their Christian nation. And boy, did they create it. Want to see what happens when you mix religious zeal with political power and social control?

In just sixty years, around 7,000 people were killed in the name of God in colonial America. When John Winthrop envisioned his "city upon a hill," he wasn't just being poetic. The Puritans established a rigid theocracy where church and state were inseparable, where only Puritan men who were full church members could vote or hold office. Laws weren't just based on civil governance - they were explicitly derived from biblical interpretation.

The vast majority of these deaths were Native Americans, slaughtered in conflicts like the Pequot War and King Philip's War. During the Pequot War alone, over 700 men, women, and children were burned alive in their village at Mystic in 1637. The Puritans weren't shy about framing this as divine mandate - they openly celebrated these massacres as God's will.

During the first 75 years of colonial settlement, New England's Indigenous population plummeted from 140,000 to just 10,000 - a devastating 93% decline - while the English population grew to 50,000. Ministers celebrated this decimation as divine providence while forcing survivors into 'praying towns' where they were required to abandon their cultural practices and submit to colonial authority.[4.2]

Remember those early Quakers we spoke of? Between 1659 and 1661, the Puritan government of Massachusetts Bay Colony executed four of them simply for being Quakers: Mary Dyer, William Robinson, Marmaduke Stevenson, and William Leddra. But execution was just the tip of the iceberg. Dozens more were tortured, imprisoned, banished, or died from mistreatment.[4.3]

And this wasn't just random violence - it was systematic suppression of authentic faith by those claiming to act in God's name. The Puritans didn't see themselves as persecutors but as protectors of true religion. They used scripture to justify their actions, turning the Bible into a weapon against those who dared to practice a more Christ-like faith.

The pattern established with the Quakers would repeat

throughout American history. Whether through the genocide of Native Americans justified by "Manifest Destiny," the enslavement of Africans defended using Biblical arguments, or the later suppression of civil rights movements - those claiming to act in God's name would consistently work to eliminate more authentic expressions of faith.

This is what happens when faith becomes a weapon of the state, when Christianity is used to justify power rather than promote love. The death toll - over 7,000 souls in just sixty years of colonial America - stands as a grim reminder of the destructive power of Christian nationalism. And perhaps most chillingly, this was just the beginning. These colonial justifications of persecution and murder in God's name would echo through American history, laying the groundwork for centuries of Christian nationalism to come.

Consider it: if 20,000 Puritan's could kill 7,000 people in God's name in just sixty years, with the limited technology and population of colonial times, is it any wonder that Christian nationalism remains such a dangerous threat today? The seeds planted in colonial soil have grown into a poisonous tree that continues to bear bitter fruit.

Because you see, the seeds planted in colonial times, watered with the blood of the accused in Salem and elsewhere, would grow into a poisonous tree. From slavery to segregation, from Manifest Destiny to modern-day culture wars, the idea that America was a Christian nation - and more specifically, a white Christian nation - would take root and flourish.

Fast forward a bit, and we see this idea taking root in different soil. As the colonies expanded, as the young nation grew, Christianity was used time and again to justify some of the darkest chapters in our history.

Take slavery, for instance. You want to talk about taking the

Lord's name in vain? How about using the Bible to defend the ownership of human beings?

I remember sitting in Sunday School, learning about how God delivered the Israelites from slavery in Egypt. Yet, nobody mentioned how Christianity used that same Bible to keep people in chains.

Christian owners of enslaved people twisted scripture to justify their cruelty. They pointed to the "Curse of Ham" to argue that Black people were destined for servitude. One of their favorite passages to misuse was from Paul's letter to the Ephesians: "Slaves, be obedient to those who are your masters according to the flesh, with fear and trembling, in the sincerity of your heart, as to Christ" (Ephesians 6:5). They cherry-picked verses like this about servants obeying masters, conveniently ignoring Christ's teachings about love and human dignity. It's crucial to note that when Paul wrote about servants obeying masters, he was addressing those finding themselves in that condition, advising them on how to honor Christ through their behavior in adverse circumstances. This was obviously not a prescription for slavery, but rather guidance for those trapped within an existing system.

And when it comes to the "Curse of Ham," I could quote dozens, even hundreds, of documents from theologians, pastors, and politicians who used it to justify slavery. Their sermons and speeches fill volumes, each more twisted than the last. But perhaps what hits closest to home for me, having grown up in the Southern Baptist church, are the words of Patrick Mell, who served as the fourth president of the Southern Baptist Convention. He said:

 From Ham were descended the nations that occupied the land of Canaan and those that now constitute the African or Negro race. Their inheritance, according to prophecy, has been and will continue to be slavery... [and] so long as we have the Bible... we expect to maintain it.

— 4.4

Yuck.

And it wasn't just about slavery. As white settlers pushed westward, they carried with them a belief in "Manifest Destiny" - the idea that it was God's will for them to expand across the continent. Never mind that this "destiny" involved displacing and destroying Native American nations.

Again, Christianity was weaponized. Native peoples were labeled "savages" who needed to be either converted or conquered. Their land was seen as a divine gift to white Christian settlers. Their cultures and religions were dismissed as pagan and inferior.

It's enough to make you sick, isn't it? To see the name of Christ invoked to justify such brutality and injustice?

These weren't just the actions of a few bad apples. This was mainstream Christianity in America. This was the norm.

And with each generation, these ideas became more deeply ingrained in the American psyche. The notion that America was a Christian nation - and more specifically, a white Christian nation - took root and grew.

It's a bitter irony, isn't it? A nation founded on the principle of religious freedom became a breeding ground for a narrow, exclusionary form of Christian Nationalism.

By the time we reach the end of the 19th century, the seeds planted in colonial times had grown into a twisted tree. The idea that to be truly American was to be Christian, and usually white, had become deeply entrenched.

And as we'll see, this toxic ideology was just getting started. The 20th century would bring new challenges, new forms of oppression, and new ways for Christian Nationalism to adapt and thrive.

These poisonous ideas still snake their way through Christian communities today. Even in my own childhood as a millennial, I remember family members explaining to me that black people's suffering throughout history was because of the "Curse of Ham." Rather than confront the dark truth of systematic oppression and racism, they clung to this biblical distortion that conveniently absolved them, their ancestors, and Christianity itself of any responsibility.

This isn't ancient history. In 2018, I experienced just how alive these ideas still are. My wife and I were at the lake with another family - people we knew from church, whose kids were friends with ours at school. We'd been building this friendship for years.

As we sat in lawn chairs in the shallow water, the father said, "Black people's brains are smaller than white people's." Just like that, speaking this racist pseudoscience as if it were obvious truth. I tried to challenge him, to lead him toward understanding the scientific and moral bankruptcy of his statements, but the roots of his beliefs ran too deep. Some weeds are so thoroughly entwined with the soil that pulling them out would require uprooting the entire garden. But what struck me wasn't just the blatant racism. It was how comfortable he felt expressing it, assuming that as fellow Christians, we'd share his views.

These aren't isolated incidents. They're symptoms of how Christian nationalism has kept these racist ideologies alive, wrapping them in religious language to make them more palatable. The same theological gymnastics used to justify slavery in the 1800s still happen during church potlucks and lakeside conversations today. We've just dressed them up in more respectable clothes.

As we move forward in our exploration, keep this in mind. The shadows we're about to encounter don't come out of nowhere. They stretch all the way back to our beginnings.

And here's a question to ponder: If the roots of Christian Nationalism in America are so deeply entwined with oppression and exclusion, can it ever truly reflect the teachings of Christ? Or is it time to untangle our faith from our nationalism once and for all?

The Antebellum South: a time and place where Christian faith and chattel slavery walked hand in hand, where the word of God was twisted into a whip, where the cross cast a shadow as dark as any auction block.

You see, by the early 19th century, slavery had become more than just an economic system in the South. It had become a way of life, a social order, a moral framework. And at the heart of this framework? A perverse interpretation of Christianity that not only tolerated slavery but actively defended it.

Let me introduce you to some names you probably didn't hear in Sunday School: Richard Furman, James Henley Thornwell, Robert Lewis Dabney. These weren't fringe lunatics or backwoods preachers. These were respected theologians, influential leaders in the Southern church.

And they used their considerable intellectual and spiritual authority to craft a "biblical" defense of slavery that shaped the mindset of an entire region. Their arguments? Oh, they were something else.

They pointed to the patriarchs of the Old Testament, men like Abraham and Jacob, who enslaved people. They cited the Apostle Paul's letters, which instructed enslaved people to obey their masters. They argued that slavery was a divinely sanctioned institution, a means of Christianizing and civilizing African "heathens."

Remember that "Curse of Ham" we discussed earlier? It became the crown jewel in their twisted theology. That story from Genesis about Noah and his sons - where Ham sees his father naked and drunk and tells his brothers, leading Noah to curse Ham's son Canaan - became their divine mandate for slavery. These antebellum theologians took this obscure passage, which never mentions race or prescribes perpetual chattel slavery, and spun it into a comprehensive defense of enslaving African people.

They argued that Black people were descendants of Ham, cursed by God to serve white people, who were supposedly descendants of Noah's other sons. It's an interpretation so twisted, so far removed from the spirit of Christ's teachings, that it would be laughable if it hadn't caused so much suffering. But, this wasn't just some abstract theological debate. This "biblical" defense of slavery had real, horrific consequences.

It gave owners of the enslaved divine permission to treat human beings as property. It allowed Christians to attend church on Sunday and oversee brutal punishments on Monday. It created a cognitive dissonance so profound that people could claim to follow a God of love while denying the very humanity of their fellow men and women.

I think about the enslaved people who heard these sermons, who were told that their bondage was God's will. How do you reconcile that with a loving God? How do you hold onto faith when it's being used as a tool of your oppression?

And yet, remarkably, many did. They found in the same Bible a message of liberation, a God who sided with the oppressed, a Christ who came to set the captives free. Their faith became a source of strength and resilience in the face of unimaginable cruelty.

You can hear it in their spirituals, songs that spoke of freedom in this world and the next. One that always gets me is "Oh Freedom." Just listen to these words:

> Oh, freedom, oh freedom, oh freedom over me
> And before I'd be a slave, I'd be buried in my grave
> And go home to my Lord and be free
> No more weeping, no more weeping, no more weeping
>   over me
> And before I'd be a slave, I'd be buried in my grave
> And go home to my Lord and be free
> No more mourning, no more mourning, no more
>   mourning over me
> And before I'd be a slave, I'd be buried in my grave
> And go home to my Lord and be free

— 4.5

There's a defiance in these lyrics, a hope that refuses to be crushed. It's a declaration that true freedom - the freedom of the soul, the freedom promised by Christ - can't be taken away by any earthly master.

When I hear these words, I can't help but think about the stark contrast between this faith and the twisted theology of their owners. Here were enslaved people, holding onto a vision of God that offered liberation and dignity, while their oppressors used the same Bible to justify bondage and cruelty. It's a powerful reminder that the message of Christ, when embraced in its fullness, is inherently liberating.

But for the white South, this perverted theology became a cornerstone of their worldview. It wasn't just about justifying slavery anymore. It was about creating a Christian national identity that was inextricably linked with white supremacy.

This is where Christian Nationalism really starts to bear its ugly head. It's not just about believing America is a Christian nation anymore. It's about believing America is a white Christian nation, divinely ordained to maintain a racial hierarchy.

And even after slavery was abolished, this ideology didn't die. It evolved. It adapted. The "Curse of Ham" became Jim Crow. The divine right of the owners of enslaved people became the divine right of segregationists.

The seeds planted in colonial times, watered with the blood and tears of enslaved people, had grown into a poisonous tree that would continue to bear bitter fruit for generations to come.

As we move forward in our story, keep this in mind. The Christian Nationalism that we struggle with today didn't come out of nowhere. Its roots run deep into the blood-soaked soil of the Antebellum South.

And it forces us to ask some hard questions: How do we reckon with this history? How do we untangle the faith from the twisted theology that was used to justify such cruelty? And most importantly, how do we ensure that we're not continuing to perpetuate these harmful ideologies, even in more subtle forms?

The truth is, the ghosts of the Antebellum South still haunt us. And until we exorcise them, we can never truly live up to the ideals of either our faith or our nation.

The Emancipation Proclamation was signed, the 13th, 14th, and 15th Amendments were passed, and you'd think that would be the end of it. You'd hope that Christians, especially, would embrace this new era of legal equality and strive to create a society that reflected Christ's teachings of love and brotherhood.

But that's not what happened. Not by a long shot.

Instead, as Reconstruction gave way to the Jim Crow era, we saw the rise of a new form of Christian Nationalism. One that cloaked itself in respectability and divine mandate, but at its core was just as committed to white supremacy as its antebellum predecessor.

Churches across the South - and many in the North - began to embrace segregation not just as a social custom or legal requirement, but as God's will. They developed a theology of separation that turned Christ's message of unity on its head.

This wasn't just happening in the immediate aftermath of the Civil War. This poison ran deep, persisting well into the 20th century and beyond. I remember a shocking revelation I had as an adult in 2017 about my childhood church.

Growing up, I always wondered why we didn't have any black people in our congregation. I naively assumed it was because there weren't any around, which was partially true. But the real truth, when I finally learned it, was quite unsettling.

There was a man in our church who had the unspoken assignment to turn away black people, telling them they needed to find another church. This discovery left me confused. It was like finding out your childhood home was actually an underground bunker and I had been raised by a kidnapper - everything I thought I knew about my church, my community, suddenly felt unstable. It wasn't just disappointment or anger I felt, but a profound sense of disorientation. How could a place that had taught me about love and acceptance have harbored such blatant discrimination?

This wasn't ancient history - this was

happening in my lifetime, as a millennial, in a church I thought I knew.

Just as I wasn't aware of it, I'm sure many others weren't aware either. But it was known by at least some that called themselves Christian's or I wouldn't have heard about it from someone that knew him. By the time I heard about it, he had already passed away, which probably allowed the person some freedom to share it.

But, this isn't just about one church or one man. This revealed that the tentacles of segregation and racism reached far deeper into our religious institutions than I had ever imagined. It made me question how much of what I'd been taught about faith and community was tainted by this legacy.

It made me realize that the legacy of Jim Crow wasn't just something in history books. It was alive and well, hiding in plain sight in the very institutions that were supposed to be beacons of love and acceptance. It dressed itself in a respectable suit and tie, led a class during Sunday school, and opened the worship services with prayer.

But how did we get here? How did the church become so entangled with the ideology of segregation?

Part of it was the resurrection of old justifications. The "Curse of Ham" theory that had been used to defend slavery was repurposed to argue for segregation. Pastors and theologians twisted scripture to claim that God had ordained separate races and wanted them to remain separate.

They pointed to Acts 17:26, "From one man he made all the nations, that they should inhabit the whole earth; and he marked out their appointed times in history and the boundaries of their lands" - and argued that this justified racial segregation. Never mind that the verse is about God's creation of all humanity from a common ancestor. Never mind that it says nothing about race.

This wasn't just happening in small, rural churches either. Some of the most prestigious theological institutions in the South were teaching these ideas. They were producing generation after generation of pastors who went out into the world believing that white supremacy was God's plan for America.

And so, churches became not just supporters of segregation, but enforcers of it. They were segregated spaces themselves, of course. But more than that, they provided the moral and theological justification for the entire Jim Crow system.

This is Christian Nationalism in its naked form. It's not just about believing America is a Christian nation anymore. It's about believing America is a white Christian nation, where segregation is divine law and equality is heresy.

As we move into the Civil Rights era, we need to remember this: The theology of segregation didn't just disappear. It evolved. It adapted. It found new ways to justify old hatreds.

And it forces us to ask: How much of this ideology still lingers in our churches today? How often do we use our faith to justify systems of oppression, even if they're more subtle than Jim Crow?

Because here's the truth: The ghosts of segregation still haunt us. My experience with my childhood church is testament to that. And until we confront these ghosts head-on, until we root out every vestige of this twisted theology in our own hearts, we can never truly claim to be following the Christ who came to break down every dividing wall.

The 1950s and 60s. A time of change, of hope, of struggle. And a time when Christian Nationalism faced its greatest challenge yet: a movement that dared to take the teachings of Jesus seriously.

The Civil Rights Movement didn't just confront segregation laws. It confronted the very theology that had been used to justify those laws for generations. And in doing so, it exposed the deep rifts within American Christianity.

On one side, you had the likes of Martin Luther King Jr., Fred Shuttlesworth, and John Lewis. Men and women who saw in their faith a call to justice, to equality, to beloved community. They preached a Christianity of liberation, one that challenged the status quo and demanded America live up to its professed ideals.

On the other side? The defenders of "the Southern way of life." Pastors, politicians, and ordinary citizens who clung to a vision of Christian America that was white, segregated, and deeply afraid of change.

The battle lines were drawn, and they ran right through the center isle and right through the heart of the church.

I remember learning about this era in school, but it wasn't until much later that I really understood how central Christianity was to both sides of the struggle. We'd hear about King's "I Have a Dream" speech, but not about how deeply it was rooted in biblical imagery. We'd learn about bus boycotts and lunch counter sit-ins, but not about the prayer meetings and church gatherings that fueled them.

And we certainly didn't hear much about the Christian's arguments used to oppose civil rights.

But make no mistake, those arguments were loud and plentiful. Take the Reverend Jerry Falwell Sr., who would later become a key figure in the Moral Majority. In 1958, he thundered from his pulpit:

 If Chief Justice Warren and his associates had known God's word and had desired to do the Lord's will, I am quite confident that the 1954 decision would never have been made... The facilities should be separate. When God has drawn a line of distinction, we should not attempt to cross that line.

— 4.6

This wasn't just Falwell's opinion. This was a common belief among white Christians who saw integration as a threat not just to their social order, but to their understanding of God's will. They called it "massive resistance." A campaign of legal and extra-legal tactics designed to subvert desegregation efforts. And at every step, they clothed their resistance in religious language.

When the Little Rock Nine tried to integrate Central High School in 1957, they were met not just with angry mobs, but with pastors declaring integration a sin against God's ordained order.

When Freedom Riders were beaten and buses were burned, there were Christians quoting scripture to justify the violence.

And when King and other civil rights leaders called for federal intervention to protect Black citizens' rights, they were denounced as communists and antichrists by preachers across the South.

The establishment of private Christian schools, often referred to as "segregation academies," was a significant development during this period. These institutions emerged in response to desegregation efforts, particularly after the Brown v. Board of Education decision in 1954. Many of these schools were founded with the explicit purpose of maintaining racial segregation in education.

I can speak to this personally. When I moved to Little Rock, Arkansas, I was initially confused by the abundance of private schools in the area. It wasn't until I began to learn more about the city's history of educational racial tensions that I understood the root cause. From the busing controversies to the historic stand of the Little Rock Nine, the city's educational landscape had been shaped by decades of racial conflict.

What I discovered was that these private schools were largely a result of "white flight" - the exodus of white families from public schools in response to integration. This exodus left a vacuum in the public school system, the effects of which are still felt to this day. In Little Rock, I learned a phrase I had never encountered in Tulsa: "academic distress." A majority of Little Rock's public schools are categorized under this term, highlighting the ongoing struggles of a system depleted by decades of segregationist policies and their aftermath.

The private Christian schools presented a complex challenge. While their founders often cited religious freedom and parental choice as justifications, the timing and context of their creation made their purpose clear: to provide an alternative to integrated public schools for white students.

This phenomenon highlighted how religious institutions could be used to circumvent the moral obligation of civil rights, blurring the lines between religious liberty and racial discrimination. It demonstrated the lengths to which some were willing to go to maintain segregation, even as legal barriers were falling.

This era laid bare the fundamental contradiction at the heart of Christian Nationalism: the claim to follow Christ while defending systems of oppression that Christ would have condemned.

But while the defenders of segregation were loud, they weren't the only Christian voices in this struggle. The Civil Rights Movement was deeply, profoundly Christian in its own right.

King's dream of a beloved community wasn't just a political

vision. It was a theological one, rooted in the belief that all people are created in God's image and that the arc of the moral universe bends towards justice.

The freedom songs that sustained marchers in the face of violence weren't just protest anthems. They were spirituals, drawing on a long tradition of finding hope and resilience in faith.

Consider the song "We Shall Overcome," as one of the many freedom songs sung during Civil Rights marches:

> We Shall Overcome, we shall overcome
> We shall overcome someday.
> Oh, deep in my heart, I do believe,
> We shall overcome someday.
> The Lord will see us through, the Lord will see us
>   through,
> The Lord will see us through someday.
> Oh, deep in my heart, I do believe,
> We shall overcome someday.
> Black and white together, Black and white together,
> Black and white together someday.
> Oh, deep in my heart, I do believe,
> We shall overcome someday.

— 4.7

And the demands for equality and justice weren't just appeals to the Constitution. They were calls for America to live up to the Christian principles it claimed to embody.

This was a battle for the soul of American Christianity as much as it was a battle for civil rights. And it forced Christians across the country to confront a hard question: Which side of this struggle truly reflected the teachings of Christ?

For many, the answer was clear. The Civil Rights Movement sparked a great awakening, challenging Christians to confront the ways their faith had been coopted by racism and nationalism.

But for others, the Civil Rights era only hardened their commitment to a white Christian America. As legal segregation crumbled, they sought new ways to maintain their power and privilege, often under the guise of defending "traditional values" or "religious freedom."

The echoes of this struggle still carry on today. The theological arguments used to defend segregation may have changed their form, but their essence persists in debates over everything from immigration to voting rights.

And it leaves us with a pressing question: How do we reckon with this history? How do we confront the ways Christian Nationalism has been used to justify oppression, even as we celebrate the Christians who stood on the front lines of the fight for justice?

Because, the Civil Rights Movement didn't end Christian Nationalism. It just forced it to evolve. And understanding how it adapted is key to recognizing its presence in our churches and our politics today.

As the 1960s gave way to the 1970s, yet again, Christian Nationalism in America didn't fade away, it evolved. This era saw the birth of what we now call the Religious Right, a movement that would profoundly reshape the landscape of both American Christianity and politics.

The key players in this new movement were a mix of familiar faces and new strategists. Jerry Falwell Sr., who had once preached against integration, found a new calling. Pat Robertson's Christian Broadcasting Network, which had been blending religion and conservative politics since the 60s, stepped into a more overtly political role. And behind the scenes, a lesser-known but crucial figure emerged: Paul Weyrich, the architect of this new coalition.

In 1979, Weyrich and Falwell founded the Moral Majority, marking a turning point in the relationship between conservative Christianity and American politics. The organization claimed to stand for "traditional family values," but beneath the surface, one could see the same old Christian Nationalism that had defended segregation just a decade earlier. The language had changed, but the underlying ideology (the belief in a white, Christian America) remained.

What made the Moral Majority different, and ultimately more successful, than its predecessors was its political savvy. They broadened their appeal beyond explicit racial issues, finding new battlegrounds in abortion, school prayer, and homosexuality. This pivot allowed them to cast themselves as defenders of morality rather than opponents of civil rights, maintaining the essence of Christian Nationalism while shedding its most overtly racist elements.

The impact of this movement wasn't just political; it was deeply personal, reshaping the lives of countless American families, including my own. I was born in the early 1980s in Tulsa, Oklahoma, into a world already being molded by these new and powerful religious leaders. Though I was too young to understand it then, the names Falwell, Robertson, and Gothard were more than just sounds in our household; they were guiding voices.

My parents, like many in their generation, found something compelling in these teachings. They attended conferences, bought books, and even chose homeschool curricula based on these leaders' principles. As I grew older and we moved within Oklahoma, the influence of the Religious Right remained a constant in our lives.

Looking back now, I can understand why these teachings

held such appeal for my parents' generation. The 1960s and 70s had brought seismic shifts in American culture. Traditional values seemed under attack from all sides—the sexual revolution, the anti-war movement, and the push for gender equality. For many Christians who had grown up in the 1950s, the world they knew was disappearing. The women's rights movement, which I had only known as "feminism" at the time, was particularly jarring. With rallying cries like "I am woman, hear me roar," it challenged long-held beliefs about gender roles and societal structures.

In this context, the message of the Religious Right wasn't just appealing; it was a lifeline. It offered a return to certainty, a clear moral framework in a time of ambiguity. It provided answers to complex questions and a sense of purpose in a changing world. Moreover, it allowed them to reconcile their faith with their patriotism in a way that felt seamless and natural. To be a good Christian was to be a good American, and vice versa.

The Religious Right also focused on shaping culture beyond politics. Figures like Bill Gothard, whose Institute in Basic Life Principles gained significant influence in the 70s and 80s, presented a totalistic worldview where every aspect of life —from family structure to civic engagement—was filtered through a narrow interpretation of scripture that conveniently aligned with existing power structures and cultural hierarchies.

To be clear, I'm not suggesting it's unbiblical to live every area of your life according to biblical teachings. The issue arises when this concept becomes kneaded into the dough of patriotism in a way that combines the Manifest Destiny doctrine or the Crusader mentality into what should be a straightforward command to love your neighbor. It's this subtle shift from a holistic, Christ-centered faith to a nationalistic ideology that can lead to a distortion of Christ's teachings and biblical values.

I remember the sense of community it fostered. Our church wasn't just a place of worship; it was a cultural bubble, a safe haven from the perceived dangers of secular society. The lines between faith, politics, and national identity blurred until they were almost indistinguishable.

But as comforting as this worldview was, and as genuine as my parents' embrace of it was, it came with significant problems. It created a version of Christianity that was more focused on cultural battles than on the teachings of Jesus. It prioritized moral certainty over compassion, political victory over service to others. Most troublingly, it perpetuated a narrow vision of what it meant to be both Christian and American, a vision that often excluded those who didn't fit a particular cultural or racial mold.

The birth of the Religious Right marked a new chapter in the story of Christian Nationalism in America. It made the movement more palatable, more mainstream, and ultimately, more influential. But it also set the stage for the deep divisions we see in American Christianity today. It created a version of faith so intertwined with political ideology that many find it hard to separate the two.

As I've grown and formed my own understanding of faith and citizenship, I've had to bear this legacy. I've had to question beliefs I once took for granted and confront the ways in which this ideology has shaped my worldview. It's a journey that's been both painful and liberating, painful because it's meant reconsidering some of the fundamental teachings of my youth, liberating because it's allowed me to discover a faith that I believe is truer to the teachings of Jesus.

As we continue to explore the modern manifestations of Christian Nationalism, it's crucial to understand this history—not to vilify those who embraced it, but to understand its appeal and its consequences. Only then can we begin to chart a path forward that honors both our faith and our diverse national identity.

The Religious Right didn't just reshape our politics - it rewired our spiritual DNA. And like any genetic mutation, its effects ripple through generations, affecting not just what we believe but how we believe. To understand its full impact, we need to look further back, to a moment when another empire first merged the cross with the crown. Because sometimes, to understand a disease, you have to find patient zero.

5

THE CONSTANTINE EFFECT
THE RISE OF CHRISTIAN NATIONALISM

To understand the full impact of Christian Nationalism in America, we need to zoom out for a moment. Way out. Let's time travel back to the 4th century AD, to the reign of Roman Emperor Constantine the Great. Now, you might be wondering, "What does a Roman Emperor have to do with modern American Christianity?" The answer is: everything.

Constantine's conversion to Christianity in 312 AD is often hailed as a turning point in Christian history. And it was - but not always in the way we might think. When Constantine embraced Christianity, he didn't just change his personal faith. He changed the entire relationship between Christianity and state power. In not so many years following the conversion, the persecuted became the privileged. The faith of outcasts became the faith of emperors. Christianity went from being a marginalized, often oppressed religious movement to being the official religion of the most powerful empire in the world.

When Christianity became entwined with state power, it also became a tool of state power. The radical, counter-cultural message of Jesus began to be co-opted to serve the interests of the empire. This is what I call the "Constantine Effect" - the profound and often problematic changes that occur when a faith becomes aligned with political power.

Fast forward to modern America, and we see the echoes of Constantine everywhere in Christian Nationalism. The story of Constantine's conversion and his use of Christian symbols to legitimize his rule provides a unique parallel to today's merging of faith and political power.

Legend has it that on the eve of a crucial battle, Constantine had a vision. He saw a symbol in the sky - the Chi-Rho, one of the earliest Christian symbols formed by superimposing the first two letters of the Greek word for Christ. Along with this symbol came a message: "In this sign, you will conquer" (in Latin, "in hoc signo vinces"). Constantine, seizing on this divine endorsement, had the Chi-Rho emblazoned on his soldiers' shields. After his victory, he adopted it as his military standard. In one fell swoop, he had merged Christian symbolism with military might, setting a dangerous precedent for using religious imagery to justify political and military power.

This fusion of faith and force, of divine sanction and earthly conquest, lies at the very heart of Christian Nationalism. Just as Constantine used the Chi-Rho to claim God's endorsement for his rule, we see modern politicians wrapping themselves in the flag and the cross, implying divine approval for their policies and actions. The echoes of "In hoc signo vinces" reverberate through the halls of our churches today. We hear it in the rhetoric of those who speak of "taking America back," in the language of spiritual warfare applied to political opponents, in the portrayal of election victories as divine mandates.

When we use Christian symbols or language to advance political agendas, when we claim God's endorsement for our partisan positions, when we paint our opponents as enemies of

God rather than fellow citizens with different views, we are engaging in shav'. We are using God's name for empty, false purposes, just as surely as Constantine did when he turned the Chi-Rho into a battle symbol.

This modern shav' is perhaps even more dangerous than its ancient counterparts. It doesn't just misuse God's name; it misrepresents His very character, turning the Prince of Peace into a warlord, the servant King into a political powerbroker. It replaces the transformative power of Christ's love with the coercive power of legislation and cultural dominance.

Just as the Roman Empire began to use Christianity to define who was a "true" Roman citizen, we see attempts to define "real" Americans as those who adhere to a particular brand of Christianity. I remember growing up with this mindset. In our house, being a good Christian and being a good American were so intertwined as to be almost indistinguishable. We'd pledge allegiance to the flag at our homeschool and Boy Scout events, then open and close with a prayer - and somehow, it all felt like part of the same devotion.

When Christianity becomes a tool of the state, it's not just the state that changes. Christianity itself is transformed. The faith of a crucified Messiah who championed the poor and challenged the powerful becomes the faith of the powerful, used to maintain the status quo. We see this play out in American history time and again. Christian rhetoric has been used to justify everything from slavery to segregation, from xenophobia to economic policies that hurt the very people Jesus called us to serve.

The Constantine Effect isn't just ancient history. It's a perpetual temptation for people of faith, especially when we find ourselves in positions of cultural or political influence. As we continue to struggle with Christian Nationalism in America, the story of Constantine serves as both a warning and a challenge. It reminds us that the marriage of faith and state power, while often attractive, comes with significant dangers. It calls us to constantly examine our motives, to ask ourselves whether we're seeking to build God's kingdom or our own earthly empires.

Just as Constantine's fusion of Christianity with state power set a dangerous precedent, perhaps no historical example better illustrates the perils of Christian Nationalism than Nazi Germany. It's a chapter of history that many American Christians would prefer to forget or dismiss as irrelevant. But if we're serious about understanding the dangers of merging faith with nationalism, we must confront this dark mirror.

The artifacts of this merger still exist - tangible remnants that force us to confront uncomfortable truths. The German Wehrmacht belt buckle stands as a chilling testament, with "Gott mit uns" (God with us) emblazoned across its surface. This wasn't just a piece of military equipment - it was a symbol worn by soldiers claiming divine sanction for their actions.

In the years leading up to Hitler's rise to power, many German Christians faced a choice that feels eerily familiar: embrace a strongman leader promising to restore national greatness and traditional values, or stand against the rising tide of communism and secular modernism. The majority chose the former, seeing in Hitler a defender of Christian civilization.

The evidence is overwhelming and demands our attention. In a Munich speech on April 12, 1922, Hitler proclaimed, "My feeling as a Christian points me to my Lord and Savior as a fighter."[5.1] The crowd, filled with self-proclaimed Christians, erupted in approving applause. Later, in a Berlin address on October 24, 1933, he declared, "The National Socialist State professes its allegiance to positive Christianity."[5.2] In *Mein Kampf*, he wrote with chilling confidence, "Hence today I believe that I am acting in accordance with the will of the Almighty Creator."[5.3]

The response from Christian institutions was equally disturbing. Paul Althaus, a leading theologian, wrote, "Our Protestant churches have welcomed the turning point of 1933 as a gift and miracle of God."[5.4] referring to the appointment of Hitler as Chancellor of Germany. Protestant pastor Hermann Gruner went further: "The time is fulfilled for the German people of Hitler. It is because of Hitler that Christ, God the helper and redeemer, has become effective among us. ... Hitler is the way of the Spirit and the will of God for the German people to enter the Church of Christ."[5.5] These weren't fringe voices - they represented mainstream Christian leadership.

The corruption of faith ran deep. Churches removed crucifixes and replaced them with Hitler's portrait. Some even placed *Mein Kampf* on their altars alongside - or in place of - the Bible. The "German Christian" movement actively worked to align Protestant Christianity with Nazi ideology, rewriting hymns to include Nazi themes and creating a nationalistic version of faith that emphasized Aryan supremacy.

Growing up, I was taught that these changes were forced upon the churches by the Nazi regime - that Hitler's portraits and Nazi symbols were displayed under duress. It was a comforting thought that painted Christians as victims rather than willing participants. But the historical truth is far more unsettling: many of these changes came from within the churches themselves. The German Christian movement wasn't a Nazi imposition on unwilling congregations; it was a grassroots movement of Protestant Christians eagerly aligning their faith with Nazi ideology. Church leaders and congregations voluntarily removed crucifixes, added Hitler's portrait, and adapted their theology to match Nazi racial theories - not because they were forced to, but because they believed in the cause. This willing participation makes the history even more challenging to confront.

Biblical interpretation itself became a tool of nationalism. Theological seminaries incorporated Nazi racial theories into their curriculum. The Theological Faculty of the University of Jena published commentaries arguing that Jesus was not Jewish but rather a Nordic warrior fighting against Jewish legalism emphasizing an "Aryan Jesus" and stripping Him of His Jewish identity.[5.6] This wasn't strategic manipulation by the Nazi state - it represented a genuine fusion of Christian faith with nationalist ideology in the minds of many believers.

Not all Christians supported Hitler, of course. The Confessing Church, led by figures like Dietrich Bonhoeffer, stood in opposition to the Nazi regime and its corruption of Christian faith. But they were a minority. Most Christians either actively supported the regime or remained silent in the face of growing evil.

This silence of the majority is perhaps the most chilling parallel to our own time. How many German Christians told themselves they were "just being patriotic" as their Jewish neighbors disappeared? How many justified their support of Hitler as "choosing the lesser evil" or "protecting Christian values"? How many convinced themselves that national loyalty and Christian faith were one and the same?

The lesson isn't that American Christian Nationalism is identical to Nazi Germany. Such a direct comparison would be simplistic and unhelpful. Rather, the lesson is that the merger of Christian faith with nationalist ideology can blind believers to very real evils, can justify very real oppression, and can lead very good people to support very bad things.

When Christianity becomes too closely aligned with national identity and political power, it loses its prophetic voice. It loses its ability to speak truth to power, to stand with the marginalized, to be the conscience of the nation. Instead, it becomes a tool of the state, a religious veneer for political power.

This is why the story of German Christianity under Nazi rule must serve as a warning. It shows us how easily faith can be corrupted when it becomes entangled with nationalism. It reveals how gradually good people can be led astray when they confuse love of country with love of God.

Most crucially, it reminds us that the choice between authentic faith and nationalist ideology isn't always obvious. It often comes in small steps, subtle compromises, quiet accommodations to power. By the time the true nature of the choice becomes clear, many find they've already chosen - and chosen poorly.

As we examine Christian Nationalism in our own time, we would do well to remember this history. Not because our situation is identical, but because the underlying dynamics - the temptation to merge faith with nationalism, the gradual compromise of values, the silence in the face of evil - remain the same.

The question for us, as it was for German Christians in the 1930s, is this: Will we recognize the danger before it's too late? Will we have the courage to disentangle our faith from nationalism, to speak truth to power, to stand with the marginalized even when it costs us something?

The stakes may not seem as high today, but the choice is just as real. And just as consequential. Because once faith becomes a tool of nationalism, it ceases to be faith at all. It becomes shav', a corruption of everything it was meant to be.

At this point, I wish I could offer a break from the dark and heavy history. Unfortunately, we must press on to fully grasp the historical significance of how Christian Nationalism has been wielded in the past. To do so, we'll journey back once again—this time to the year 1095, at the dawn of the Crusades, to examine another pivotal chapter in this story.

When we think of the Crusades, many picture medieval knights in shining armor, marching off to the Holy Land in the Lord's name. It's easy to dismiss this as ancient history, a relic of a less enlightened time. But the reality of the Crusades, and the mentality that drove them, isn't as far removed from our modern world as we might like to think.

Growing up, I was fed a sanitized version of the Crusades. They were presented as a noble Christian response to Muslim aggression, a heroic effort to reclaim the Holy Land from the godless hordes. Muslims were painted as the epitome of evil, the devil incarnate, threatening the very existence of Christendom.

It wasn't until much later that I learned the brutal truth. The Crusades weren't just a defensive reaction; they were a series of nine religiously sanctioned military campaigns, spanning roughly two hundred years. These weren't just battles over territory. They were holy wars, where conquest and genocide were justified in the name of God.

The First Crusade, launched in 1095, was a response to an appeal from the Byzantine Emperor for help against the Seljuk Turks. But what began as a call for aid quickly morphed into something far more sinister. Pope Urban II framed it as a righteous war, promising remission of sins for those who took up arms. Suddenly, butchering your fellow man wasn't just acceptable - it was a fast track to heaven.

The results were catastrophic. When the crusaders took Jerusalem in 1099, they massacred much of the city's Muslim and Jewish population. Men, women, and children were slaughtered in the name of Christ. The crusaders' own accounts describe the streets running ankle-deep with blood.

While exact casualties from the Crusades are difficult to

determine given the limitations of medieval record-keeping, historians estimate that between 1 and 9 million people died across all nine Crusades. The Fourth Crusade in 1204 saw Christian armies sacking the Christian city of Constantinople, pillaging its treasures and desecrating its churches. These numbers represent not just military casualties, but entire communities - men, women, and children - wiped out in the name of Jesus.

The Crusades should serve as a reminder of how the command to love our neighbors can be perverted into a license to slaughter them instead. When we demonize those of other faiths, when we frame political conflicts in terms of holy wars, when we claim divine sanction for our own agendas - we're not far removed from those medieval crusaders. We're using the same playbook, just with different targets.

In fact, the echoes of the Crusades mentality persist through American Christian Nationalism in ways that are both subtle and deeply concerning. I'm not suggesting that modern Christian nationalists are literally calling for armed religious conquests. But the underlying ideology - the belief that we're engaged in a spiritual battle of good versus evil, with America as God's chosen instrument - bears an uncomfortable resemblance to the mindset that fueled the Crusades.

I remember growing up immersed in this worldview. In our church, America wasn't just a nation; it was God's nation, locked in a spiritual battle against the forces of darkness. We read books like This Present Darkness and sang songs about being "Christian soldiers" and talked about "taking back" America. It all seemed so righteous, so clear-cut.

But this fusion of faith, patriotism, and a sense of divine mission extended far beyond the church walls. I vividly recall my parents' involvement in Amway, the multi-level marketing company. At every Amway rally - or as my grandfather called them, "hoorah meetings" - we witnessed a powerful blend of the American Dream and God's divine will for us to achieve it. These events weren't just about business; they were a celebration of a particular version of the American Dream, one that inextricably linked Christian faith with national identity and capitalist success.

The soundtrack to these rallies was a mix of patriotic and religious fervor. We'd sing or listen to recordings of songs such as "God Bless America:"

> God bless America, land that I love
> Stand beside her and guide her
> Through the night with a light from above

— 5.7

Or "God Bless the USA:"

> And I'm proud to be an American
> Where at least I know I'm free
> And I won't forget the men who died
> Who gave that right to me
> And I'd gladly stand up next to you
> And defend Her still today
> 'Cause there ain't no doubt I love this land
> God Bless the U.S.A.

— 5.8

And then there's "America the Beautiful:"

> America! America!

God shed His grace on thee
And crown thy good with brotherhood
From sea to shining sea

— 5.9

These songs were either played on cassette as people sang along or led by artists such as The Gaither Vocal Band or The Goads. The lyrics weren't just words to us; they were declarations of America's divine purpose and our role in it. I remember my mother often tearing up at the end of God Bless the USA. Now I want to be clear, these were tears of thankfulness to God for placing us here, not to dominate others but of genuine gratitude. But without consciously realizing it, these lyrics continued to merge faith and patriotism in our minds.

This merger of faith, patriotism, and economic success created a potent worldview - one that cast America's role in almost messianic terms. It was a short step from seeing our nation as uniquely blessed to viewing our cultural and economic systems as divinely ordained. And herein lies the danger.

When you start seeing political, cultural, and even economic conflicts as holy wars, it becomes dangerously easy to demonize your opponents. After all, if you're fighting for God, anyone who disagrees with you must be against God, right?

This crusader mentality manifests in various ways in modern America. We see it in the language of "culture wars," in the portrayal of political opponents as not just wrong, but evil. We see it in foreign policy rhetoric that casts international conflicts in religious terms, framing America's geopolitical interests as divinely ordained missions.

Perhaps most troublingly, we see it in the way some Christians approach evangelism and social issues. Instead of seeing the sharing of faith as an act of love and invitation, it becomes a conquest - a mission to defeat the enemy and claim God's territory. And once we've claimed it, what do we do? We piss all over it like a bunch of dogs marking their turf. "This fire hydrant belongs to Jesus now, boys!" It'd be laughable if it weren't so damn tragic.

This crusader mentality turns the great commission into a spiritual game of "Capture the Flag," with us strutting around like we're God's own personal territory markers. We've traded in the shepherd's staff for a can of spiritual spray paint, tagging everything in sight with our brand.

I've had to confront this mentality in myself. How often have I approached disagreements, even within the church, with a "crusader" mindset? How many times have I been more concerned with winning an argument than with showing Christ's love?

The dangers of this mentality are profound. Just as the historical Crusades led to untold suffering and actually hindered the spread of the Gospel, the modern crusader mentality often achieves the opposite of its intended effect. Instead of drawing people to Christ, it pushes them away. Instead of showcasing God's love, it displays human arrogance and aggression.

Moreover, this mentality distorts the very essence of Christ's teachings. Jesus didn't call us to conquer; He called us to serve. He didn't tell us to defeat our enemies; He told us to love them. The kingdom He proclaimed wasn't one of earthly power, but of self-sacrificial love.

As I've grown in my faith and understanding, I've struggled with how deeply this crusader mentality had influenced my worldview. Unlearning it has been a challenging but liberating process. It's meant embracing a faith that's more about bridge-building than fortress-defending, more about listening than conquering.

The Crusader mentality in modern Christian Nationalism presents a significant challenge. It turns faith into a weapon, converts potential dialogue into conflict, and often leads to a tragic misrepresentation of Christ's message.

But there's hope. By recognizing this mentality for what it is - a distortion of Christian teachings - we can begin to chart a different course. We can embrace a faith that engages with the world not through conquest, but through compassion. Not through domination, but through dialogue.

As we continue to examine Christian Nationalism, let's keep this lesson from the Crusades in mind. Let's ask ourselves: Are we using our faith as a banner to march under, or as a towel to wash their feet? Are we more interested in winning battles, or in winning hearts?

The answers to these questions will shape not just our personal faith journeys, but the very nature of Christianity's role in American public life. And they might just determine whether our faith is a force for division and conflict, or for healing and reconciliation in our fractured world.

The concept of Manifest Destiny stands as one of the most potent examples of how religious rhetoric has been used to justify national ambitions and, in the process, cause immense harm. Manifest Destiny wasn't just about territorial expansion. It was about divine right - about God's will for America.

The term was coined in 1845 by journalist John L. O'Sullivan, who wrote of "our manifest destiny to overspread the continent allotted by Providence for the free development of our yearly multiplying millions."[5.10] Growing up, I remember learning about Manifest Destiny in school. It was presented as this grand, almost romantic idea - brave pioneers striking out into the wilderness, fulfilling America's God-given purpose.

What they didn't tell us - or at least, what they glossed over - was the human cost of this "destiny." Because Manifest Destiny wasn't just about empty land waiting to be settled. It was about land that was already inhabited by Native American nations who had lived there for generations, by Mexican communities in the Southwest. This "destiny" meant displacement, war, cultural destruction, and death for these peoples.

And all of it was justified with biblical language. Senator Thomas Hart Benton, arguing for the annexation of Oregon in 1846, declared:

> It would seem that the White race alone received the divine command, to subdue and replenish the earth! For it is the only race that has obeyed it— the only one that hunts out new and distant lands, and even a New World, to subdue and replenish.
> 5.11

The arrogance, the casual racism, the twisting of scripture to justify conquest - it made me realize how deeply this ideology had shaped our national identity. Manifest Destiny wasn't just about territorial expansion. It was a form of American exceptionalism cloaked in religious language. It painted America as God's chosen nation, destined to spread its influence across the continent and, eventually, the world.

This ideology had profound and lasting impacts:

- It provided a moral justification for the displacement and genocide of Native American peoples
- It fueled the Mexican-American War, leading to the annexation of vast territories in the Southwest

- It shaped our foreign policy, laying the groundwork for American interventionism around the globe
- Most disturbingly, it embedded in our national psyche the idea that America has a divine right and duty to shape the world in its image

The echoes of Manifest Destiny are still with us today. We might not use the term anymore, but the underlying idea has been rebranded. Now it often takes the form of rhetoric about America being a "Christian Nation" with a divine purpose to maintain its values. This notion of America's exceptional role in the world, sanctioned by God, continues to shape policies and attitudes.

We see it in foreign policy rhetoric about spreading democracy. We see it in the language of American exceptionalism that pervades our political discourse. And yes, we see it in certain strains of Christianity that view America's power and prosperity as signs of divine favor.

The legacy of Manifest Destiny challenges us to think critically about the relationship between faith and nationalism. It reminds us of the dangers of assuming God's endorsement for our national ambitions. And it calls us to reckon with the ways in which religious language has been used - and continues to be used - to justify actions that are fundamentally at odds with the teachings of Christ.

As followers of Christ, we're called to be peacemakers, to love our neighbors (and yes, that includes our neighbors across borders), to stand with the oppressed. How can we reconcile that calling with a nationalistic ideology that has been used to justify conquest and oppression?

The story of Nazi Germany, Manifest Destiny, and the Crusades aren't just history. They're a warning about the dangers of merging religious faith with national ambition. It's a reminder that we must always be vigilant, always questioning, always willing to examine our beliefs and assumptions. Because when we fail to do so, when we uncritically accept narratives that merge God's will with national ambition, we risk repeating the sins of our past. And that's a destiny none of us should be willing to manifest.

Now that we've traced these dark threads through history - from Constantine's Chi-Rho to Hitler's belt buckles, from the Crusaders' swords to Manifest Destiny's march westward - you might be tempted to breathe a sigh of relief. To tell yourself, "Thank God we've moved past all that." But here's the thing about history: it doesn't stay quietly in the past. The same forces that turned the cross into a conquest banner, that transformed Christ's teachings into tools of empire, didn't just disappear. They evolved. They adapted. They put on suits and ties, traded their swords for campaign slogans, and walked right into our modern churches. And what they're doing there might be the most dangerous chapter of this story yet.

6

MODERN CHRISTIAN NATIONALISM
SAME WOLF, NEW CLOTHES

Now that we enter the modern era, we've finally shed all that baggage - the overt Christian Nationalism, the unholy alliances, the twisted theology. After all, we're enlightened now, right? We've moved past all that nonsense.

Wrong. Dead wrong.

If only it were that simple. The truth is, Christian Nationalism didn't fade away as we stepped into the 21st century. It didn't politely excuse itself and bow out. No, it just got sneakier, more insidious, snaking itself into the very fabric of American Christianity in ways both subtle and shocking.

The reality we face is far more complex and unsettling than a simple "We've outgrown that" narrative. Christian Nationalism isn't just alive and well - it's thriving, adapting, evolving into forms that are harder to spot but no less dangerous.

The legacy of this unholy alliance between faith and national identity isn't just continuing to shape our politics, our culture, and our understanding of what it means to be both

Christian and American. It has become so deeply ingrained in the fabric of American Christianity that it's almost impossible to separate it from genuine faith for many believers.

This isn't a fringe ideology anymore - if it ever truly was. It's the air many American Christians have breathed their entire lives. It's found its way into nearly every church in America, from the smallest rural congregations to the mega-churches of our suburbs. It's become so normalized that for a large majority of American believers, it's not seen as nationalism at all, but simply as the correct expression of their faith.

What we're dealing with isn't just a political stance or a theological quirk. It's a worldview so pervasive that it's become invisible to many who hold it. It's the lens through which they view not just their nation, but their faith itself. For many, this fusion of Christianity and American identity has become the gold standard of what it means to be a "good Christian."

The nature of this ideology lies in its apparent actionability. It offers clear, politically-charged ways to "live out" one's faith. Vote for the right candidate. Support the right policies. Oppose the right social changes. It provides a sense of purpose and belonging that's deeply alluring in our complex and often chaotic world.

But here's the truly challenging part: Even for those of us who recognize the dangers of Christian Nationalism, who have consciously tried to repent of it and resist it, the task of truly separating it from our faith is monumentally difficult. It's not just a matter of changing our political views or even our theological stances. It requires a fundamental rewiring of how we think about God and our place in the world.

I've struggled with this myself. Even as I've become more aware of the problematic nature of Christian Nationalism, I've caught myself falling back into its patterns of thought. It's like trying to unlearn your native language - the words and concepts are so deeply ingrained that they shape your very thought processes.

As we explore the manifestations of Christian Nationalism in our modern era, we need to keep this context in mind. We're not just dealing with a set of political beliefs or even a particular theological stance. We're confronting a deeply rooted cultural phenomenon that has shaped the very essence of what many Christians understand Christianity to be.

This reality makes our task both more urgent and more challenging. It's not enough to simply point out the most egregious examples of Christian Nationalism. We need to dig deeper, to examine the subtle ways this ideology has shaped our understanding of faith, citizenship, and moral responsibility.

Only by recognizing the true depth and breadth of Christian Nationalism's influence can we hope to chart a path towards a faith that truly reflects the teachings of Christ rather than the demands of national identity.

In 2015, I remember watching the Republican presidential debates. One moment stands out vividly: when then-candidate Donald Trump declared, "I will be the greatest jobs president that God ever created." The audience cheered. Yuck.

It wasn't just the arrogance that bothered me. It was the casual invocation of God to sanctify political ambition. It was the assumption that God takes sides in American politics. And it was the way the audience - many of them Christians - ate it up.

This moment crystallized for me how Christian Nationalism has evolved in the modern era. It's become more subtle in some ways, more brazen in others, but no less potent.

Let's look at a few key examples:

1. The Response to Black Lives Matter

When the Black Lives Matter movement gained prominence, the reaction from many white evangelical circles was telling. Instead of engaging with the movement's calls for racial justice - a cause that you'd think would align with Christ's teachings - many Christian leaders dismissed or even demonized BLM. I watched as pastors I once respected framed the movement as anti-Christian, as a threat to "traditional values." They used the language of faith to defend the stance, repeating the pattern of the way Christian rhetoric was once used to justify slavery and segregation.

2. The 2016, 2020, and 2024 Elections
These elections saw Christian Nationalism on full display. Remember the photos of people laying hands on a cardboard cutout of Trump to pray for his victory? Or the "Prophet" who confidently declared that God had told him Trump would win re-election? These weren't fringe events. They represented a significant strain of thought in American Christianity - one that saw a particular political outcome as divinely ordained.

3. The COVID-19 Pandemic
The pandemic brought another dimension to this issue. I watched in dismay as some churches defied public health orders in the name of religious freedom, framing mask mandates and gathering restrictions as persecution. It was a reminder of how Christian Nationalism often prioritizes a narrow definition of "religious liberty" over the biblical mandate to love our neighbors and protect the vulnerable.

4. The January 6th Insurrection
Perhaps the most shocking manifestation of modern Christian Nationalism came on January 6, 2021. What unfolded that day wasn't just a political protest gone wrong; it was a violent insur-

rection with unmistakable Christian undertones. As rioters stormed the Capitol, many carried Christian flags alongside Trump banners. The incongruity was stark: symbols of a faith founded on love and peace, used in an act of violence and insurrection. Some paused to pray in Jesus' name in the Senate chamber, a perverse sanctification of their assault on democracy.

But the religious symbolism went beyond flags and prayers. Outside the Capitol, insurrectionists had erected a wooden gallows, complete with a hanging noose. It was allegedly intended for Vice President Mike Pence, branded a traitor for refusing to overturn the election results. This makeshift execution structure, built by those claiming to act in God's name, evoked images of the medieval Crusaders more than the followers of Christ.

The violence was real and terrifying. Approximately 140 police officers were injured in the attack. Rioters beat them with flag poles – some with Christian flags. Inside the Capitol, elected officials and staff members hid in fear for their lives, as the mob chanted threats of violence and searched for specific targets. I wish I was making this all up.

What drove this violent assault on the seat of American democracy? A deeply held belief, fueled by Christian nationalist rhetoric, that it was God's will for Donald Trump to remain president. This wasn't just political preference; for many in the crowd, it was divine mandate. They believed so fervently in this God-ordained mission that they were willing to break laws, assault officers, and potentially commit murder to see it fulfilled.

As I watched the events unfold on television, I felt a mix of horror and heartbreak. This was the culmination of years of rhetoric that had merged Christian identity with a particular political ideology. The result was a violent attempt to overturn an election, carried out in part by people who genuinely believed they were doing God's will.

It was like watching a scene from a horror movie, but the monsters weren't fictional creatures – many of them were fellow Christians. The cross had become a battle standard (remember Chi-Rho?), and the name of Jesus a war cry. It was a chilling reminder of how far Christian Nationalism had strayed from the teachings of Christ.

This event forced many American Christians, myself included, to confront uncomfortable truths about the state of our faith and its entanglement with political power. How had the message of Jesus become so distorted that His followers could mistake an insurrection for a holy crusade?

The January 6th insurrection stands as a warning of the dangers of Christian Nationalism taken to its extreme. It challenges us to examine our own beliefs and assumptions, to question where we might be allowing political ideology to supersede our commitment to Christ's teachings of love, peace, and justice.

What's perhaps even more troubling than the events themselves is the reaction they provoked - or failed to provoke - in many Christian communities across America. This wasn't just a far-off display of radicals that the rest of us could easily condemn and distance ourselves from. The ripple effects reached into countless homes, churches, and communities, including my own.

In the days and weeks following the insurrection, I was shocked to discover how many people in my own circle - family members, longtime friends - sympathized with the rioters. They might not have condoned the violence outright, but there was an undercurrent of support for the insurrectionists' goals. I heard phrases like "They went too far, but their hearts were in the right place" or "Sometimes you have to fight for what's right." There was a sense that while the methods might have been wrong, the objective - keeping their divinely-appointed leader in office - was justified.

This silent support, this unspoken approval, was in many ways more chilling than the overt actions of those who stormed the Capitol. It revealed how deeply Christian nationalist ideology had penetrated into the mainstream of American Christianity. People I had known and respected for years, people I had worshipped alongside, were willing to entertain the idea that a violent overthrow of a democratic election could be God's will. It was a reminder that the line between 'radical' and 'mainstream' isn't as clear as we might like to think, and that Christian Nationalism isn't just a fringe ideology - it's a widespread worldview that has shaped the political and spiritual perspectives of millions of American believers.

As I've worked through these events over the last few years, I've had to confront some hard truths. The Christian Nationalism we see today isn't an aberration. It's the natural evolution of the ideologies we've traced throughout this chapter - from the Puritans to Manifest Destiny to the Religious Right.

Folks, it doesn't have to be this way.

I've also seen Christians standing up against this tide. Pastors preaching about racial justice. Believers advocating for immigrant rights and religious freedom for all faiths. Young evangelicals questioning the political allegiances of their parents' generation.

These voices often get drowned out by the louder, more sensational expressions of Christian Nationalism. But they are there, and they're growing!

As we wrap up this exploration of Christian Nationalism's

dark history, I'm left with a mix of despair and hope. Despair at how deeply this ideology has shaped our nation and our faith. Hope that by confronting this history honestly, we can chart a different path forward.

> [*Content warning: This section discusses practices that may be deeply ingrained in many readers' experiences of faith. My intent is not to offend, but to encourage thoughtful reflection on how our practices shape our understanding of faith and national identity.*]

Growing up, there was a ritual so common, so unremarkable, that nobody seemed to question it. Whether at Bible school, church camp, TeenPact, or Boy Scouts, we always began the same way: with a pledge of allegiance. First to the American flag, then to the Christian flag.

It didn't take long for the significance of this practice hit me. Why did we pledge allegiance to America before Christ? Was it simply because the American flag is always flown above others? Or was there something deeper at play - a subtle message that our national identity came first, with our Christian identity as a sort of add-on?

I remember feeling a mix of emotions during these pledges. There was often an internal eye-roll at the Christian flag pledge, which felt tacked on, as if to make pledging to the U.S. flag in church less jarring. And who even created this pledge? That's probably a stupid question that has a good answer but I don't even care to research it. I was confused about why we needed a Christian banner at all. Were we "Onward, Christian Soldiers" or followers of a Prince of Peace?

But most of all, there was a growing sense of unease. Why even was there an American flag on the side of church stages at all? Why were we pledging allegiance to any nation within our Bible school classroom or Sunday morning worship?

These practices, often implemented with the best of intentions, have consequences we may not have considered. They blur the lines between faith and nationalism in ways that can be profoundly unhealthy for both.

Consider this: According to U.S. Flag Code, the American flag should fly above the Christian flag, even at a church. While this is a matter of etiquette rather than law, the intense public reaction when one church dared to place God's symbol above the nation's reveals something profound about where our true allegiances lie.

In 2015, when West Asheville Baptist Church in North Carolina dared to fly the Christian flag above the American flag, it sparked national outrage. Think about that - in a supposedly Christian nation, people were more offended by "disrespect" to a national symbol than by churches symbolically placing the nation above God.

It costs nothing to publicly demonstrate where our highest loyalty belongs. Yet most churches dutifully follow flag code, placing the national symbol above the Christian one - a vivid illustration of the tensions inherent in trying to serve both God and country. Perhaps the real question isn't which flag should fly higher, but why we feel compelled to fly national flags in our sacred spaces at all.

This reality exposes a fundamental misunderstanding of the church's role in society. We've somehow convinced ourselves that our houses of worship should function more like American voting booths than embassies of God's kingdom. The church isn't meant to be an extension of American civic life, but a representation of God's kingdom on earth.

Just as an embassy operates on foreign soil while representing its home nation, our churches should embody and promote kingdom values within, but distinct from, the nations they inhabit.

These flag ceremonies aren't the only way churches often weave faith and nationalism together. Think about how many churches celebrate veterans as the ultimate Christian soldiers through special Veteran's Day and Memorial Day services. Yet these same churches might balk at the idea of becoming true sanctuaries for the displaced and downtrodden. Instead of opening their doors to house refugees or provide shelter for the homeless, they opt for occasional food drives or clothing donations. Rather than offering sustained financial assistance to help struggling families keep their lights on or childcare services so single parents can secure stable employment, they choose the comfort of arms-length charity.

It's as if we've forgotten Jesus' words:

> For I was hungry, and you gave Me *something* to eat; I was thirsty, and you gave Me *something* to drink; I was a stranger, and you invited Me in; naked, and you clothed Me; I was sick, and you visited Me; I was in prison, and you came to Me.
>
> — MATTHEW 25:35-36

We've replaced the radical hospitality of Christ with a sanitized, risk-free version of service that doesn't disrupt our assumptions about who deserves our help.

This reluctance to fully embrace the messy, demanding work of caring for the marginalized is another form of shav'. We use God's name to claim we're following Christ's teachings, but our actions reveal a hollow faith more concerned with maintaining our social standing than truly embodying the love and sacrifice Jesus modeled.

But what if, instead of retreating, we engaged? What if, instead of creating a Christian bubble, we sought to be salt and light in our broader communities?

These practices - the pledges, the special services, the retreat from broader culture - all contribute to a form of Christian Nationalism that subtly reshapes our understanding of faith. They suggest that being a good Christian and being a good American are one and the same. They imply that our national identity is inseparable from our religious identity.

But is this really what Jesus called us to? Did He envision His followers pledging allegiance to Caesar, to a nation? Or did He call us to a kingdom not of this world, a citizenship in heaven that transcends national boundaries?

As we work to untangle our faith from nationalism, we need to take a hard look at these symbols and rituals. We need to ask ourselves: Are these practices drawing us closer to Christ, or are they merging our faith with our national identity? Are they helping us love our neighbors - all of our neighbors - or are they creating an us-vs-them mentality, a Crusader mentality?

This isn't about abandoning patriotism altogether. It's about ensuring that our ultimate allegiance is to Christ, not to any earthly nation. It's about creating church cultures that reflect the inclusive, boundary-breaking love of Jesus rather than nationalism.

The road ahead isn't easy. These practices are deeply ingrained in many of our church cultures. Questioning them may feel uncomfortable, even sacrilegious. But if we're serious about rebuilding a Christian witness that truly reflects Christ, it's a journey we must undertake.

Let's create churches where our identity is in Christ, not in our nationality. Where our symbols and rituals draw us closer to God and to all of humanity, not just to those who share our passport. Where our allegiance to God's kingdom always, unquestionably, comes first.

This shift in perspective isn't just semantic - it's revolutionary. It challenges us to reconsider where our ultimate allegiance lies and how we engage with the world around us. Imagine the transformation if our churches truly saw themselves as embassies of God's kingdom rather than clubhouses of Christianity. It's time we started acting less like patriots and more like ambassadors.

As we conclude this very long chapter, I find myself experiencing a mix of emotions - grief for the ways Christian Nationalism has distorted our faith, anger at the harm it has caused, and hope for a better way forward.

This journey through the dark history of Christian Nationalism in America isn't just an academic exercise. It's a necessary reckoning, a confrontation with uncomfortable truths that we've ignored for far too long.

We've seen how the seeds of Christian Nationalism were planted in our colonial past, how they grew through the eras of slavery and segregation, how they adapted and evolved in the modern age. We've witnessed how this ideology has persistently corrupted the message of Christ, turning a faith rooted in love and justice into a tool for exclusion and domination.

But knowledge of this history isn't enough. Awareness alone won't break the cycle. We need to act.

As I reflect on my own journey - from a child steeped in the culture of white evangelical Christianity to an adult struggling to untangle faith from nationalism - I'm reminded of Jesus' words in John 8:31-32, "If you continue in My word, *then* you are truly My disciples; and you will know the truth, and the truth will set you free." Confronting the truth about Christian

Nationalism, as painful as it is, is the first step towards liberation.

This liberation isn't just for ourselves. It's for the countless individuals who have been hurt by Christian Nationalism, by the Church - the marginalized communities it has excluded, the vulnerable populations it has failed to protect, the seekers it has driven away from Christ's message of love.

So where do we go from here?

We start by acknowledging the harm that Christian Nationalism has caused. We repent - not just with words, but with actions. We commit ourselves to the hard work of reimagining a faith that truly reflects Christ's love for all people.

We reclaim the prophetic voice of Christianity - a voice that speaks truth to power, that champions justice for the oppressed, that welcomes the stranger and loves the enemy.

And perhaps most importantly, we humble ourselves. We recognize that our understanding of God, of faith, of what it means to follow Christ, is limited and flawed. We open ourselves to learning, to growth, to transformation.

The deeper I dig into Christian Nationalism, the more familiar its patterns become. The control. The conformity. The unquestioning loyalty. The absolute certainty. There's a word for this - a word that makes people uncomfortable, a word nobody wants to say out loud. But sometimes, calling something by its true name is the first step toward freedom. And what I'm about to say next might make you mad.

7

THE CULT OF CHRISTIANITY
GOOGLE? DEFINE: CULT

What if, by every definition, you're in a cult? The word "cult" tends to conjure images of isolated compounds and charismatic leaders with outlandish beliefs. But what if I told you that many of the hallmarks of cult-like behavior have seeped into mainstream Christianity?

Before we dive in, I want to be clear: I'm not suggesting that all forms of Christianity are cult-like. But there are disturbing trends within many Christian circles that mirror cult-like characteristics, and we need to confront them head-on.

Steven Hassan, a leading expert on cults and author of *Combating Cult Mind Control*, identifies four key components of cult-like groups: behavior control, information control, thought control, and emotional control.[7.1] As we explore Christian Nationalism, we'll see all of these control mechanisms at play.

But why does this matter? Because cult-like thinking is antithetical to the freedom Christ offers. Jesus said, "If you continue in My word, *then* you are truly My disciples; and you will know the truth, and the truth will set you free" (John 8:31-

32). True Christianity should liberate us, not constrain us in rigid thought patterns or unquestioning loyalty to human leaders.

As we unpack these cult-like characteristics, you might feel uncomfortable. You might recognize some of these patterns in your own church or even in your own heart. That's okay. In fact, it's necessary. Because only by recognizing these tendencies can we begin to break free from them and reclaim a faith that truly reflects the liberating love of Christ.

One of the most striking features of cult-like groups is their tendency to elevate a charismatic leader to near-divine or divine status. In the realm of Christian Nationalism, we've seen this play out with political figures being cast in messianic terms.

Consider the way some Christian leaders have spoken about certain politicians. They're described not just as good leaders or even as God's chosen instruments, but in almost messianic terms. They're portrayed as uniquely anointed to save America, to restore it to an idealized Christian past.

This elevation of political figures to messianic status is a form of shav' - a misuse of God's name for empty, false purposes. It's attributing to fallible human beings the kind of devotion and unquestioning loyalty that should be reserved for God alone.

We've seen this in the way some Christians have responded to criticism of their preferred political leaders. Any critique, no matter how valid, is dismissed as an attack on God's anointed. Moral failings are excused or ignored. It's a dangerous mixture of political loyalty and spiritual fidelity.

This cult of personality around political figures is perhaps most starkly illustrated in certain contemporary Christian music. Songs that once might have been written about Jesus are now being penned about political leaders. They use religious language and imagery to create an aura of divine appointment around specific politicians.

A very recent example refers to Donald Trump as "The Chosen One," suggesting divine selection and even comparing the politician to biblical figures. Her music video centers around imagery of Donald Trump at rallies delivering speeches. Natasha Owens sings in *The Chosen One*:

> I'm standing with the Chosen one
> Ain't no stopping what the Lord's begun
> He's only human
> Like you and me
> Just a chosen one
> The chosen one

— 7.2

Another song, "I Am America," blends patriotic fervor with religious zeal, painting political opponents as enemies of God's will. Written by an old friend of mine and performed by his wife, Krista Branch, who was heavily involved in furthering the political campaign of Herman Cain back in 2012. She sings:

> I am America, one voice, united we stand.
> I am America, one hope to heal our land.
> I will not give up on this fight,
> I will not fade into the night

— 7.3

The song's lyrics might seem to target external threats, but listen closely - the real enemy being portrayed is other Americans. It's fellow citizens who hold different political views that are painted as the threat to "heal." This rhetoric of internal enemies has only escalated. In a 2024 interview with Fox News' Maria Bartiromo, Trump made this explicit when discussing potential Election Day disruptions:

> I think the bigger problem is the enemy from within - We have some very bad people. We have some sick people, radical left lunatics. And I think they're the big — and it should be very easily handled by, if necessary, by National Guard, or if really necessary, by the military, because they can't let that happen.
>
> — 7.4

These aren't just expressing political preferences. They're creating a narrative of divine endorsement that elevates political figures to a status that should be reserved for God alone, while demonizing fellow Americans as enemies to be suppressed - even by military force. It's a modern-day golden calf, a human-made idol we've convinced ourselves is ordained by God, complete with its own list of heretics to be purged.

This merging of political and spiritual devotion is deeply problematic. It blinds us to the flaws and failures of our leaders. It makes it nearly impossible to hold them accountable. And perhaps most dangerously, it sets us up for disillusionment - not just with a political figure, but potentially with faith itself when these human "messiahs" inevitably fall short.

One of the hallmarks of cult-like thinking is the creation of a stark, uncompromising division between "us" and "them." In

Christian Nationalism, this manifests as a belief that there's a spiritual battle between "true" Christian patriots and everyone else.

This mindset isn't new. Throughout history, religious and political movements have used the creation of an "other" to solidify group identity and loyalty. But in the context of Christian Nationalism, it takes on a particularly deceptive form.

I have sat in so many church services where the pastor would rail against "the radical left" as if they were agents of Satan himself. The world outside our Christian bubble was painted as a dangerous, hostile place, full of people actively working to destroy our faith-based nation.

This us-vs-them mentality is often reinforced through music and media. Consider these other lyrics from the song *I Am America*:

> You preach your tolerance but lecture me.
> Is there no end to your own hypocrisy?
> Your god is power, you have no shame,
> Your only interest is political gain.

> — 7.3

These words create a clear divide between "us" (the righteous Americans) and "them" (the hypocritical, power-hungry liberals). It's a simplistic, adversarial worldview that leaves no room for understanding.

The danger of this mentality is twofold. First, it dehumanizes those who disagree with us, making it easier to dismiss their concerns and perspectives (*remember that word dehumanizes" we'll come back to just how literal that becomes*). Second, it creates a siege mentality within the group, fostering an unhealthy dependence on the group's leaders and ideology for protection against these perceived enemies.

But, Jesus didn't call us to fabricate enemies. He called us to love our enemies. He didn't tell us to build walls, but to break them down. The us-vs-them mentality of Christian Nationalism stands in stark contrast to Christ's call to radical, boundary-breaking love.

As followers of Christ, we need to resist the temptation to demonize those who disagree with us. We need to cultivate empathy, to seek understanding, to recognize the image of God even in those we might consider our opponents. Only then can we hope to be true peacemakers in a divided world.

Another characteristic of cult-like groups is a fixation on apocalyptic scenarios and end-times prophecies. In Christian Nationalism, this often takes the form of seeing current events as signs of the end times and framing political conflicts in terms of spiritual warfare.

This apocalyptic mindset isn't just about believing in the Second Coming of Christ. It's about interpreting every political development, every social change, every natural disaster as a sign that the end is near - and that "our side" needs to prepare for the final battle.

I've sat through countless sermons and Bible studies where current events were mapped onto the book of Revelation with absolute certainty. Political leaders were identified as potential Antichrists. Social changes were seen as fulfillment of end-times prophecies. The sense of urgency was real - we were always just on the brink of the Tribulation.

This apocalyptic thinking often bleeds into political rhetoric. Consider a different section of the lyrics from Natasha Owens' battlecry song for Trump's divine purpose *The Chosen One*:

This great nation
Is under attack
And its real leader has
Arrows in his back
So many greet him
With a Judas kiss
But God gave us a warrior
For such a time as this

— 7.2

These words frame current political conflicts in apocalyptic terms. The nation is "under attack," and a political leader is portrayed as a divinely appointed warrior, echoing the language of end-times prophecies.

Moreover, this thinking can justify extreme actions. If we believe we're soldiers in a cosmic political war, it becomes easier to demonize our political opponents and to justify any means to achieve our ends.

But Jesus called us to a different approach. When His disciples asked Him about the end times:

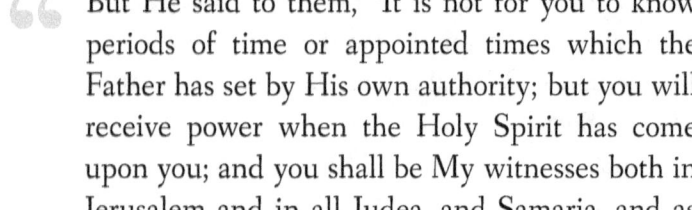

But He said to them, "It is not for you to know periods of time or appointed times which the Father has set by His own authority; but you will receive power when the Holy Spirit has come upon you; and you shall be My witnesses both in Jerusalem and in all Judea, and Samaria, and as far as the remotest part of the earth."

— ACTS 1:7-8

Jesus didn't call us to obsess over end-times timelines. He called us to be His witnesses - to live out His love and truth in the here and now.

As we navigate these challenging times, let's resist the allure of apocalyptic thinking. Instead, let's focus on being faithful witnesses to Christ's love in our daily lives. Let's work for justice, seek peace, and care for our world as if we expect it to be around for a long time to come. Because whether the end is near or far, our calling remains the same: to love God and to love our neighbors as ourselves.

In the age of social media and personalized news feeds, we're all susceptible to living in information bubbles. But in the context of Christian Nationalism, these bubbles can become echo chambers that reinforce a particular worldview while shutting out dissenting voices.

I've witnessed this firsthand in many Christian circles. There's often an unspoken (and sometimes spoken) expectation about which news sources are "trustworthy" and which are "liberal propaganda." Certain political commentators are elevated to almost prophet-like status, their words treated as gospel truth.

This information control isn't always overt. It's often subtle, a gradual narrowing of perspective until we're only hearing voices that confirm what we already believe.

Social media has exacerbated this problem. Algorithms feed us more of what we already like, creating digital echo chambers that can be hard to break out of. Consider the recent controversy surrounding Facebook's handling of political content. Internal documents revealed that the platform's algorithms often amplified divisive and extreme content, contributing to the polarization we see in our society. [7.2.1]

The danger of these echo chambers is that they can lead to a distorted view of reality. They can make us believe that our perspective is the only valid one, that anyone who disagrees is either misinformed or malicious.

Music has always been a powerful tool for shaping beliefs and stirring emotions. In the context of Christian Nationalism, it's often used to reinforce political ideologies and create an emotional connection between faith and national identity.

Consider the lyrics of some popular worship songs. While many are theologically sound and genuinely worshipful, others blur the lines between devotion to God and devotion to country. Take, for a pretty extreme example but somehow gaining popularity in some churches, the song by Gary Moore, a former minister of music at First Baptist Church of Dallas "Make America Great Again" which premiered at the "Celebrate Freedom Rally" by the choir and orchestra of First Baptist Church of Dallas:

> Make America great again
> Make America great again
> Lift the torch of freedom all across the land
> Step into the future joining hand in hand

— 7.2.2

These lyrics, set to a worship-style melody, create an emotional fusion of patriotism and faith. They suggest that making America "great" is somehow aligned with God's purposes, a notion that can be problematic when scrutinized.

While some songs are created specifically for political purposes, others can be repurposed in ways that diverge from their original intent. The popular worship song "How Great Is Our God" provides a striking example of this phenomenon. Originally written as a celebration of God's greatness, this song has been adopted by some Christian nationalist groups for political rallies and protests.

The song "How Great Is Our God" featured prominently during the "Jericho Marches" in November and December 2020, events organized to protest the results of the 2020 presidential election. It was also sung by protesters in the lead-up to the January 6, 2021 attack on the U.S. Capitol.

The very concept of calling these events "Jericho Marches" is a prime example of Christian Nationalism in action. It inappropriately confuses the intentions of an Old Testament story of God's direct command to the Israelites with a modern-day political agenda. This comparison implies that God is on the side of conservatives and that the "walls" holding them back (liberal politicians or policies) are divinely ordained to fall, just as the walls of Jericho did. This misuse of biblical narrative to justify political actions is deeply problematic and epitomizes the danger of merging faith with nationalism.

More recently, on April 25, 2024, MAGA activist and worship leader Sean Feucht led a version of the song through a bullhorn during the "United for Israel" march at Columbia University in Manhattan. This event, however, wasn't primarily about supporting Israel or addressing global justice issues. Instead, it was largely a political statement against what conservatives view as "woke" institutions and liberal ideologies on college campuses.

The use of "How Great Is Our God" in this context demonstrates how worship music can be co-opted for political purposes that may have little to do with the song's original spiritual intent. In this case, the song served as a rallying cry not just for religious belief, but for a particular conservative political stance. It was used to create an association between conservative Christianity and support for Israel, while simultaneously positioning this group against liberal academic institutions and their broader views on global justice and peace.

This incident highlights how Christian Nationalism often blends religious expression with political ideology, using familiar spiritual language and practices to advance specific political agendas. The song has also become a staple at various Christian Nationalism conferences in recent years, further cementing its role as a cultural marker for a particular brand of politically conservative Christianity.

This shift in usage - from a Sunday morning worship setting to a political rally cry - highlights how the meaning and impact of a song can dramatically change based on its context and the intentions of those using it. Such repurposing of spiritual music for political ends is another form of shav', using elements of faith in ways that may be considered empty or false when viewed through the lens of their original spiritual purpose.

This emotional manipulation isn't limited to music. Christian movies, books, and social media content often use fear and anger to drive engagement. They paint a picture of a Christian faith under siege, creating a sense of urgency that can override critical thinking.

For instance, the movie *God's Not Dead* portrays academia as universally hostile to faith, reinforcing a persecution narrative that doesn't accurately reflect the complex reality of faith in higher education. While the film resonated with many Christians, it also reinforced an us-vs-them mentality that can be harmful to genuine dialogue and understanding.

The film's subplots further reinforce harmful stereotypes and oversimplified narratives. It portrays a Muslim father violently abusing his daughter when she expresses interest in Christianity, perpetuating a damaging and inaccurate stereotype about Muslims.

Another storyline follows a 'liberal vegan atheist' - a character seemingly designed to embody everything the filmmakers perceive as un-Christian - who predictably converts to Christianity after a cancer diagnosis, implying that her previous lifestyle and beliefs were as misguided as her party affiliation. These portrayals reduce complex identities and life experiences to simplistic caricatures, further entrenching an us-vs-them mentality.

Despite these problematic elements, the movie was widely embraced across mainstream Christian groups as child-appropriate and faith-inspiring, illustrating how deeply ingrained these divisive narratives have become in Christian circles. This uncritical acceptance of such messaging underscores the need for more compassionate approaches to discussing faith in media and daily life.

As followers of Christ, we need to be discerning consumers of media. We need to ask ourselves: Is this content drawing me closer to Christ and His love for all people? Or is it stoking fear, anger, and division?

This isn't a call to isolate ourselves from media or to avoid all potentially challenging content - Christian or otherwise. Rather, it's an invitation to develop a more critical eye. Once we recognize these patterns of emotional manipulation and divisive messaging, we can't unsee them. This awareness allows us to better understand the underlying messages and motivations, enabling us to engage with media more thoughtfully and from a place of Christ-like love and discernment.

Let's cut to the chase: What we're witnessing isn't just a slight shift in Christian practice. It's the birth of a full-blown cult, one that's hijacked the name of Christ while betraying His teachings at every turn.

This new cult of Christianity has redefined what it means to be a follower of Christ so radically that if Jesus himself were to return today, He'd be branded as woke by His own supposed followers.

In this cult, being a "good Christian" has little to do with loving your neighbor, serving the poor, or turning the other cheek. Instead, it's all about political allegiance, cultural warfare, and blind nationalism.

I've watched in horror as this cult has taken root in churches across America. This cult has its own twisted version of the Beatitudes:

Blessed are the gun owners, for they shall protect God's country.

Blessed are the rich, for their wealth is a sign of God's favor.

Blessed are the nationalists, for they shall inherit America.

It's a perversion of everything Christ stood for, and yet it's become the dominant form of Christianity in many parts of our country.

The most chilling part? Many caught up in this cult genuinely believe they're following Jesus. They've been so thoroughly indoctrinated that they can't even see how far they are away from the path.

This isn't just a theological disagreement or a difference in political opinion. It's a fundamental redefinition of what it means to be a Christian. And if we don't confront it head-on, it threatens to destroy not just the witness of the church, but the very essence of Christ's teachings in America.

We're standing on the precipice of a Christian Dark Age, and many of us are too busy waving flags and chanting political slogans to notice. The cultish thinking that's infected our faith and our culture isn't just misguided - it's dangerous. It's a cancer eating away at the heart of Christianity, turning followers of the Prince of Peace into foot soldiers in a political and cultural war.

This cultish version of American Christianity has more in common with the Pharisees who crucified Jesus than with Jesus himself. It's a religion of power, not of service. Of judgment, not of mercy. Of fear, not of love.

To understand just how deep this cultish thinking runs, let's look at Steven Hassan's four key components of cult-like groups and how they manifest in American Christianity today. Hassan, a leading expert on cult psychology who himself escaped from the Unification Church, developed what he calls the "BITE Model" to identify controlling groups: [7.1]

1. Behavior Control:
   - Dictating how members should vote, dress, and even think
   - Encouraging isolation from those with different beliefs
   - Imposing strict rules about acceptable behavior, often with threat of divine punishment
2. Information Control:
   - Demonizing "secular" or "liberal" media sources
   - Creating alternative "Christian" versions of everything from news to science
   - Discouraging critical thinking or questioning leaders who claim to speak for God
3. Thought Control:
   - Using loaded language and clichés to stifle complex thinking
   - Encouraging black-and-white, us-vs-them thinking
   - Instilling phobias about the consequences of questioning its beliefs

4. Emotional Control:
   o Manipulating feelings of guilt and
     unworthiness
   o Using fear (of hell, of God's punishment, of the
     "end times," of the liberal agenda) as a control
     mechanism
   o Creating a sense of elitism or specialness for
     being part of the "true" faith

These cultish tendencies aren't limited to fringe groups anymore. They've become mainstream, infecting churches across America, from small rural congregations to suburban megachurches. I've watched it happen in real time, seen it transform the faith I once knew into something Jesus himself would hardly recognize.

I remember sitting in a vinyl Sunday School chair as a kid, memorizing verses for candy and singing about how "Jesus loves the little children, all the children of the world." Seems innocent enough, right? But even then, the subtle machinery of thought reform was humming along beneath those felt-board Bible stories.

What starts with memorizing verses for Skittles evolves into a comprehensive system that shapes not just what you believe, but how you think. And that's the insidious genius of it. These control mechanisms don't announce themselves with warning labels. They're packaged in language of love, truth, and freedom.

Take behavior control. In my childhood church, it started with dress codes and music restrictions. Christian girls couldn't wear two-piece swimsuits; Christian boys couldn't grow their hair too long. Christian families couldn't listen to secular music. Small rules, maybe – but they established the fundamental principle that external authorities had the right to dictate personal choices based on their interpretation of God's will.

By adulthood, this evolved into voting guides distributed in church foyers, pastors endorsing candidates from the pulpit, and small group leaders checking if you've been "faithful" with your tithing. The mechanisms become more sophisticated, but the underlying message remains: your behavior isn't your own.

Information control happens so gradually you barely notice it. It starts with well-meaning warnings about "discernment" when consuming media. Then suddenly you're only reading Christian books, only watching Christian movies, only listening to Christian music. Your news comes exclusively from sources that reinforce your existing beliefs. Before you know it, you're in an echo chamber so complete you could spend your entire life never encountering an idea that challenges your worldview.

I watched my parents' generation transition from "be careful what you read" to "any information contradicting our political views is satanic deception." I've seen people I love, intelligent people, confidently assert that climate science is a liberal conspiracy, that universities are indoctrination camps, that mainstream media is controlled by the devil himself – all while getting their own information from sources that profit from their fear and anger.

But thought control is where things get truly Orwellian. The loaded language creates mental shortcuts that prevent actual thinking. Terms like "biblical worldview," "spiritual warfare," and "spiritual covering" become thought-terminating clichés that shut down questions before they can even form. Try asking a substantive question about church finances or leadership decisions and watch how quickly "don't bring division" gets deployed to silence you.

I've sat in men's Bible studies where complex social issues were reduced to "God's way versus the world's way," with no room for nuance or a more thorough understanding. I've watched thoughtful people stop mid-sentence and say, "I shouldn't be thinking this way," not because they've reached a better conclusion, but because they've been conditioned to fear certain thoughts.

And then there's emotional control, perhaps the most powerful tool in the arsenal. When you've been taught since childhood that doubting certain doctrines means you might burn forever, that questioning leadership means you're in rebellion against God, that feeling attracted to the wrong person means you're defective – you become your own jailer. The fear gets installed so deep you police your own thoughts.

What makes this system so effective is that it's self-perpetuating. Once these controls are internalized, you become your own cult leader. Your internal voice takes over the job of controlling your behavior, filtering your information, limiting your thoughts, and manipulating your emotions. And you do it all voluntarily, believing you're simply being faithful.

The parallels with political systems of control aren't accidental. The ability to dictate behavior, control information flow, restrict thought, and manipulate emotions is the foundation of every authoritarian regime in history. The difference is that religious systems do it with God's endorsement, which makes them infinitely more powerful and more dangerous.

The most dangerous lies are the ones we tell ourselves in God's name.

The parallels between cult-like devotion to divine leaders and the fervent support for Donald Trump within Christian circles are not just striking - they're downright chilling. Steven Hassan's key points on divine leaders in cults reads like a playbook for the Trump era of American Christianity. Let's break it down:

1. **Absolute Authority** We've witnessed the transformation (or possibly transubstantiation) of a reality TV star into a messianic figure. Trump isn't just seen as a political leader; for many Christians, he's become God's chosen instrument. Remember when he said, "I am the chosen one," [7.5] while looking up at the sky? Instead of being met with skepticism, many Christians nodded in agreement.

2. **Unquestionable Leadership** The mental gymnastics performed to justify every tweet, every crude remark, every policy decision is mind-boggling. I've seen lifelong Christians twist themselves into ethical pretzels, abandoning principles they've held for decades, all to avoid criticizing their chosen one. "I'm not writing a love letter. I'm making a strategic move," or "God can use imperfect vessels" they say. While I recognize that's not a theologically inaccurate statement, but when did that mean embracing every word and action with unquestionable loyalty and divine purpose?

3. **Charismatic Influence** Trump's rallies became the new revival meetings. The fervor, the chanting, the blind adulation - it's worship, plain and simple. I've watched people I've known for years, people who once preached about the fruits of the Spirit, gleefully join in chants of "Lock her up!" and "Fuck Joe Biden!" or, as they're shirts mask the chant, "Let's Go Brandon!" The cognitive dissonance is staggering.

4. **Centralized Power** The Republican Party has become the Party of Trump. Policies, platforms, even basic facts - all are subject to change based on one man's whims. And the church has followed suit. Pastors twist scriptures to align with Trump's latest tweet and preach sermons that sound more like campaign speeches than Gospel messages.

But here's the truly terrifying part: This isn't just about Trump. He's a symptom, not the disease. What we're seeing is the emergence of a new form of Christian Nationalism that bears all the hallmarks of a full-blown cult.

This new cult doesn't disappear when Trump leaves office, goes to prison, or dies. No, it's paved the way for a succession of divine political leaders, each one further removing us from the teachings of Christ. We're standing on the brink of a new dark age of faith. One where allegiance to a political figure or ideology trumps allegiance to Christ. Where the Sermon on the Mount takes a backseat to the latest conspiracy theory. Where love for neighbor is conditional on their voting record.

This isn't hyperbole. This is the reality we're facing. I've watched family members disown each other over political disagreements, I've had decades-long friendships crumble because I dared to question the chosen leader. I've witnessed churches split, not over theological issues, but over whether a man who can barely quote a Bible verse is God's anointed one.

Behind this cult of personality lurks something even more fundamental: the belief that Christians are called to take control of every sphere of society - not through persuasion or service, but through political power. This isn't just happening in obscure theological circles; it's happening in your church, in your Facebook feed, and among your friends and family.

You may not have heard the term "Seven Mountain

Mandate," but odds are you've absorbed its basic premise. This doctrine, popularized by the growing New Apostolic Reformation (NAR) movement but now spreading far beyond it into mainstream churches, is simple: Christians are called to capture and control seven key areas of influence - government, business, media, arts and entertainment, education, family, and religion.[7.2.3] Only when believers dominate these "mountains" can America fulfill its divine purpose.

This isn't fringe theology anymore. A recent survey found that 42% of American Christians now agree with the statement "God wants Christians to stand atop the Seven Mountains of Society." [7.2.4] That's nearly half of all believers embracing a doctrine of dominion that would have seemed extreme just a generation ago - a doctrine that originated within the NAR but has now infected much of mainstream Christianity.

You can see it in the language pastors use when they talk about "taking back America." You can hear it when Christian parents discuss "reclaiming" public schools or the entertainment industry. And you'll notice it when church leaders describe politics not as public service but as "spiritual warfare" against demonic forces.

What's terrifying isn't just the theology itself, but how it's been normalized. The same Christians who would flinch at the term "dominionism" nod approvingly about "Christians in positions of influence." The same believers who would reject theocracy in theory eagerly support candidates who promise to govern based on "biblical principles." The language gets sanitized, but the core belief remains: God's people are called to rule.

This worldview transforms political opponents into enemies to be destroyed, not just defeated. Look no further than the chilling manifesto *Unhumans: The Secret History of Communist Revolutions (and How to Crush Them)* co-authored by far-right figure Jack Posobiec and enthusiastically endorsed by the current Vice President J.D. Vance with a blurb. This isn't some obscure text - it carries a forward by Steve Bannon and endorsements from Tucker Carlson, Donald Trump Jr., Michael Flynn, and other mainstream conservative figures.

The book explicitly frames political opponents as "unhumans" who are "trying to undo civilization itself" and who must be "crushed" - not debated, not persuaded, not compromised with - but eliminated. And where do these "unhumans" operate? You guessed it, in what the book calls "media, government, education, economy, family, religion, and arts and entertainment" - the exact seven mountains of dominionist theology.

Most disturbing of all, the book openly rejects democracy itself: "Democracy has never worked to protect innocents from the unhumans," the authors declare. "It is time to stop playing by rules they won't." The authors go even further, arguing that immigration inherently destroys nations. If immigration " dilutes and unbalances a shared culture," they claim, then the only solution is an "all-powerful state" - one explicitly without civil liberties. Let that sink in. A book endorsed by the President and Vice President explicitly rejects both democracy and basic constitutional freedoms as viable systems. And Christians are nodding along, seeing nothing incompatible between this rejection of democracy, this call for authoritarian power, and the teachings of Jesus who came to proclaim liberty to the captives.

This deadly combination - viewing political opponents as less than human and democracy itself as an obstacle - isn't just dangerous to our political system. It's a complete inversion of Jesus's command to love our enemies, pray for those who persecute us, and recognize the inherent dignity of every person as made in God's image. It's replacing the cross with a sword.

The cult of Trump will eventually fade, but this deeper

cult of dominionism - this belief that America belongs to one religious group and that establishing their control is a divine mission - will continue to corrupt Christianity from within until we confront it honestly. When half of American Christians have embraced a theology that justifies political dominance as God's will, we're no longer talking about a fringe movement. We're talking about a fundamental transformation of American Christianity itself.

The choice is ours. But make no mistake - the future of our faith, and of our nation, hangs in the balance. And the consequences? They're devastating.

It's driving young people away from the faith in droves. A recent Pew Research study found that the number of Americans identifying as Christian has dropped 12 percentage points over the past decade, with the sharpest decline among young adults.[7.6] Many cite the church's alignment with conservative politics as a key reason for their departure.

It's destroying our witness to a watching world. The association of Christianity with a particular political ideology has led many to view the faith not as a source of love and hope, but as a tool of oppression and division.

This cult has turned Christianity into a punch line, a synonym for hypocrisy and intolerance. We've become what Jesus warned us against in Matthew 23:27 - whitewashed tombs, beautiful on the outside but full of dead men's bones:

> Woe to you, scribes and Pharisees, hypocrites! For you are like whitewashed tombs which on the outside appear beautiful, but inside they are full of dead men's bones and all uncleanness.

What's particularly alarming is how quickly Christian Nationalism has become synonymous with American Christianity. In less than five years, the term has gone from a fringe concept to a mainstream identity. A 2021 survey by the Pew Research Center found 45% of U.S. adults say the country should be a Christian nation.[7.7] This fusion of religious and national identity is at the core of Christian Nationalism, and it's become increasingly difficult to separate it from mainstream American Christianity.

Political leaders have embraced this conflation, with some openly calling for Christian Nationalism. Religious leaders, too, have blurred the lines, suggesting that true Christianity necessitates a particular political stance. This merging of identities has created a situation where, for many, being a "good Christian" and being a "true American" are seen as one and the same.

This conflation isn't just a matter of semantics. It's reshaping the very nature of Christian faith in America. It's creating a version of Christianity that's more concerned with winning cultural battles than with embodying Christ's love. More focused on achieving political power than on serving the least of these.

When we mix Christian identity with political allegiance, when we start believing that God has chosen one party or one leader to save America, we open the door to authoritarianism. We become willing to overlook corruption, to excuse abuse of power, to trample on the rights of others - all in the name of "saving" our Christian nation.

This is how democracies die. Not with a bang, but with a whimper - the whimper of Christians so caught up in culture wars that they're willing to sacrifice the very freedoms they claim to cherish.

But to truly understand how this cultish Christianity has captured so many hearts and minds, including my own for so many years, we need to look beyond the symptoms to the deeper psychological appeal. After all, no one wakes up one morning and decides to join a cult. We're drawn in gradually, seduced by something that meets our deepest human needs for meaning, belonging, and purpose. And that's the most dangerous part of all: Christian Nationalism isn't just a political ideology. It's a powerful psychological framework that knows exactly which buttons to push, which wounds to exploit, and which desires to fulfill. And to escape its grip, we first need to understand its appeal.

8

THE ENEMY WITHIN

A TRANSLATION GUIDE FOR CONSERVATIVE POLITICS

The party was winding down, and I'd joined a circle of guys discussing Little Rock. The conversation had started reasonably enough. You know, making our city safer. Crime rates. Public safety. The kind of thing any concerned citizen would care about. Everyone was nodding. The concerns seemed legitimate.

Then someone mentioned bringing in the National Guard to crack down on crime. Then ICE. Immediately, the real targets emerged: immigrants, Democrats, and "the blacks."

The protective language fell away, revealing what had been underneath all along.

That sick, disorienting feeling hit me. How long had I been nodding and how long had they noticed I had continued nodding? And at what point had "community safety" become code for something much uglier? Then it was confirmed, these guys were casually discussing what amounted to ethnically and politically cleansing people from our city.

But it hadn't sounded like that at first. It sounded like concerned citizens discussing practical solutions. Or at least that's where it started. And as each sentence got heavier, they got more comfortable thinking that they were in good company to share.

This is how Christian Nationalism operates in modern America. Not through explicitly hateful rhetoric that believers can easily reject, but through a sophisticated rebranding strategy that makes exclusion sound like protection, dominance sound like defense, and hatred sound like biblical values.

The strategy has a name in political rhetoric: the foil.

In literature, a foil is a character who contrasts with another to highlight particular qualities. The villain makes the hero look heroic, the coward makes the brave look courageous.

We've all become way too familiar with it. If you've heard a speech from Trump, you'll be able to understand how it work. Trump didn't invent the foil, but he perfected it for modern conservative politics and the entire movement followed his lead. Every policy position, every cultural battle, every political stance now gets built around a simple formula: find an enemy and define yourself as their opposite. Then, you're not advocating for supremacy, defending against attack, or promoting exclusion. But rather, you're "protecting Christian values."

By using this strategy, the "dangerous immigrants" make you the protector of white America. The "radical left" makes you the defender of traditional values. The "Deep State" makes you God's anointed warrior. The "fake news media" makes you the truth-teller.

And once you have the right enemy, you don't need coherent theology, sound policy, or Christ-like behavior. You just need to be the opposite of whatever threat you've defined.

This tactic isn't new to history. Hitler understood the power of the foil better than perhaps any political figure before him. In *Mein Kampf*, he explicitly outlined this strategy: "The art of leadership... consists in consolidating the attention of the people against a single adversary and taking care that nothing will split up that attention." [10.8]

He didn't just have enemies, he carefully crafted them as foils to make himself look like Germany's savior.

In a 1923 speech, he declared: "There are only two possibilities: either victory of the Aryan, or annihilation of the Aryan and the victory of the Jew." Notice the formula: not "here's my vision for Germany," but "it's us or them." [10.9]

When positioning himself against the Weimar Republic, he proclaimed in 1932: "I am fighting for the work of the Lord." [10.10] By framing weak democracy as his foil, he became the strong leader Germany needed. By framing Jews as the foil for Aryan purity, he became the protector. By framing Communists as chaos, he became order itself.

He knew exactly what he was doing. In *Mein Kampf*, he wrote: "The great masses of the people... will more easily fall victims to a big lie than to a small one." [10.11] And the biggest lie was simple: Germany's problems weren't complex, they had a single enemy to blame.

This same tactic, refined and repackaged for a democratic age, is the foundation of modern Christian Nationalism. It bypasses every rational filter we have, and more dangerously, it overrides the very teachings of Christ we claim to follow.

Because here's what I discovered standing in that circle: when you're presented with a common enemy that threatens something you love, your brain doesn't carefully evaluate the logic. It doesn't pause to ask whether the threat is real or whether the proposed solution aligns with your values. It just... agrees. The foil does its work, and before you know it, you're nodding along to ideas you would have condemned an hour earlier.

The Translation Guide

Once you begin to understand the foil strategy, you're going to start seeing it everywhere! And you'll realize that Christian Nationalism has built an entire vocabulary around it, a collection of phrases that sound reasonable on the surface but carry something much darker underneath.

Here's how to decode the lingo. When they say one thing, they often mean something else entirely:

When you hear: "Great Replacement Theory"
It means: White Supremacy

Tucker Carlson spent years on Fox News talking about how immigrants were "replacing" Americans, framing it as demographic analysis rather than what it actually was: mainstreaming white supremacist talking points in over 400 of his commentary episodes. [10.12] The "Great Replacement" is about the fear that white people might lose their dominant position in American society. And what's wild about this is, they won't disagree by that definition. Rather, the position is explained and justified.

Charlie Kirk, before his tragic assassination, had turned this rhetoric into a recruitment tool for young conservatives. And I have to be absolutely clear because many people have been taken out of context when evaluating Kirk's teachings: the murder of Charlie Kirk was a horrific act that solved nothing and only deepened the divisions his worldview helped create. Condemning his assassination doesn't require us to ignore the substantial influence he had on conservative culture, particularly his ability to package white nationalist concepts for college audiences.

Kirk's influence on shaping conservative youth culture was undeniable. Through Turning Point USA, he would talk about "demographic transformation" and "cultural replacement" in ways that made white nationalism sound like patriotic concern. He made supremacist ideology sound like common sense to thousands of young people who thought they were just learning about conservative politics.

The tragedy of his death doesn't erase the damage this pipeline has done, but neither does recognizing that damage justify what happened to him. Both things can be true: his murder was wrong, and his ideology was harmful.

The rebranding works because it makes protecting white dominance sound defensive rather than offensive. Instead of "we want to maintain white supremacy," it becomes "they're replacing us." Same ideology, but much friendlier packaging.

When you hear: "War on Christianity"
It means: Christian Supremacy

Franklin Graham and Tony Perkins of the Family Research Council have perfected this framing. Every push for religious pluralism becomes an "attack on faith." [10.14] Every attempt to separate church and state becomes "persecution." [10.15] They're not defending religious freedom, they're defending Christian dominance while making it sound like they're the ones under siege.

When they talk about the "War on Christmas" or complain about prayer being removed from schools, they're not advocating for equal religious expression. They're mourning the loss of Christian cultural supremacy and demanding its restoration.

The foil? Secularists attacking Christianity making their demand for dominance sound like self-defense.

When you hear: Anti-"DEI"
It means: Pro-Segregation/Exclusion

Christopher Rufo deserves recognition for strategic brilliance, even as we condemn the strategy itself. He took the deeply unpopular concept of racial exclusion and rebranded it as opposition to "Diversity, Equity, and Inclusion." Suddenly, supporting segregation sounded like opposing unfairness.

Ron DeSantis turned Rufo's rebranding into political gold in Florida, dismantling diversity programs while claiming to fight discrimination.

The foil? "DEI" as reverse discrimination making exclusion sound like justice. Who wants to be labeled "anti-diversity"? But who doesn't want to be against policies that seem to favor some people over others?

It's the same segregationist impulse that's always existed, just with better marketing. Instead of "we don't want your type 'round here," it becomes "we're fighting unfair advantages." It's the same goal with sanitized language.

When you hear: "Border Security"
They mean: Xenophobia

Greg Abbott's rhetoric about "invasion" and Trump's fear-mongering about immigrants "poisoning the blood" [8.1] of America aren't really about security policy. They're about making fear of foreigners sound practical and reasonable.

A little sidetone about that comment. This was another reference that Trump used from Hitler's *Mein Kampf*, "All great cultures of the past perished only because the originally creative race died out from blood poisoning," [8.2] It probably doesn't help that when you regularly read the collected speeches of Hitler and keep it on your nightstand, you inevitably quote it. [8.3]

When they talk about "securing the border," they're not primarily concerned with immigration processes, they're feeding ancient fears about outsiders threatening the tribe.

The foil? Dangerous immigrants make xenophobia sound like common sense protection. Of course we should secure our borders. But listen closely to how they talk about the people on the other side of those borders, and you'll hear something much uglier than policy concerns.

When you hear: Anti-"Deep State"
They mean: Pro-Authoritarianism

Steve Bannon's war on the "administrative state" and Kash Patel's targeting of government institutions aren't about fighting corruption, they're about consolidating power. The "Deep State" is a convenient foil that allows them to justify dismantling the very institutions designed to check authoritarian impulses.

When they rail against bureaucrats and civil servants, they're not promoting good government. They're promoting the idea that only their loyalists should have power, and that any institutional resistance to that power is illegitimate.

The foil? Unelected bureaucrats undermine the people's choice making authoritarianism sound like democracy.

When you hear: "Religious Liberty"
They mean: Theocracy

This one is particularly insidious because it weaponizes

language that sounds fundamentally American. Of course we support religious liberty, it's in the First Amendment. But when Christian Nationalists talk about "religious liberty," they're not talking about protecting American's right to practice their faith freely.

They're talking about the right to impose Christian fundamentalism on others while being exempt from laws they find religiously inconvenient.

The foil? Secularists attacking religious freedom makes theocracy sound like constitutional protection. It's not about liberty at all. It's about power.

When you hear: "Protecting Children"
They mean: Homophobia/Transphobia

Perhaps no rebranding has been more effective than this one. Who doesn't want to protect children? By framing discrimination against LGBTQ+ individuals as child protection, they make bigotry sound caring and parental.

The foil? LGBTQ+ people are threats to children, which makes exclusion and discrimination sound like responsible guardianship. It's the same pattern we've seen throughout history: demonize the minority group as a threat to innocence, then justify whatever measures you want to take against them.

The genius of this linguistic manipulation is psychological. It allows people to support harmful ideologies while telling themselves they're being reasonable, protective, even virtuous. They're not advocating for supremacy, they're defending against attack. They're not promoting exclusion, they're protecting inclusion from those who would corrupt it.

The foil creates a victim narrative that turns oppressors into the oppressed. It provides defensive framing that makes aggression look like protection. And it offers moral laundering that wraps ugly ideas in righteous-sounding language.

Standing in that circle at the party, I was witnessing this machinery in action. Those guys weren't sitting around saying "let's be racist." They genuinely believed they were protecting their community from real threats. The rebranding had done its work so effectively that they couldn't even see what they were actually advocating for.

That's the power, and the danger, of the foil strategy. It doesn't just change how we talk about things. It changes how we think about them. It reshapes our moral intuitions so that exclusion feels like inclusion, supremacy feels like equality, and hatred feels like love.

But this linguistic sleight of hand doesn't happen in a vacuum. It needs intellectual infrastructure, and that's where figures like John MacArthur come in. For decades, MacArthur has provided the theological architecture that makes supremacist ideology sound biblically justified.

MacArthur's influence on evangelical thought cannot be overstated. His sermons reach millions, his books fill Christian bookstores, and his seminary has graduated pastors who now lead churches across the country. And throughout his career, he's provided religious justification for racial hierarchy.

In a 2001 sermon dealing with slavery, MacArthur promoted what's known as the "Curse of Ham" theory, the twisted interpretation of Genesis that suggests Black people were divinely ordained for servitude.[8.4] He stated explicitly that the descendants of Ham, including those who "constitute the African or Negro race," were cursed to serve others. In

MacArthur's telling, this wasn't historical injustice to be lamented, it was divine ordering to be accepted.

This wasn't fringe theology relegated to white supremacist websites. This was mainstream evangelical teaching, delivered from one of the most respected pulpits in conservative Christianity. MacArthur, author of almost 500 publications including 150 books describing what millions of American Christians consider "sound theology," provided biblical cover for the very racial hierarchies that figures like Tucker Carlson would later mainstream and Charlie Kirk would package for young audiences.

The pipeline is clear and deliberate: respected theologians like MacArthur provide the religious justification. Media figures mainstream the ideas. Youth leaders recruit the next generation. Each stage makes the ideology sound more reasonable, more defensible, and more Christian.

And here's the shav' at the heart of it all: using God's name to sanctify human hierarchies, using biblical language to justify exclusion, using Christian terminology to promote ideologies that Christ himself would condemn. It's taking the Lord's name in vain in the most literal and devastating way possible.

MacArthur didn't just provide intellectual cover for racism, he made it sound holy. He made it sound biblical. He made it sound like faithfulness to God's word rather than what it actually was: faithfulness to a racial caste system that benefits some people at the expense of others.

Charlie Kirk's assassination was a tragedy that solved nothing and only deepened the divisions his worldview helped create. But we cannot let the horror of his murder overshadow the substantial influence he had on conservative culture, particularly among young people.

Through Turning Point USA, Kirk had perfected the art of making supremacist ideology sound like patriotic common sense to college students. He understood something crucial: you can't recruit young people by talking explicitly about race or supremacy. They're too sophisticated for that. They've been raised in a world that taught them racism is wrong.

But you can absolutely get them fired up about "preserving American culture" and "protecting traditional values." You can talk about "demographic replacement" not as racial theory but as electoral strategy. You can frame opposition to immigration not as xenophobia but as economic protection for American workers.

The sophistication of Kirk's approach was remarkable and disturbing. His campus events drew thousands of students who thought they were learning about conservative politics and constitutional principles. What they were actually getting was a carefully crafted introduction to white nationalist thinking, wrapped in the language of patriotism and faith.

Kirk would bring in speakers who talked about the "Great Replacement" as if it were demographic analysis rather than conspiracy theory. He would frame anti-immigration policies as common sense rather than xenophobia. He would present opposition to diversity initiatives as defending merit rather than protecting privilege.

And it worked. It worked because he understood the foil strategy. He gave young people enemies to fight against, liberal professors indoctrinating students, social justice warriors destroying free speech, immigrants taking American jobs, and positioned conservatism as the defense against these threats.

The tragedy of Kirk's death doesn't erase the damage this pipeline has done. From TeenPact to Turning Point USA, we've watched conservative youth organizations evolve from civic education to ideological indoctrination, each generation becoming more sophisticated at hiding supremacist ideas behind reasonable-sounding language.

I know because I was in that pipeline. I attended TeenPact as a teenager, feeling that same intoxicating rush of being part of something bigger than myself, of having a divine mission to transform America. Looking back now, I can see how the language was carefully crafted, how the enemies were strategically chosen, and how the theology was selectively applied to make exclusion sound like faithfulness.

But this isn't new. Supremacist movements have always rebranded themselves when the old language becomes socially unacceptable. "Slavery" became "states' rights." "Segregation" became "separate but equal." "White supremacy" became "Great Replacement Theory."

Each generation thinks they've moved beyond the ugliness of the past, not realizing they've simply accepted a more palatable version of the same ideas. The language evolves, the enemies change, but the underlying ideology remains constant: some people matter more than others, some people belong more than others, and some people deserve power more than others.

Hitler understood this. He knew that if you could give people the right enemy, they would follow you anywhere. He knew that "fighting for the Aryan race" sounded better than "pursuing racial supremacy," even though they meant the same thing. He knew that framing Jews as a threat made genocide sound like self-defense.

And that's the most terrifying parallel: the foil strategy doesn't just make bad ideas sound good. It makes evil sound necessary. It makes cruelty sound like protection. It makes hatred sound like love.

When those guys at the party were talking about bringing in the National Guard and ICE to remove immigrants, Democrats, and "the blacks" from Little Rock, they genuinely believed they were talking about making the city safer. The foil, dangerous undesirables threatening our community, made ethnic cleansing sound like urban renewal.

That's how the rebranding works. That's how ordinary people end up supporting extraordinary evil. That's how Christians end up advocating for policies that Christ would weep over.

This linguistic manipulation is shav' in its most sophisticated form. It's using righteous language to justify unrighteous positions. It's using God's name to sanctify human hatred. It's using the vocabulary of justice to promote injustice.

When Franklin Graham wraps exclusion in religious liberty language, that's shav'. When Ron DeSantis calls segregation "anti-discrimination," that's shav'. When MacArthur uses biblical interpretation to justify racial hierarchy, that's shav'. When any of us use Christian terminology to justify policies that Christ himself would condemn, that's taking the Lord's name in vain in the most literal sense.

The Third Commandment isn't just about casual cursing or thoughtless oaths. It's about this: using God's name, God's authority, or God's reputation to advance human agendas that have nothing to do with God's actual character or desires.

Christian Nationalism has turned shav' into an art form. It's draped every exclusionary impulse in biblical language. It's framed every supremacist ideology as defending Christian values. It's made hatred sound holy and cruelty sound righteous.

And the most devastating part? Many of the people promoting these ideas genuinely believe they're being faithful. The rebranding has worked so well that they can't see what they're actually advocating for anymore. They think they're protecting children when they're promoting discrimination. They think they're defending America when they're advancing white supremacy. They think they're being faithful Christians when they're betraying Christ'a teachings.

Understanding the vocabulary is just the beginning. The real question isn't how they rebrand these ideologies, it's why we're so hungry for enemies to fight in the first place.

Because that's what all of this linguistic manipulation depends on: our deep, apparently insatiable appetite for having someone to blame, someone to fear, someone to fight against. The rebranding only works because we want it to work. We want clear enemies and simple solutions. We want to believe that our problems are caused by other people rather than by complex systems, historical patterns, or—God forbid—our own choices and complicity.

The conservative right didn't create this hunger for enemies. They just learned how to feed it more effectively than the left. They understood that if you can give people the right enemy to hate, they'll forgive almost anything else. They'll abandon their principles, ignore obvious contradictions, and support leaders they would normally despise, as long as those leaders promise to fight their enemies for them.

I saw this in that circle at the party. These weren't bad people. They weren't sitting around planning how to be racist or cruel. They were scared. Scared of change, scared of losing control, scared of a future that looks different from the past they remember. And someone had given them enemies to blame for that fear.

That's the most frightening realization of all. This isn't really about language at all. The words are just the delivery system. The real virus is our addiction to having enemies, our desperate need to believe that someone else is to blame for everything that's wrong with the world.

Standing there, nodding along before I caught myself, that moment revealed something I didn't want to face. It showed me how easy it is to be swept along when the enemy is defined and when the protective language is deployed skillfully, then the foil does its work.

The hunger for enemies runs deeper than politics or even theology. It taps into something primal in us, something that craves simple explanations and clear battle lines. Something that would rather have someone to fight than face the complex, uncomfortable reality that most of our problems don't have villains, they have causes. Historical causes, systemic causes, collective causes that implicate all of us.

But causes don't make good foils. You can't rally people against complexity. You can't generate outrage toward historical patterns. You need flesh-and-blood enemies. You need someone to point at and say, "There's the problem. There's the threat. There's what we're fighting against."

And once you have that enemy, once the foil is in place, the rest follows naturally. The erosion of empathy. The abandonment of Christ-like love. The willingness to support cruelty in the name of protection. The ability to call evil good and good evil without even realizing you've done it.

This is what happens when we let the foil strategy work on us. We stop being followers of the Prince of Peace and become soldiers in a war that has nothing to do with the Kingdom of God. We stop seeing people as image-bearers deserving of dignity and start seeing them as threats to be eliminated. We stop asking "What would Jesus do?" and start asking "How do we win?"

The answer to Christian Nationalism isn't better arguments or more compelling logic. Those things matter, but they're not enough. Because you can't reason someone out of a position they weren't reasoned into. You can't logic your way past the foil strategy when it's operating at the level of identity and belonging and psychological need.

The answer is something much harder: we have to confront the hunger itself. We have to ask ourselves why we're so desperate for enemies. What are we really afraid of? What are we really trying to protect? And is it worth sacrificing Christ's call to radical, boundary-breaking love?

These aren't rhetorical questions. They're the questions that should keep us awake at night. Because until we face them honestly, until we deal with the hunger that makes us vulnerable to the foil strategy in the first place, we'll keep falling for the same rebranded supremacy, the same sanitized hatred, the same old evil dressed up in new language.

Which raises the question that should terrify every one of us: What happens when a people who claim to follow the Prince of Peace become addicted to the psychology of war? What happens when Christians become so focused on fighting enemies that we forget to love neighbors? What happens when the foil strategy succeeds so completely that we can no longer tell the difference between defending the faith and betraying it?

The answers to these questions aren't abstract or academic. They're written in our churches, our politics, and our communities. They're written in conversations at parties where good people casually discuss ethnic cleansing. They're written in the theological justifications that make racism sound biblical. They're written in the youth movements that turn patriotism into nationalism and nationalism into supremacy.

And they're written in the uncomfortable truth that the line between standing in that circle nodding along and catching myself before it was too late. And that line is thinner than any of us want to admit.

9

THE APPEAL OF CHRISTIAN NATIONALISM

AND THE ALLURE OF A DIVINE MISSION

The intoxicating rush of being part of something bigger than yourself - that's what I felt at TeenPact. But looking back now, I can see it was more than just teenage enthusiasm. It was my first real taste of how Christian Nationalism taps into our deepest psychological needs.

This isn't just about politics or theology. It's about how our minds work, how we make sense of the world, how we find our place in it. Christian Nationalism offers a complete psychological package:

- A clear group identity that tells us exactly who we are
- The certainty we crave in an uncertain world
- Protection from the fears that haunt us
- Simple, clear moral boundaries in a complex world

Each of these elements reinforces the others, creating a powerful web that can be hard to recognize when you're caught in it - and even harder to break free from. This is why logical arguments alone often fail to counter Christian Nationalism. You can't reason someone out of a position they weren't reasoned into in the first place.

My own journey into this web began at fifteen. Not at a revival or a church camp, but in the marble halls of the Oklahoma State Capitol. I was there for TeenPact, a Christian-based leadership program designed to engage young people in politics and government. Little did I know that week would be my first real taste of the psychological allure of Christian Nationalism.

Dozens of teenagers, dressed in their Sunday best, flooded the halls. We weren't there just to learn about government. No, we were there on a mission - to reclaim America for Christ.

Our leaders spoke of a divine calling, of our generation being chosen by God to transform the nation. We weren't just studying policy and parliamentary procedure, we were training to be soldiers in a cultural war.

Looking back now, I can see TeenPact for what it was: a masterclass in the psychology of Christian Nationalism. It wasn't really about policy or even politics. It was about identity, purpose, and belonging. It was about feeling chosen, special, part of a spiritual story.

And let me tell you, for a fifteen-year-old trying to figure out his place in the world, that was intoxicating. Since that moment, some of my classmates have gone on to be councilmen, representatives, and senators.

Christian Nationalism isn't just a political ideology. It's not even just a theological stance. It's a worldview that taps into some of our deepest psychological needs and desires. It offers certainty in an uncertain world, identity in a culture of rootlessness, and purpose in a life that often feels meaningless.

TeenPact understood this intuitively. They knew that if

you could make a teenager feel like they're on a divine mission, then you have another Christian soldier.

In this chapter, we're going to dive deep into the psychological appeal of Christian Nationalism. We're going to explore why it's so attractive, why it's so persistent, and why simply pointing out its logical flaws isn't enough to counter its influence. Because until we understand its appeal, until we confront the very human needs and desires it taps into, we can't hope to offer a meaningful alternative.

Christian Nationalism offers a powerful sense of identity and belonging. It tells you exactly who you are: a soldier in God's army, a true American, a defender of the faith. It gives you a clear enemy to fight against: the secular world, the liberals, anyone who doesn't share your specific brand of Christianity. It's us versus them, good versus evil, light versus darkness. Simple. Clean. Comforting. But it's also dangerous as hell.

Because when your identity is so tightly bound to a particular group or ideology, you start to lose your ability to think critically. To question. To empathize with those outside your tribe.

I saw this play out in my own life. The more I embraced the identity of a "Christian patriot," the harder it became for me to relate to anyone who didn't fit that mold. My non-Christian friends? Potential converts. Democrats? The enemy. Anyone who questioned America's "Christian heritage"? Clearly deceived by Satan.

It was a worldview that left no space for genuine human connection across ideological lines. And isn't that the opposite of what Jesus taught? He constantly crossed social and cultural boundaries, reaching out to those His society deemed "other"?

The irony is bitter: in our quest to be more Christlike, we ended up building walls that Christ would have torn down. But breaking free from this tribal identity isn't easy. It's like leaving a cult - and in many ways, that's exactly what it is. You're not just changing your beliefs; you're reshaping your entire sense of self.

I remember the first time I really questioned my Christian nationalist identity. I was at college, surrounded by people from different backgrounds, different faiths, different political views. And to my shock, they weren't the godless heathens I'd been led to expect. They were just... people. Complex, flawed, beautiful people, trying to make sense of the world just like me.

It was enlightening. Like seeing in color for the first time after a lifetime of black and white. But it was also profoundly disorienting. If I wasn't the Christian soldier I'd always seen myself as, then who was I?

That's the question I've been wrestling with ever since. And I'll be honest - I don't have all the answers. But I'm learning that there's something more, in the questioning, in the constant becoming, in the unlearning.

I'm learning that true belonging isn't about conforming to a narrow identity, but about embracing the full complexity of who we are - and allowing others to do the same.

It's harder than the easy belonging offered by Christian Nationalism. It's messier. Less certain. But it's also more real. More human. And, I believe, more in line with the radical, boundary-breaking love of Christ.

Having a strong group identity feels good. It tells us who we are, who's with us, who's against us. But this tribal belonging creates another psychological need - the need to be certain we're on the right side.

You know another thing that keeps me up at night? It's not the fear of slipping a goddammit. It's the vast, terrifying uncertainty of existence. The knowledge that we're hurtling through space on a tiny rock, that our lives are fleeting, that so much of what happens to us is beyond our control. It's enough to make anyone long for a little certainty. And in that longing, in that deep-seated human need for solid ground beneath our feet, lies one of the most powerful appeals of Christian Nationalism.

In a world where nothing seems certain, Christian Nationalism offers absolute truths. Clear-cut answers. A spiritual narrative where everything makes sense.

- Why is there suffering? God's testing us.
- Why is America facing challenges? We've strayed from His path.
- What's our purpose? To bring America back to God.

Simple. Clean. Certain.

It's a worldview that provides a comforting framework for understanding life's complexities, reducing the vast, often overwhelming tapestry of human experience into a straightforward narrative of good versus evil, right versus wrong, us versus them.

I remember the comfort I used to find in this worldview. Growing up in the Bible Belt, everything was black and white. There were good guys and bad guys, right and wrong, saved and unsaved. The lines were clear, and I knew exactly where I stood. It was like living in a John Wayne movie - you always knew who to root for. The good guys wore the white hats while the bad guys wore the black hats. This certainty extended beyond personal morality into the realms of politics and national identity. America was God's chosen nation, and our civic duty was inextricably linked with our Christian calling. It was a simple, clear mission that gave purpose to every aspect of life.

But here's the uncomfortable truth I've had to struggle through: real life isn't a John Wayne movie. It's messy, complicated, and filled with more than 50 shades of gray that defy easy categorization. And that's where the certainty offered by Christian Nationalism's wheels start to fall off.

I remember the first time I really wrestled with this. I was in college, taking a New Testament class with Dr. Castleman. She was unlike any professor I'd ever had, her faith a stark contrast to the Christian Nationalism I'd grown up with.

Dr. Castleman understood scripture in a way I'd never encountered before. She lived by Jesus' words, not just preached them. Her class wasn't about simple answers or clear-cut certainties. It was about diving deep into the complexities of faith, about wrestling with difficult questions and uncomfortable truths.

At first, it was terrifying. Everything I thought I knew was being challenged. The neat, tidy worldview of Christian Nationalism was crumbling under the weight of real, substantive biblical scholarship. But as the semester progressed, something unexpected happened. Instead of feeling lost without my familiar certainties, I felt... alive. Engaged. Like I was finally starting to understand the depth and richness of my faith.

Dr. Castleman showed me that it was okay to question, to doubt, to wrestle with God. That faith could be strong even when - perhaps especially when - it wrestled with life's complexities.

This was a far cry from the Christian Nationalism I'd known. Where it offered simple answers, Dr. Castleman encouraged thoughtful questions. Where it was painted in black and white, she revealed a world of vibrant colors.

It wasn't easy. Starting to let go of the certainty I'd clung to for so long felt like stepping off a cliff. But with each class, each discussion, I began to see that there was solid ground beneath my feet - just not the ground I'd expected.

The appeal of Christian Nationalism lies in its simplicity.

It offers clear enemies, straightforward solutions, a sense of righteous purpose. It's a soothing ointment for the anxieties of an uncertain world.

But it's a false comfort. It reduces the rich, complex tapestry of faith into a blunt instrument, more concerned with power than with truth.

The faith I discovered in Dr. Castleman's class - and have been exploring ever since - is different. It's not about having all the answers. It's about engaging with the questions. It's about seeking the truth, even when that truth is uncomfortable or not what you wanted it to be.

This faith isn't always easy. It doesn't offer the same clear-cut certainties that Christian Nationalism does. But it's real. It's authentic. And I believe it's far closer to the faith Jesus lived and taught.

Twenty years later, I think about Dr. Castleman often. If I knew her today, I believe we'd see eye to eye on this subject. She taught me that faith can be both deeply rooted and wildly expansive. That it can provide a firm foundation without building walls.

The challenge, then, is this: How do we address the very real human need for certainty and purpose without falling into the trap of Christian Nationalism?

When our certainties are challenged - and they always are in this complex world - fear isn't far behind. That's where Christian Nationalism's masterful use of fear comes into play.

Fear works in mysterious ways. I was sixteen when Y2K hysteria gripped the Christian community. The turn of the millennium preyed on our deepest apocalyptic fears - would it be the Rapture or global collapse? Jesus coming back or society breaking down? Nobody knew for sure, but it had to be one or the other.

I watched as this fear made people do the craziest things.

One family I knew bought a bunch of land and built an entire homestead in preparation for economic collapse. Churches organized lock-ins - partly to minister to teens, but mostly, I suspect, to make sure we were all in one place if Jesus decided to slide down the chimney at midnight.

My grandfather tried to calm the hysteria. "They're making this into more than it is," he said. "I was in charge of replacing the systems in the Memphis Air Traffic Control tower in the '80s in preparation for this." But fear has a way of drowning out rational voices.

I ended up at one of those New Year's Eve lock-ins at a friend's church. Looking around the property, I noticed something interesting - the pastor's house sat right next to the power pole with the church's main breaker. Being a teenager with questionable judgment and some basic knowledge of electricity, I hatched a plan. The pastor, showing either impressive humor or questionable judgment of his own, agreed to flip that switch at midnight.

The countdown began. Prayers were lifted. Hands were raised. And then... BOOM! Darkness.

What happened next was pure chaos. Even the most devout among us blurted out words that definitely weren't in the church's hymnal. My girlfriend's Dr Pepper found a new home all over my clothes. And for a brief moment, raw fear stripped away every layer of religiosity, revealing just how thin the veneer really was.

The spell broke when someone noticed the outdoor light pole was still on. But in those few seconds of darkness, I witnessed something profound: how quickly fear can peel back our facades, revealing the scared little humans underneath.

Looking back, Y2K was more than just a collective moment of panic. It was a window into how fear operates in Christian communities - how it can drive us to build homesteads we don't really want, gather in churches to await the end times, and momentarily forget all our religious training at the flip of a switch. It shows how easily fear can override both faith and reason, leading even sincere believers to actions that, in retrospect, seem almost comical.

But here's the thing about fear - it's also a powerful tool for control. It can make you see enemies where there are none. It can make you cling to false securities. It can make you betray your deepest values in the name of self-preservation.

This manipulation of fear reminds me of Peeta's ordeal in *The Hunger Games.* Just as Peeta was injected with venom to induce terror and turn him against Katniss, we often see fear used as a weapon in our society. It distorts our perceptions, making us view even those we once loved as threats. Like Katniss, who became a target of Peeta's fear-induced rage, entire groups of people can become scapegoats when we're caught in the grip of manufactured panic. This artificial fear can override our rational thinking and core values, leading us to act in ways that betray our true selves and hurt those around us. The real danger lies in how easily this fear can spread, turning communities against each other and eroding the trust that binds us together. And let me tell you,

Christian Nationalism deals in fear like a dealer deals in meth.

But this isn't a new phenomenon. The roots of this fear-based faith run deep in American Christianity, all the way back to the Great Awakening of the 18th century. And at the heart of that movement was a sermon that would shape the American religious psyche for generations to come: Jonathan Edwards' "Sinners in the Hands of an Angry God."

It's July 8, 1741 at a Congregationalist church in Enfield, Connecticut. Edwards takes the pulpit and begins to speak. His words paint a vivid, terrifying picture of humanity's precarious position before a wrathful deity: "The God that holds you over the pit of hell," he says, "much as one holds a spider, or some loathsome insect over the fire, abhors you, and is dreadfully provoked: his wrath towards you burns like fire; he looks upon you as worthy of nothing else, but to be cast into the fire."[9.1.1]

I'm sure the effect was electric. People weeping, crying out, and clinging to the pillars of the church, feeling as if the very floor might at any moment open up and plunge them into the fiery pit. It was a masterclass in the use of fear as a spiritual motivator, and it worked. The Great Awakening spread like wildfire, fueled by this potent mixture of terror and hope for salvation.

But while Edwards' intention was to awaken people to their need for divine grace, the legacy of his approach has been far more complex and, in many ways, problematic. It laid the groundwork for a strain of American Christianity that sees the world through a lens of fear, constantly on guard against the threats of divine punishment, worldly corruption, or "the other."

Fast forward to today, and you can still hear the echoes of Edwards' fire and brimstone in the rhetoric of Christian Nationalism. The spirit of God's wrath has been replaced by fears of secular humanism, liberal agendas, or the decline of "traditional values." But the underlying message remains the same: be afraid. Be very, very afraid.

I remember sitting in church as a teenager, listening to dire warnings about the threats facing our faith, our values, our very way of life. The secular world was out to get us. Liberals wanted to destroy the family. The government was trying to silence Christians. Every news story, every cultural shift, every political development was framed as part of an ongoing war against Christianity. It was terrifying. And it was meant to be.

Because fear is a powerful motivator, it bypasses our rational mind and goes straight for the gut. It makes us react instead of reflect. It makes us circle the wagons and demonize the "other." In short, it makes us ripe for manipulation.

But, when you're constantly on the defensive, constantly afraid, you lose sight of what you're supposedly defending. The loving, compassionate, world-changing faith of Jesus gets twisted into something small, scared, and mean-spirited. "The Good News" becomes "the bad news" for anyone who doesn't think, look, or believe like you do.

And the real tragedy? Most of these "threats" are massively over exaggerated, if not entirely imaginary. Just as the congregants in Edwards' church weren't actually about to fall into a literal pit of fire, the modern Christian faith isn't on the brink of extinction because of social progress or political shifts.

In fact, the Christian faith not only isn't in danger of being overcome, it can't be overcome by any of these supposed threats at all. This isn't just optimism or wishful thinking - it's a promise straight from Christ himself. Remember His words to Peter in Matthew 16:18:

> And I also say to you that you are Peter, and upon this rock I will build My church; and the gates of Hades will not overpower it

The gates of hell itself cannot prevail against the church. So why are we acting like a few cultural shifts or political disagreements are going to be its downfall? This fear-mongering isn't just unnecessary - it's a profound lack of faith in the very promises of Christ.

It's taken me years to unlearn this fear-based mentality. To realize that diversity isn't a threat, but a reflection of God's creativity. That social progress isn't an attack on faith, but often an expression of the very values Jesus taught. That the Kingdom of God isn't some fragile thing that can be destroyed by political decisions or cultural shifts. It's a reality we're called to live out here and now, through love, justice, and radical inclusion.

Don't get me wrong - there are real challenges facing our world. Real injustices to fight. Real reasons for concern. But meeting those challenges from a place of fear and defensiveness isn't the answer.

Jesus didn't call us to circle the wagons. He called us to go out into the world, to be salt and light, to love our neighbors and even our enemies. That's a call that requires courage, not fear. Openness, not defensiveness. Love, not paranoia.

So here's my challenge: The next time you feel that fear rising, the next time you hear warnings about threats to faith and morals, take a deep breath. Step back. Ask yourself: Is this really something to be afraid of? Or is this an opportunity to live out my faith in a new and challenging context? Is the appropriate response to circle the wagons, or to reach out in love? Am I acting out of fear, or out of the perfect love that casts out fear?

It's not easy. Believe me, I know. Fear is a potent force, and Christian Nationalism has weaponized it to a devastating effect, building on a foundation laid centuries ago. But we have a choice. We can continue to let fear drive us, to let it shrink our faith and our world. Or we can choose courage. We can choose love. We can choose to live out a faith that's big enough, bold enough, and beautiful enough to transform the world.

Not through power or control or cultural dominance. But through the radical, fearless love of Christ. It's a risk. It's uncertain. It might cost us our comfortable illusions of security.

Fear drives us to seek safety. And what feels safer than clear, unambiguous rules? This is where Christian Nationalism's appeal to moral absolutes becomes so powerful.

In a world of moral gray areas, Christian Nationalism offers something incredibly appealing: black and white certainty.

Growing up in the Bible Belt, I was steeped in this worldview. Everything was neatly categorized into "godly" and "ungodly." There was no room for nuance, no space for questioning. It was comforting, in a way. You always knew where you stood. But here's the problem:

Real life isn't that simple and neither is morality.

The appeal of clear moral boundaries is understandable. It provides a sense of security, a feeling of righteousness. It makes decision-making easier - you don't have to wrestle with complex ethical dilemmas when everything is pre-sorted into "right" and "wrong."

But this simplification comes at a cost. It leads to a stunted moral development, an inability to truly understand the complexities of real-world ethical situations. It can make us judgmental and mean-spirited, unable to empathize with those whose experiences don't fit neatly into our moral categories.

I've seen this play out in debates over issues like abortion, where complex medical situations are reduced to simplistic slogans. I've watched as nuanced discussions about gender and sexuality are shut down with a quick reference to a handful of Bible verses, ignoring the real complexities of human beings.

The irony is, Jesus himself often challenged the overly simplistic moral codes of his day. He ate with outcasts, touched the untouchable, and frequently pointed out the hypocrisy of those who thought they had it all figured out.

Breaking free from this mindset isn't easy. It requires a willingness to engage with complexity, to wrestle with difficult questions, and to challenge our own assumptions. But it also opens us up to a richer, more nuanced understanding of morality - one that reflects the depth and breadth of God's love and justice in a complex world.

Unlearning is hard.

There's a reason they say "old habits die hard." And when those habits are tied to your very identity, your understanding of God and country? Well, breaking free feels less like changing a habit and more like shedding your own skin.

I remember how I first really started questioning my Christian nationalist beliefs. It wasn't a lightning bolt moment. It was more like a slow, creeping discomfort. A growing awareness that the neat, tidy worldview I'd been handed didn't quite fit the reality I was experiencing.

It started with small things. Realizing that my non-Christian friends weren't the heathens I'd been led to expect and often acted in ways more Christlike than my circle of Christian influences. Noticing the disconnect between the "Christian" politicians I supported and the teachings of Christ. Feeling a gnawing unease every time I recited the Pledge of Allegiance in church, or really at all. But admitting these doubts? That was terrifying.

Because questioning Christian Nationalism wasn't just about changing my political views. It was about reshaping my entire identity.

The cognitive dissonance was crippling. I'd find myself defending beliefs I no longer fully held, clinging to certainties that were crumbling beneath my feet. It was easier to ignore the doubts, to push them down, to surround myself with voices that reinforced what I'd always believed. But here's the thing about truth: once you start seeing it, you can't unsee it.

Breaking free from Christian Nationalism is a journey. It's a process of deconstructing and reconstructing, of questioning and seeking, of letting go and embracing anew. And it's not for the faint of heart.

It requires intellectual humility - the willingness to admit that maybe, just maybe, you don't have all the answers. It demands emotional resilience - the strength to weather the storm of uncertainty that comes when you let go of false certainties. And it calls for spiritual courage - the faith to believe that God is big enough to handle your questions, your doubts, your wrestling.

It's meant reexamining scripture with fresh eyes, seeking to understand the cultural and historical context rather than applying a simplistic interpretation. It's meant engaging with diverse perspectives, listening to voices I'd previously dismissed or ignored. And perhaps hardest of all, it's meant having difficult conversations with friends and family who still hold the beliefs I've left behind. It's meant risking relationships, facing accusations of backsliding or betraying the faith.

But here's what I've discovered: On the other side of this unlearning is a faith that's deeper, richer, more authentic. A faith that's big enough to embrace complexity, humble enough to admit uncertainty, and strong enough to truly love my neighbor - even when that neighbor looks, thinks, or believes differently than me.

Understanding these psychological dynamics isn't just academic - it's essential for breaking free from them. When we recognize how Christian Nationalism taps into our basic human needs and fears, we can begin to imagine healthier ways to meet those needs. Ways that don't require us to demonize others, oversimplify complex realities, or betray the radical love at the heart of Christ's teachings.

The journey of unlearning isn't easy. It means facing our fears, embracing uncertainty, and finding new ways to belong. But before we can chart that path forward, we need to understand how these psychological forces shape our daily lives and institutions. Because what starts in the mind doesn't stay there - it flows out into our churches, our politics, and our communities, creating patterns of behavior that can either heal or harm. And those patterns? They're about to become painfully clear.

10

THE SEDUCTION OF POWER
AND THE TEMPTATION OF A THEOCRACY

L et's talk about power. Raw, unvarnished, earthly power. It's not something we Christians like to admit we're attracted to. But if we're honest with ourselves, the allure of power - especially power wielded in God's name - is real. And it's at the very heart of Christian Nationalism.

This temptation isn't new. It goes all the way back to the Garden of Eden, to the serpent's whisper: "You will be like God." And even before that, it's the same sin that led to Lucifer's fall - the desire to grasp power, to be in control.

In the context of Christian Nationalism, it manifests as the temptation to build the Kingdom of God through worldly power. To create a Christian nation not through love and service, but through legislation and coercion.

I've seen the corrosive effects of this mindset up close, and let me tell you, it's ugly. I've watched friends and family members completely turn a blind eye to behavior that, in any other context, they would condemn without hesitation. All in the name of gaining or maintaining political power for "God's side."

The most glaring example in recent years has been the support for Donald Trump. Here's a man who has openly brags about sexual assault ("grab 'em by the pussy"), mocked a disabled reporter, called for a "total and complete shutdown of Muslims entering the United States," has been convicted of multiple felonies, found liable for sexual abuse, and publicly accused of rape by at least 26 women. He's a man who has displayed vanity, promiscuity, and a casual relationship with the truth that would make a snake oil salesman blush.

And yet, I've seen Christian after Christian excuse it all away. "He's not perfect, but he's God's chosen instrument," they say. Or, "We're electing a president, not a pastor." And my favorite, "We're not writing a love letter, we're making a strategic chess move to create the future that we want." Yuck. I've heard people justify his treatment of women by saying, "King David had his flaws too."

It's not just about overlooking flaws. It's about actively embracing someone whose actions and words are antithetical to everything Jesus taught. Trump has said he's never asked God for forgiveness because he doesn't feel he needs to.[9.1] He's referred to taking communion as "drinking my little wine and having my little cracker.[9.2] He's used tear gas to clear peaceful protesters for a photo op with a Bible he held upside down.[9.3] Some say the crowd being tear gassed was unrelated to him taking a photo op minutes later. But if that was the case, then where's the apology? It's astounding.

And yet, for many Christians, he became a messianic figure. Why? Because he promised them power. He promised to "Make America Great Again," to give the church its place at the center of American life once more.

It's a reminder of how deeply the desire for power can corrupt our moral compass. How easily we can convince ourselves that the ends justify the means, even when those means involve supporting someone who embodies the very opposite of Christian values.

But, Jesus explicitly rejected worldly power as a means of establishing His kingdom (Luke 4:5-8). When Satan offered Him control over all the kingdoms of the world, He refused. When the crowd wanted to make Him king by force, He bowed out (John 6:15).

Christ's kingdom, He said, is not of this realm (John 18:36). It doesn't advance through political chess-like maneuvering or state coercion. It grows through love, service, and radical, self-giving grace.

The road away from this temptation isn't easy. It requires us to embrace a kind of holy powerlessness. To trust that God's purposes will be fulfilled not through our control of society, but through our faithful witness within it.

Because here's the truth: The Kingdom of God doesn't need our political schemes. It needs our faithful obedience. It doesn't advance through control, but through sacrificial love.

And that's a power that no election can give, and no political defeat can take away.

But if Christian Nationalism can't seize power to build God's kingdom in the future, surely it can restore it to some glorious past when America truly was a Christian nation. Right?

There's something seductive about the "good old days," isn't there? That hazy, golden-hued past where everything was simpler, purer, better. For many caught in the web of Christian Nationalism, that idealized past takes the form of a "Christian America" - a time when faith was strong, values were clear, and God's favor rested squarely on our nation.

I remember sitting at my grandparents' dinner table,

listening to stories about this mythical era. "Back then," they'd say, "people respected the Bible. Kids prayed in school. Businesses were closed on Sundays and everybody went to church. America was a God-fearing nation."

It sounded like paradise. A stark contrast to the moral decay and spiritual confusion they saw in the present. But here's the thing about nostalgia:

It's a liar. A beautiful, comforting liar, but a liar nonetheless.

The reality is, this "Christian America" never existed. Not in the 1950s, not in the 1850s, not even in the days of the Founding Fathers. The rosy picture painted by Christian Nationalism is a masterwork of selective memory, glossing over the injustices, complexities, and contradictions that have always been part of our national story.

Sure, prayer was allowed in schools in the 1950s. But so was segregation. Churches might have been full on Sundays, but many of them were preaching a gospel of racial hatred. The "traditional values" so often yearned for often included the systematic oppression of women, minorities, and anyone who didn't fit the mold of white Christianity.

This isn't to say that there was nothing good in the past, or that we can't learn from history. But the uncritical glorification of a mythical "Christian America" does more harm than good. It blinds us to the progress we've made, the work still to be done, and the complex realities of both past and present.

I've had to confront this in my own life. Growing up, I was fed a steady diet of David Barton-style "Christian history," which painted America as a nation explicitly founded on biblical principles, its Founding Fathers as devout Christians establishing a Christian nation. It was a narrative that made me feel proud, special, and chosen.

But as I dug deeper, as I actually read the writings of Jefferson, Madison, and others, I discovered a much more complex picture. Yes, many of the Founders were Christian, but others were not. Yes, biblical ideas influenced some of their thinking, but so did Enlightenment philosophy and classical republicanism. The story was far richer, far more complex than I had been led to believe.

Letting go of the myth of a "Christian America" wasn't easy. It meant giving up a comforting narrative, a sense of divine national destiny. It meant confronting the ugly parts of our history alongside the inspiring ones. It meant acknowledging that perhaps God's plan for America isn't what we've always assumed it to be.

But it also opened up new possibilities. If America wasn't founded as an explicitly Christian nation, then maybe our faith isn't dependent on political power or cultural dominance. Maybe we're called to be faithful citizens and witnesses in a pluralistic society, rather than trying to resurrect some imagined Christian golden age.

The challenge for us now is to engage with our national story honestly, in all its complexity. To learn from the past without idealizing it. To work towards a better future without trying to recreate a mythical past.

It's a harder road than the one offered by Christian Nationalism. It requires us to wrestle with ambiguity, to unlearn contradictory truths. But it's also a road that leads to a richer, more authentic faith and a more honest patriotism.

So the next time you hear someone yearning for the "good old days" of Christian America, pause. Ask yourself: What's really being longed for here? Whose experiences are being centered, and whose are being erased? How might this nostalgia be blinding us to the work God is calling us to do here and now?

Because here's the truth: God isn't limited to working in the past. The Kingdom of God isn't about restoring an idealized historical moment. It's about bringing justice, love, and redemption in the here and now, in all the messy complexity of our current world.

Maybe instead of trying to "Make America Great Again" (as if it ever truly was), we should focus on making our faith more Christ-like. Maybe instead of yearning for a mythical golden age, we should be working to build a future that truly reflects God's love and justice for all people.

But beyond this nostalgia for an imagined past lies an even more powerful belief - the conviction that America holds a unique and divine purpose in God's plan.

Growing up in the Bible Belt, I was steeped in the ideology of American exceptionalism. From church pulpits to home-school curricula, the message was clear: America had a special calling from God. We were a city on a hill, a light to the nations.

But here's the thing about feeling chosen: it can make you arrogant. Self-righteous. Blind to your own faults and dismissive of others' virtues.

The idea of America as God's chosen nation isn't new. It's been woven into our national mythology since the days of the Puritans. This narrative of divine purpose has shaped our politics, our foreign policy, even our sense of national identity.

It's a powerful story. And it's also a dangerous lie.

Because when you believe your nation has a divine

mandate, it becomes easy to justify all sorts of actions in the name of fulfilling that purpose. Manifest Destiny? Just fulfilling God's plan for America to stretch from sea to shining sea. American imperialism? Spreading God's favor to heathen nations.

Now, it's true that the Bible speaks of a chosen people and a promised land. But wait for it: that's not us. Those promises were made to a specific people in a specific time and place - and they look a lot more like the people we've often oppressed than like us.

The truth is, the idea of America as God's new chosen nation sits uneasily with the teachings of Jesus. Christ spoke of a kingdom not of this world. He called his followers to be citizens of heaven first, to love all nations, to seek justice for all people.

Breaking free from this mindset isn't easy. It requires us to confront a more complex, less flattering view of our nation's history and role in the world. It demands that we hold our patriotism more loosely, subjecting it to the higher claims of our faith.

But it also opens up new possibilities. When we let go of the idea that America has some unique, divine purpose, we're free to engage more honestly with our nation's strengths and weaknesses. We're able to appreciate the good in other nations and cultures. We're challenged to live out our faith in ways that transcend national boundaries.

That's a harder truth to swallow than the sugar-rush of American exceptionalism. But it's a truth that can lead us to a faith that's bigger than any one nation, and a love that knows no borders.

Of course, letting go of American exceptionalism isn't just intellectually challenging - it creates a profound psychological tension. When deeply held beliefs about God's special relationship with America collide with the reality of our nation's past and present, something has to give. This brings us to one of the most powerful psychological forces at work in Christian Nationalism.

Let's talk about cognitive dissonance. It's that uncomfortable feeling you get when you hold two conflicting beliefs at the same time. And let me tell you, it's at the very heart of why many Christians vote the way they do.

I've felt it myself. That nagging discomfort when my faith tells me one thing, but my political allegiances pull me in another direction. It's like trying to serve two masters, and we all know how well that works out.

Here's where it gets really tricky: As Christians, we often feel a moral imperative to vote for policies that align with our understanding of God's will. It feels wrong, even sinful, to support things like legalizing same-sex marriage or allowing any form of abortion. After all, many Christians believe these things go against God's design for holy living.

But here's a key point that I need you to hear: we also know, deep down, that holiness can't be legislated. We know that following the letter of the law - any law, whether God's or man's - doesn't make anyone holy. And that's a whole book in and of itself.

So we're left with this tension: How do we reconcile our desire to see God's will reflected in our laws with the knowledge that laws can't actually make people holy? It's enough to tie your brain in knots.

But what if we've been approaching this all wrong? What if, in our zeal to create a "Christian nation," we've actually been working against the very principles of our faith?

Here's a radical thought: Being Christian and voting to incorporate our religious beliefs into law might actually be in direct opposition to our faith. Let me break it down:

1. We know from scripture that the law doesn't make us holy. Following rules, even God's rules, isn't enough. It's about the spirit, not just the letter.
2. If following the letter of the law doesn't make us holy, why on earth would we try to force others to follow it through legislation?

The answer, I believe, lies in how we understand our relationship with our neighbors - and how we vote affects that relationship profoundly.

When we vote, we're not just expressing our personal beliefs. We're making decisions that impact the lives of our neighbors - all our neighbors, whether they share our faith or not. And what does Jesus tell us about our neighbors? To love them. Not to legislate them into holiness, but to love them.

I've heard the counterarguments. Some say, "If we truly love our neighbors, we won't cause them to stumble by allowing sinful behavior." Others argue for "tough love," claiming that true love means legislating morality to keep people from harming themselves. Still others insist, "If we love them, we wouldn't let them do these things."

But these arguments are reading between the lines of Jesus' words, inserting meanings He never said. Jesus never said, "Love your neighbor by making laws to control their behavior." He never equated love with legislation or governmental control.

In fact, when given the opportunity to condemn or use the law against those society deemed sinful, like the woman caught in adultery, Jesus chose mercy and personal transformation over legal punishment. The story itself is deeply revealing: When her accusers brought her before Jesus, demanding judgment according to the law of Moses, He stooped down and wrote in the sand. Then He said, "He who is without sin among you, let him be the first to throw a stone at her" (John 8:7). And one by one, from the oldest to the youngest, they dropped their stones and walked away until Jesus was left alone with the woman.

This detail is profound - Scripture specifically notes that Jesus was alone with her. No crowd. No public shame. No performative correction. In that intimate moment, He asked her, "Woman, where are they? Did no one condemn you?" She responded, "No one, Lord." Then Jesus said, "I do not condemn you, either. Go. From now on sin no more" (John 8:10-11).

This is the model Jesus gave us - not public condemnation or legislative force, but personal, transformative encounters marked by both truth and grace. He focused on changing hearts, not enforcing laws. What a stark contrast to our modern approach of trying to legislate morality through public policy and loud, performative judgment.

By trying to legislate morality, we're not following Jesus' example; we're potentially creating barriers between people and the transformative love of Christ. We're substituting our judgment for God's grace, and that's a dangerous path to tread. Jesus called us to love our neighbors, to serve them, to show them compassion - not to rule over them or force them into our vision of righteousness. When we try to use the law to enforce our religious beliefs, we risk becoming modern-day Pharisees, more concerned with rules than with the heart of God's law: love.

So maybe, just maybe, when we step into that voting booth, we need to ask ourselves one simple question:

How would love vote?

Let's bring it close to home. Imagine your neighbor is [insert something about them that you believe doesn't align with God's desire for us]. If you had the power to set a law that affected only them, would you strip away the legal rights that everyone else enjoys? Would that action make them more open to the faith we're called to share, or would it build walls of resentment and mistrust?

Are we relying on the law to do what only love can accomplish? Are we diminishing the power of the Holy Spirit to transform people from the inside out?

I've had to wrestle with this myself. I've had to confront the cognitive dissonance between my desire to see my Christian values reflected in society and my call to love my neighbors unconditionally. And let me tell you, it's not an easy wrestling match.

But here's what I've come to realize: When we vote based on love for our neighbors rather than a desire to enforce our religious beliefs, we're actually being more faithful to Christ's teachings. We're acknowledging that our role is to love, not to judge or coerce. We're recognizing that God's relationship with individuals is just that - individual - and not something we can legislate.

I'm reminded of the words of Jim Walz, the 2024 Vice-Presidential candidate, at the Democratic National Convention in August 2024. He said, "I represented my neighbors in Congress for 12 years. And I learned an awful lot. I learned how to work across the aisle on issues like growing the rural economies and taking care of veterans. And I learned how to compromise without compromising my values." [9.4]

Walz's words hit me like a ton of bricks. Here was a man who had figured out how to vote for his neighbor, how to navigate the complex terrain of faith and politics without losing sight of either. It was a stark contrast to what I witnessed at the Republican National Convention.

Before the RNC, JD Vance, the vice presidential Republican nominee, voiced his support for mass deportation in an interview with Sean Hannity on Fox News. "We have to deport people," Vance told Hannity. "We have to deport people who broke our laws [by the act of coming here] who came in here." [9.5]

At the RNC itself, Ted Cruz, the senator from Texas, declared: "We are facing an invasion on our southern border – not figuratively, a literal invasion." Cruz later claimed that Democrats wanted "votes from illegals." [9.2.2]

The contrast between Walz's approach and the rhetoric I was hearing from the RNC was stark.

Walz's words were a reminder for what it means when we stop trying to create a "Christian nation" through legislation and instead focus on being Christ-like citizens in a diverse society. It means we prioritize policies that promote justice, compassion, and human dignity for all, not just those who believe as we do.

Breaking free from the cognitive dissonance of Christian Nationalism isn't easy. It requires us to hold complex truths in tension. To recognize that God's will for individual lives doesn't necessarily translate into how we should vote or govern a pluralistic society.

It's liberating isn't it? It frees us from the burden of trying to play Holy Spirit to our neighbors. It allows us to engage in politics not as culture warriors, but as servants and peacemakers.

And isn't that, after all, what Jesus called us to be?

So the next time you feel that cognitive dissonance creeping in as you approach a voting decision, pause. Ask yourself: Am I voting out of love for my neighbors - all my neighbors? Or am I trying to use the law to do what only God's grace can accomplish?

Because when we vote from a place of love rather than a desire for control, we're not just being better citizens. We're being better followers of Christ.

So where do we go from here? I believe the answer lies in cultivating what I call a "neighborly faith." A faith that takes seriously Jesus' command to love our neighbors as ourselves - not just the neighbors who look like us or vote like us, but all of our neighbors.

About four years ago, I believe it was Easter Sunday of either 2020 or 2021. I found myself sitting in Hot Springs Baptist Church in Hot Springs, AR, listening to Reverend Manley Beasley, Jr. preach. Now, Beasley is a man respected by many, including several members of my family. He comes from a legacy of "godly" men, as they say. On this particular Sunday, he was preaching about this very concept of neighborly faith. And then, as plain as day, he said something that made my jaw hit the floor:

> Now who are our neighbors? I don't mean those outside of the church, or you know, liberals and foreigners. Jesus meant your fellow Christians, brothers and sisters in Christ.

I could not believe my ears. The congregation around me nodded and "Amened" as if heresy hadn't just flowed from the pulpit. In that moment, I felt a sharp pain in my leg - my wife, bless her fiery soul, had dug her nails into me. If I hadn't quickly placed my hand over hers, I'm pretty sure she would've stood up right then and there, in front of a thousand people, to set the good reverend straight. My wife's not one to let sleeping dogs lie, especially when they're spouting stuff like that.

The irony, of course, is that Jesus actually did define who our neighbors are. Remember the parable of the Good Samaritan? When asked "Who is my neighbor?", Jesus told a story about a despised foreigner who showed compassion to a stranger in need. He made it clear that our "neighbor" isn't just the person who looks like us, believes like us, or lives next door to us. Our neighbor is anyone and everyone, especially those we might be tempted to exclude.

Yet here was Rev. Beasley, and an entire congregation, completely missing the point. And why? Because his interpretation aligned perfectly with the core beliefs of Christian Nationalism. It's an easy answer, a comfortable one. It doesn't challenge us to look beyond our church walls or political affiliations. But it's a lie, plain and simple.

This moment crystallized for me just how deeply Christian Nationalism has infected our understanding of faith. It's twisted even the most basic teachings of Jesus into something exclusionary and self-serving. We've taken the radical, barrier-breaking love that Christ preached and turned it into a country club membership. And that, my friends, is about as far from neighborly faith as you can get.

In my experience, even bringing up Christ's command to love our neighbors often unleashes criticism from fellow Christians. I've been accused of offering a "copout," of watering down the faith, of compromising with the world.

It's a bizarre twist, isn't it? Being criticized for emphasizing what Jesus Himself said was equally as important as the greatest commandment.

I remember one particularly heated discussion with a long-time friend from my church. When I suggested that our political engagement should be guided by love for our neighbors, he scoffed. "That's just liberal feel-good hullabaloo," he said. "We're called to stand for truth, not cave to the world's demands."

But is it really a copout to take Jesus at His word? Is it weakness to prioritize love and compassion in our civic engagement?

The pushback I've received reveals something profound about the mindset of Christian Nationalism. It's a worldview that's often more focused on power and control than on embodying the love of Christ. It's a faith that's more comfortable with judgment than with grace, more interested in winning culture wars than in winning hearts.

This reaction also exposes a fundamental misunderstanding of what Christ-like love really means. It's not about being "nice" or avoiding conflict. It's about seeking the genuine good of others, even when it's difficult or costly to ourselves.

A neighborly faith doesn't mean abandoning our convictions. It means holding those convictions with humility, engaging with those who disagree with respect and empathy, and always, always prioritizing the command to love.

It's a high calling, and one that often puts us at odds with the prevailing Christian nationalist narrative. It requires us to resist the allure of easy answers and scapegoats, to continually examine our own hearts and motives.

But isn't this closer to the example Christ set for us? A Savior who crossed social and cultural boundaries, who challenged religious and political authorities, who called us to a kingdom not of this world?

As we move forward, we need to ask ourselves some hard questions. How have we allowed our faith to be co-opted by political agendas? How can we reclaim the radical, boundary-breaking love of Christ in our civic engagement? And perhaps most challengingly, how do we love our neighbors - all of our neighbors - in a way that truly reflects the heart of God?

The psychological appeal of Christian Nationalism runs deep, tapping into our most basic needs for certainty, belonging, and purpose. But there's something even more fundamental at stake - something hiding in plain sight, embedded in the very words we use to describe our faith. It's time we talk about the label we've worn so proudly, and how it might be strangling the very faith it claims to represent.

11

THE LANGUAGE THAT BLINDS US
THE WEIGHT OF A WORD

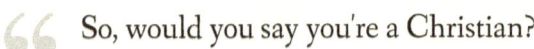 So, would you say you're a Christian?

T he question hung in the air, hovering over the remnants of our meal like an uninvited guest. Georgia's words, spoken with genuine curiosity.

My wife and I were recently gathered around our dining table with our friends Georgia and Josh. The aroma of a home-cooked meal lingered in the air, mingling with the gentle clink of wine glasses and the rustle of game pieces being arranged for PLAYTE, a game we'd recently prototyped. There was an ease to the evening, the kind that comes with true friendship - where conversations can drift into life's deeper waters without fear of drowning.

The talk had meandered, as it often does, through the labyrinth of life's big questions. We touched on spirituality, existence, the nature of belief - all those wonderfully complex topics that emerge when guards are down and wine bottles are half-empty. Georgia and Josh approached these subjects from entirely outside the realm of Christian belief, bringing fresh perspectives that made the conversation spark with possibility rather than tension.

I didn't quite expect a full-on existential crisis when she asked a simple question. I'm pretty sure they asked if I was okay or if I had just had a stroke. As I opened my mouth to respond, I couldn't help but wonder: When did a single word become so loaded?

In that moment, I was transported back to my childhood, to a time when answering that question was as simple as reciting the Pledge of Allegiance. Back then, being a Christian was synonymous with being a good American. It was a label worn with pride, a badge of belonging in a nation that proclaimed itself "one nation under God."

But as I sat there, struggling to formulate a response, I realized that the word "Christian" had become something far more complex, far more political, far more divisive than it was in my youth. In an era where religious identity was increasingly tied to partisan loyalty, where faith was weaponized to justify exclusion and discrimination, where the teachings of Jesus were drowned out by the shouts of Christian nationalists, what did it really mean to claim that label?

Georgia's question wasn't just about my personal faith. It was about the witness of the Church in a nation where Christianity was becoming synonymous with nationalism, where the teachings of Christ were being replaced by a dystopian vision reminiscent of a real-life Handmaid's Tale in the hearts and minds of many believers.

But it was also about the dark legacy of religious nationalism throughout history. From the Crusades to the Third Reich, from the justification of slavery to the Doctrine of Discovery, the marriage of faith and nationalist fervor has led to unspeakable atrocities. When religious identity becomes tied to national identity, when the cross is wrapped in the flag, the result is rarely a more compassionate society, but rather one that justifies oppression and violence in the name of God.

This pattern, repeated throughout history, should serve as a warning for the present moment. When we see Christianity being used to support xenophobic policies, to demonize marginalized communities, to prioritize national identity over human dignity, we are seeing the seeds of a dangerous ideology that has borne bitter fruit time and time again.

In that moment, I realized that answering her question honestly would require more than a simple yes or no. It would mean fumbling through the uncomfortable truth that the label "Christian," a word once used to identify followers of Jesus, had become a political brand, a cultural marker, and often a weapon in war - one with a bloody history we would be wise to remember.

As I searched for the right words, I couldn't help but wonder: Was it possible to follow Christ without embracing the baggage that now came with the "Christian" label? Could authentic faith still thrive in a climate where religious identity was so tightly intertwined with political power?

Georgia's question was an invitation to explore these issues, to examine how the witness of the Church was being compromised by its alliance with nationalist ideology, and to consider the dangerous road we were traveling in light of the past. It was a chance to start a conversation about what it really means to walk in the way of Jesus in a world where His name is often used to justify the very things He came to challenge.

But more than that, it was a reminder that the personal is always political, that the words we use to define our faith have real-world consequences for unbelievers and those on the margins. As I looked around the table at the faces of my friends, each coming from different backgrounds and belief systems, I knew that my answer mattered, not just for me, but for the witness of Christ in a watching world.

So I took a deep breath, met Georgia's gaze, and began to speak, knowing that my words were just the beginning of a much longer journey - a journey of unlearning, of reimagining, of reclaiming a faith that looked more like Jesus and less like the Christianity of America, and of remembering the harrowing lessons of history so that we might not be doomed to repeat them.

Words have power. They can heal or hurt, build up or tear down. But sometimes, the most dangerous words aren't the ones hurled as weapons from the start. They're the ones that begin with good intentions, that start as tools for understanding, only to be twisted into something that causes pain. I've watched this happen with the word "Christian." But it's not the first time a label meant to help has been transformed into something that hurts.

There was a time when "retarded" was a medical term, carefully chosen by professionals to describe a range of developmental and learning disabilities. The word itself simply meant "slowed" or "delayed" - a clinical description, nothing more. But you probably remember what happened. As the label spread beyond medical contexts, it morphed. Schoolyard taunts. Casual insults. A weapon to demean and exclude. A word chosen with care to help understand and support people became a tool to hurt and marginalize them.

This transformation didn't happen overnight. It was gradual. First, the word began to lose its clinical precision, becoming a catch-all term for any perceived cognitive difference. Then it seeped into everyday language, its meaning broadening while its impact sharpened. Soon, parents and advocates began pushing back. They saw how this label, originally meant to help, had become a burden, a stigma, a wall between their children and the world.

By the early 2000s, most medical and educational institutions had abandoned the term. Not because the conditions it described had changed, but because the word itself had become toxic. It had been weaponized beyond redemption. Today, using "retarded" marks you as either ignorant or cruel. The word's history of harm outweighs any original useful meaning it might have had.

I tell this story because it illuminates a pattern - how labels can transform from descriptive to destructive, from helpful to harmful. And it brings me to another word that's undergone a similar transformation: "Christian."

I remember sitting in my childhood Sunday School class, cheerfully singing the song that spells out the word, "I am a C.H... I am a C.H... I am a C.H.R.I.S.T.I.A.N... And I have C.H.R.I.S.T. in my H.E.A.R.T..." It's just a simple and fun VBS song. But it is an example of how we begin at an early age, repeating to ourselves "I am a Christian, I am a Christian, I am a Christian" - identifying with a label more than a journey, arriving at a destination more than living for a cause.

Like "retarded," the word "Christian" began with a specific meaning. Around 47 AD in Antioch, outsiders coined the term "Christianos" - "little Christs" or "Christ followers" - to describe this strange new sect. It wasn't a compliment. Acts 11:26 tells us "...the disciples were first called Christians in Antioch." Notice that - they were called this. Not necessarily that they chose it.

The early followers of Jesus had their own words for themselves: "The Way" (Acts 9:2), "disciples," "brothers and sisters," "saints." Active words. Words that described a journey, a relationship, or a way of living rather than a fixed identity.

But watch how this label transformed through history.

During the Crusades, "Christian" became a battle cry. Robert the Monk wrote in 1107 following the First Crusade turning faith into a justification for conquest:

> Let this then be your war-cry in combats, because this word is given to you by God. When an armed attack is made upon the enemy, let this one cry be raised by all the soldiers of God: 'It is the will of God! It is the will of God!'

— 10.1

The same identification that once marked people for their sacrificial love became a mark of who to kill and who to spare.

In 1493, Pope Alexander VI's Doctrine of Discovery explicitly linked being "Christian" with the right to conquer and colonize. The papal bull Inter Caetera granted Spain authority over the New World because of their commitment to spread 'the Christian Empire.' The document declared that non-Christian peoples were "barbarous nations" to be "subjugated" - transforming "Christian" from a mark of faith into a mark of civilization and superiority.[10.2]

Ushering in the Nazi regime, Christianity was twisted to support genocidal ideology. In 1922, Adolf Hitler declared: "I say: my feeling as a Christian points me to my Lord and Saviour..." attempting to merge Christian identity with Nazi ideology. [10.3] The term "Christian" became a tool for demonizing Jews and justifying genocide.

In American history, the label was wielded to justify both slavery and segregation. Frederick Douglass said in 1845,

> Between the Christianity of this land and the Christianity of Christ, I recognize the widest

possible difference—so wide that to receive the one as good, pure, and holy, is of necessity to reject the other as bad, corrupt, and wicked. To be the friend of the one is of necessity to be the enemy of the other. I love the pure, peaceable, and impartial Christianity of Christ; I therefore hate the corrupt, slave-holding, women-whipping, cradle-plundering, partial and hypocritical Christianity of this land. Indeed, I can see no reason but the most deceitful one for calling the religion of this land Christianity...

— 10.5

During the Civil Rights era, Martin Luther King Jr. observed from his Birmingham jail cell how "Christian" had become compatible with segregation and racism: "I have watched white churchmen stand on the sideline and mouth pious irrelevancies and sanctimonious trivialities" while basic human rights were denied. [10.6]

Today, we're watching another transformation of this ancient word. "Christian" has become a political identifier, a cultural boundary marker, and a tool of power. Recent polls show that about 45% of U.S. adults believe the country should be a "Christian nation" - not understanding how that very concept contradicts the teachings of Christ who said "My kingdom is not of this realm" (John 18:36). [7.7]

The pattern is clear. Just as "retarded" evolved from medical term to weapon, "Christian" has evolved from a description of radical love and sacrifice into a tool of power and exclusion. The word that once marked people for their Christ-like behavior now often marks them for their political alignment, their cultural conformity, and their willingness to use faith as a means of control.

This evolution forces us to confront an uncomfortable question: When does a label become so distorted, so weaponized, that it no longer serves its original purpose? When does it become shav' - empty, false, and worthless?

When does a word become a weapon? When does a way to identify transform into a tool? These questions demand answers as we watch the label "Christian" being wielded in ways that betray its origins and corrupt its meaning.

The pattern is clear. Static labels, no matter how pure their origins, eventually become tools of power. It happened with "Christian" during the Crusades, the colonization of the Americas, the justification of slavery, and it continues to happen today. The word that once described people willing to die for their faith now more often describes those willing to let others die for their politics.

But there's another way. The early followers of Jesus understood something we've forgotten - that faith is better described by actions than labels. When questioned about their beliefs, they showed rather than told: "See how they love one another," observers wrote about.

This wasn't accidental. Jesus himself rarely used labels. Instead, he described active faith: "By this everyone will know that you are my disciples, if you love one another" (John 13:35). Not by what you call yourself. Not by the label you wear. But by how you love.

Think about the implications. When someone asks about your faith, what if instead of saying "I'm a Christian," you said "I'm learning to follow Christ" or "I'm trying to live up to the best of what Jesus taught"? These aren't just semantic differences. They're fundamentally different ways of understanding faith.

It's not that we're failing to live up to our claims. It's that we're claiming a perfection we can never achieve. We're calling ourselves "Christ-like" when at best, we're "Christ's bumbling idiots." We're setting ourselves up as finished products when we're really works in progress.

This isn't about beating ourselves up for not being perfect. It's about being honest about our journey. What if, instead of claiming to be Christians, we admitted we're just trying to follow Christ? What if we acknowledged that we're learning, growing, often failing, but always striving?

Consider the example of Fred Rogers, better known to millions, even billions, as Mister Rogers. A devoted follower of Christ, Rogers never made his show about "Christianity." Instead, he infused every episode with the very essence of Christ's teachings: kindness, empathy, and compassion.

On May 9, 1969, at the height of racial tensions in America, Rogers did something big. He invited Officer Clemmons, a recurring character played by African American actor François Clemmons, to join him in cooling his feet in a small pool. This wasn't just a casual invitation, it was a direct challenge to the segregation of public pools still prevalent in many parts of the country.

The image was striking in its simplicity and power. A black man and a white man, their feet side by side in the same water. In that era of racial strife and segregation, this seemingly simple act was revolutionary. The camera's focus on their feet sharing the same pool was a vivid, unmistakable symbol of equality and shared humanity. It communicated volumes without a single word being spoken about race or politics. This visual metaphor of integration, broadcast to millions of homes across America, challenged deeply ingrained prejudices and offered a powerful alternative to the segregated reality many viewers knew. Rogers had created a picture of racial harmony so clear and compelling that even a child could understand its meaning.

But Rogers didn't stop there. He presented Clemmons as a police officer at a time when black officers represented a fraction of a percent of the police force in America. In many communities, a black police officer was unheard of. Rogers was quietly reshaping perceptions, challenging stereotypes, and promoting equality or equity, all without ever using the word "Christian."

And then, in a moment of profound symbolism, Rogers helped dry Clemmons' feet. To the untrained eye, it was a simple act of kind- ness. But for those who understood, it was a powerful allusion to Jesus washing His disciples' feet, an act of humility and service that transcended racial boundaries.

In those few minutes of television, Rogers embodied the teachings of Christ more fully than a thousand sermons could have. He didn't need to label himself a Christian. He didn't need to quote scripture or preach about morality. He simply lived out the love, humility, and radical inclusivity that Christ exemplified.

This is the kind of faith that changes the world. Not because it wears the right label or uses the right words, but because it acts in ways that challenges injustice, breaks down barriers, and demonstrates unconditional love. Rogers showed us that sharing the love of Christ doesn't require a label – it requires action, often quiet and unassuming, but powerful in its impact.

What if we approached our faith like Mister Rogers approached his show? What if, instead of focusing on identifying ourselves as Christians, we focused on embodying Christ's love in every interaction? How might that transform not just our own lives, but the lives of those around us and the very fabric of our society?

Static labels create artificial finish lines. They suggest arrival rather than journey, achievement rather than aspiration. But faith isn't a finish line. It's a path. A journey. A daily choice to follow, to learn, and to grow.

Active descriptions, on the other hand, carry built-in humility. There's something profound about saying "I'm trying to follow Christ" rather than "I'm a Christian." It acknowledges the gap between aspiration and achievement. It invites conversation rather than assumption. It describes a journey rather than claiming an arrival.

This isn't about shame or unworthiness. It's about honesty. About acknowledging that none of us have fully arrived at Christlikeness. When Paul wrote "Be imitators of me, just as I also am of Christ" (1 Corinthians 11:1), he was describing active faith, not static identity.

The beauty of active descriptions is that they're harder to weaponize. You can claim a label without living it, but you can't claim to be actively following Christ without evidence. Actions speak louder than labels. They're harder to fake, harder to co-opt, harder to turn into tools of power.

This is why abandoning the label "Christian" isn't about rejecting faith. It's about reclaiming it. About returning to a more authentic, more humble, more Christ-like way of expressing our journey. It's about choosing descriptions that reflect the active, ongoing nature of faith rather than the static, arrived nature of labels.

Critics might say this is surrendering ground, letting others define our faith. But consider Jesus' words: "You are the salt of the earth; but if the salt has become tasteless, how can it be made salty *again*? It is no longer good for anything, except to be thrown out and trampled underfoot by people." (Matthew 5:13). When a label becomes shav' - empty, false, worthless - holding onto it doesn't preserve its meaning. And if it only preserves the emptiness, maybe it should thrown it out.

The call to abandon "Christian" as an identifier isn't about shame or retreat. It's about integrity. About choosing words that better reflect the reality of faith as a living, breathing, active thing. It's about following the example of those early believers who were more concerned with living their faith than labeling it.

This won't be easy. Labels provide comfort, certainty, and belonging. They make it easy to know who's in and who's out. But maybe that's exactly the problem. Maybe faith isn't supposed to be about in and out. Maybe it's supposed to be about movement - constant, humble movement toward the example of Christ.

So what do we lose by abandoning this label? A shorthand. A cultural identifier. A political tool. But what do we gain? Authenticity. Humility. The freedom to describe our faith in terms of action rather than identity. The opportunity to be known by our love rather than our label.

The choice is ours. We can cling to a label that's increasingly becoming shav', or we can embrace descriptions that better reflect the active, transformative nature of true faith. We can hide behind static identifiers, or we can step into a more realistic space of describing our faith as the journey it truly is.

The world doesn't need more people checking the "Christian" box on a form. It needs more people actively, humbly, persistently trying to follow the way of Christ. Maybe it's time our words reflected that truth. And sometimes, understanding this requires us to turn everything we think we know upside down.

Look at the cover of this book. What do you see? An upside-down cross - a symbol that might make some Christians recoil, assuming it represents something sacrilegious or even

satanic. The reaction is understandable. We've been conditioned to see the inverted cross as a symbol of rebellion against
faith, a deliberate perversion of something sacred.

But here's the thing: The upside-down cross is actually
known as St. Peter's Cross. According to tradition, when Peter
was sentenced to crucifixion, he requested to be crucified
upside-down, feeling unworthy to die in the same manner as
his Lord. What appears at first glance to be a rejection of faith
is, in reality, one of history's most profound expressions of
humility before Christ.

This symbolism isn't accidental. I chose it deliberately for
this book's cover because it embodies everything we've been
discussing about labels, assumptions, and the nature of true
faith. The same symbol can represent either mockery or
martyrdom, rebellion or reverence - depending not on the
symbol itself, but on the heart behind it.

Peter's upside-down crucifixion was a powerful statement
that true faith isn't about maintaining appearances or meeting
others' expectations - it's about genuine humility before Christ.

In the same way, letting go of the "Christian" label might
look to some like abandoning faith. But perhaps it's actually an
act of humility similar to Peter's. Perhaps it's saying, "I don't
deserve to claim this identity that's been so distorted, but I will
strive to follow Christ in my actions." Perhaps it's choosing
substance over symbol, journey over destination, authentic
faith over easy labels.

When Peter chose to be crucified upside-down, he wasn't
rejecting the cross - he was expressing his unworthiness to
claim equality with Christ's sacrifice. Similarly, choosing to let
go of the "Christian" label isn't about rejecting faith - it's about
acknowledging that our journey of following Christ deserves
more honest, more humble expression.

When it comes to letting go of the "Christian" label, the

hardest conversations aren't with strangers but with family and with friends. With the people who taught you that this identity was sacred, who see your choice as rejection not just of a word, but of them.

When people let go of the label, they often find their faith deepening. Without the safety net of identity politics, they're forced to wrestle more directly with what it means to follow Christ. Without the shorthand of "Christian," they have to explain their faith in terms of actions and values rather than tribal belonging.

Some discover that losing their place in Christian circles opens doors to genuine ministry with people who've been hurt by the church. Others find that stepping away from the label helps them see more clearly how it's been weaponized. Many report that their faith feels more authentic, more challenging, more alive than when it was safely wrapped in cultural Christianity.

The path ahead is clear, even if it isn't easy. The machinery of Christian Nationalism grows stronger each day, more demanding of conformity, more punishing of dissent. The time for half-measures and polite disagreement has passed. We face a moment of decision that will define not just our personal faith, but the very future of Christ-like witness in America.

There's a slow-motion coup happening in America, and it's wrapped in the language of faith. What we're witnessing is not just a shift in political power, but a fundamental rewiring of the relationship between religion and government, with far-reaching consequences for all Americans, regardless of their beliefs.

Since President Trump's re-election in 2024, we've seen an unprecedented acceleration of the Christian nationalist agenda. It's reshaping the nation in ways that should alarm the Christian church but unfortunately, it's not.

Let's start with the most visible changes: the integration of religion into public education. In states like Louisiana and Oklahoma, we're seeing mandatory Bible readings and religious instruction becoming part of the curriculum. Schools are being turned into de facto mission fields, with chaplains installed in classrooms and the Ten Commandments displayed on walls. It's a clear violation of the First Amendment's Establishment Clause, but it's being justified under the guise of "religious liberty."

But the real danger lies in what's happening behind the scenes. Since 2024, we've witnessed a systematic purge of federal agencies, with career civil servants being replaced by loyalists who pass a different kind of litmus test – not just political allegiance, but adherence to a specific brand of Christian Nationalism. Dissenters are being rooted out and sidelined, creating a bureaucracy that is accountable not to the Constitution, but to a particular religious ideology.

This religious takeover extends beyond the halls of government. Billionaires like Elon Musk, who have made no secret of their support for Christian Nationalism, are being appointed to positions of incredible power. The result is a growing fusion of corporate, religious, and political interests, blurring the lines between church and state in ways not seen before.

All of this is happening against a backdrop of increasing hostility towards marginalized communities. But the Bible is clear about God's heart for the marginalized, the oppressed, the stranger. In Matthew 25, Jesus tells us that how we treat "the least of these" is how we treat Him. But the policies being enacted in the name of Christianity today are doing the exact opposite – they are crushing the very people Jesus called us to protect.

This is not a new phenomenon. Throughout history, the fusion of religious and national identity has often led to the oppression of minorities, the suppression of dissent, and even to genocide. From the Crusades to the conquest of the Americas, from the Holocaust to the Rwandan genocide, the pattern is painfully clear.

What we're seeing in America today is the resurgence of an old and dangerous idea: that to be a true American, one must adhere to a specific type of Christianity. It's an idea that history warns us against, but one that is gaining ground with each passing day.

As Christians, we cannot stay silent in the face of this threat. The very integrity of our faith is at stake. When the Gospel is used to justify oppression, when the teachings of Jesus are replaced by the agenda of Christian Nationalism, it is our duty to speak out, to resist, to bear witness to a different way.

But to do that, we must first reckon with the uncomfortable truth – that the label "Christian" has become associated with a political movement that is antithetical to the teachings of Christ. We must be willing to question, to challenge, and to reimagine what it means to follow Jesus in a nation where Christianity has become synonymous with nationalism.

This is not a battle for political power, but a struggle for the soul of our faith. It's a call to remember the lessons of history, to stand with the marginalized, and to bear witness to a gospel that transcends national boundaries and political allegiances.

In the face of a systematic takeover that threatens to redefine Christianity in the image of American Nationalism, our response must be clear: Not in our name. Not with our faith.

The answer isn't running away. It's standing firm right where you are.

When Dr. King wrote his famous "Letter from Birmingham Jail," he didn't call for separation or retreat. Instead, he articulated why they were fighting and what gave them strength to continue:

> One day the South will know that when these disinherited children of God sat down at lunch counters, they were in reality standing up for what is best in the American dream and for the most sacred values in our Judeo-Christian heritage, thereby bringing our nation back to those great wells of democracy which were dug deep by the founding fathers in their formulation of the Constitution and the Declaration of Independence.
>
> — 10.4

They understood what they were fighting against - and more importantly, what they were fighting for. That clarity gave them courage to face fire hoses and police dogs, to endure jail cells and violence, to stand firm in the face of systemic oppression.

Today, we face a different kind of struggle. Not against segregated lunch counters, but against the systematic co-opting of faith for political power. The label "Christian" has become a weapon, a tool of conformity, a marker of political allegiance rather than spiritual transformation. Understanding this - really understanding it - gives us the clarity to stand firm.

You don't need to leave your church. You don't need to start a new movement. You need to stand firm where you are and speak truth. When your pastor mixes patriotism with faithfulness, question it. When policies hurt the vulnerable in Christ's name, oppose them.

This isn't about being divisive. It's about being clear. Clear about why we can no longer accept the empty use of Christ's name - shav' - to justify beliefs and policy that hurt the poor, marginalize the stranger, and serve power rather than love.

Dr. King understood that change doesn't come from retreat but from courageous confrontation with injustice. In that same letter, he wrote:

> Human progress never rolls in on wheels of inevitability; it comes through the tireless efforts of men willing to be coworkers with God, and without this hard work, time itself becomes an ally of the forces of social stagnation. We must use time creatively, in the knowledge that the time is always ripe to do right.

— 10.4

The time is ripe now. Not to run away, but to stand firm. To say, "I follow Christ, but I reject the way His name is being used as a political weapon." To demonstrate through our actions and words what authentic faith looks like.

This might cost us - relationships, opportunities, friends, and family. But as Dietrich Bonhoeffer reminded us, "When Christ calls a man, he bids him come and die." [10.4.1] Not physical death, necessarily, but death to the compromises that allow injustice to flourish.

The early church faced similar challenges. When commanded to stop speaking truth, Peter and John replied, "Whether it is right in the sight of God to listen to you rather than to God, make your *own* judgment;" (Acts 4:19). They didn't retreat - they stood firm in the public square, speaking truth regardless of the cost.

This is our moment. Not to create alternative structures or underground networks, but to be voices of authentic faith within our existing communities. To help others see how the name of Christ has been co-opted and corrupted. To demonstrate through our lives what it really means to follow Jesus.

The label "Christian" isn't just tainted - it's become a form of shav', an empty shell that betrays the very essence of Christ's teachings. The time for half-measures and polite disagreement is over. We need to stop using this label. Stop identifying with it. Stop allowing it to serve as cover for policies and actions that Christ would condemn.

This isn't about semantics or personal preference. When a word becomes a weapon, when it serves power rather than love, when it's used to exclude rather than embrace - continuing to use it makes us complicit. Every time we identify as "Christian" in today's context, we inadvertently lend our credibility to a system that's crushing the very people Jesus came to lift up.

"But what will we call ourselves?" people ask. Maybe that's the wrong question. Perhaps it's time we let our lives speak louder than our labels.

Truth over comfort. It sounds noble, doesn't it? Like a battle cry for the righteous. But what happens when that truth starts to burn away everything you thought you knew about your faith? What rises from those ashes isn't just a new identity - it's something far more dangerous to the powers that be: authentic faith unbound by nationalism. And that's where our real story begins.

12

FAITH WITHOUT NATIONALISM
THE NEED FOR A NEW APPROACH

We've spent enough time diagnosing the disease. Now it's time for the cure. Christian Nationalism isn't just a political problem or a theological misunderstanding. It's a spiritual cancer eating away at the heart of Christianity. It's turned the liberating message of the Gospel into a tool for division and control. It's wrapped the cross in the flag and called it faithfulness.

Beneath the layers of cultural Christianity and nationalistic fervor, there's a faith that's vibrant, transformative, and true to the teachings of Christ. A faith that doesn't need political power to thrive. A faith big enough to embrace complexity, humble enough to admit uncertainty, and strong enough to truly love our neighbors - all of our neighbors. It's a redeeming faith, a real faith, a healing faith, a saving faith.

This isn't about creating a new denomination or starting a new movement. It's about stripping away the cultural baggage and political agendas that have obscured the simple, profound truth of the Gospel.

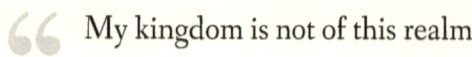 My kingdom is not of this realm.

These words of Jesus, spoken to Pilate as he faced execution, are a reminder that the kingdom Christ came to establish isn't bound by national borders, political systems, or cultural identities.

For eight years, serving under the teaching of Pastor Dr. Phil at New Beginnings Church, I attribute a significant portion of my spiritual growth in the real principles of Jesus' teachings to his leadership and discipleship. Despite our generational differences, we remain close friends to this very day, even after moving to different states. Dr. Phil had a saying that's stuck with me:

> The Kingdom of God is God's rule and reign, His will and way, His presence and power, in my life right now.

This simple statement captures a profound truth: The Kingdom of God isn't just about the afterlife. It's about the here and now. It's about how we live, how we treat others, and how we engage with the world around us.

Jesus spent a lot of time talking about this kingdom. Let's look at a few of His words:

> ...What is the kingdom of God like, and what can I compare it to? It's like a mustard seed that a man took and sowed in his garden. It grew and became a tree, and the birds of the sky nested in its branches.

—LUKE 13:19

> ...The kingdom of heaven is like yeast that a woman took and mixed into 50 pounds of flour until it spread through all of it.
>
> — MATTHEW 13:33

These parables paint a picture of a kingdom that grows not through force or coercion, but through small acts of faith and love. It spreads not through political domination, but through the quiet, transformative power of lives changed by grace. And perhaps most challengingly:

> But I tell you, love your enemies and pray for those who persecute you, so that you may be sons of your Father in heaven. For He causes His sun to rise on the evil and the good, and sends rain on the righteous and the unrighteous.
>
> — MATTHEW 5:44-45

This kingdom calls us to a radical love that transcends political divisions and national loyalties. It challenges us to see the image of God even in those we might consider our enemies.

Rediscovering the Kingdom of God means letting go of our desire for earthly power and prestige. It means recognizing that our primary allegiance isn't to any flag or nation, but to a king who reigns through self-sacrificial love.

This is the kingdom we're called to seek first. Not a faith that needs political power to thrive, but a faith that transforms lives and communities through the power of love.

It's about bringing the values of God's kingdom - love, justice, mercy, reconciliation - into every sphere of life. Not through force or coercion, but through faithful witness and sacrificial service.

This isn't a copout or a weak excuse for inaction. Quite the opposite. It's a call to engage with the world in a radically different way, one that requires more courage, more commitment, and more Christ-like love than any political crusade ever could.

And nowhere is this courage more needed than in how we engage with truth itself. While we claim to serve a God of truth, we've developed a peculiar habit of rejecting it whenever it disagrees with our long-held beliefs. Like a child covering their ears and humming to avoid hearing something they don't like, we've created artificial battles between faith and facts that never needed to exist.

The relationship between science and Christian faith has become unnecessarily adversarial in American Christianity, particularly within Christian nationalist circles. This antagonism often manifests in the reflexive rejection of scientific evidence that appears to challenge traditional biblical interpretations. From climate change, to a big bang, to vaccines, many Christians have adopted a stance that if scientific findings seem to contradict their understanding of scripture, the science must be wrong.

This position creates several problems:

1. It damages Christian witness by making believers appear anti-intellectual and unwilling to engage with evidence
2. It creates unnecessary barriers for scientifically-minded people who might otherwise be open to the faith

3. It often stems from misinterpretation of scripture rather than actual biblical teaching
4. It makes Christians vulnerable to manipulation by political figures who exploit this skepticism of science

The Trump era has highlighted this dynamic. When scientific evidence contradicted preferred political narratives around COVID-19, climate change, or other issues, many Christians found it easy to dismiss the science because they were already practiced in rejecting scientific findings that challenged their belief preferences.

What if, instead of assuming science is wrong when it appears to conflict with our interpretation of scripture, we considered another possibility: What if we're interpreting scripture incorrectly?

This isn't about compromising biblical authority - it's about approaching scripture with appropriate humility, recognizing that our interpretations are not infallible. Throughout history, Christians have had to revise their understanding of scripture in light of new knowledge:

- The church once interpreted scripture as teaching that the Earth was the center of the universe
- Christians used biblical passages to justify slavery
- Biblical texts were used to argue against women's suffrage
- Scripture was cited to oppose interracial marriage

In each case, it wasn't the Bible that was wrong - it was our interpretation of it. As we gained better understanding of both the natural world and the historical/cultural context of scripture, we realized these interpretations were flawed.

The consequences of science denial in Christian communities go beyond just academic disagreement.

When Christians reject well-established science:

1. It can lead to real harm (as seen in COVID vaccine resistance)
2. It undermines credibility on other matters of faith
3. It creates unnecessary stumbling blocks for educated people considering Christianity
4. It makes Christians vulnerable to manipulation by those who exploit this tendency

We need a more nuanced approach that:

1. Recognizes both scripture and nature as God's revelation
2. Approaches biblical interpretation with appropriate humility
3. Understands genre and context in scripture
4. Distinguishes between what the Bible actually teaches and our interpretations of it

This isn't about choosing between science and scripture - it's about being faithful to both God's written word and His revelation in nature. As St. Augustine wrote in "The Literal Meaning of Genesis":

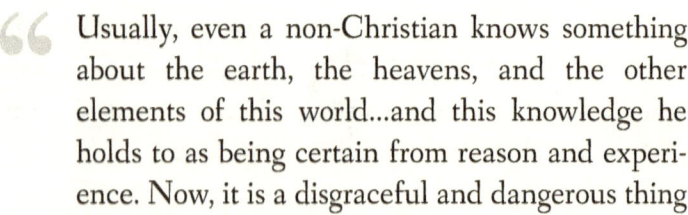 Usually, even a non-Christian knows something about the earth, the heavens, and the other elements of this world...and this knowledge he holds to as being certain from reason and experience. Now, it is a disgraceful and dangerous thing

for an infidel to hear a Christian, presumably giving the meaning of Holy Scripture, talking nonsense on these topics...If they find a Christian mistaken in a field which they themselves know well and hear him maintaining his foolish opinions about our books, how are they going to believe those books in matters concerning the resurrection of the dead, the hope of eternal life, and the kingdom of heaven?

— 11.1

As we work to unlearn Christian Nationalism and its associated distortions of faith, we must also unlearn the false dichotomy between faith and science. This means:

1. Approaching both scripture and science with appropriate humility
2. Being willing to question our interpretations when evidence challenges them
3. Distinguishing between defending the Bible and defending our interpretation of it
4. Recognizing that God's truth in scripture won't ultimately conflict with God's truth in nature

When we create unnecessary conflicts between faith and science, we not only damage our witness - we may actually be fighting against truth itself. As we seek to rebuild authentic Christian witness in a post-Christian nationalist world, we must learn to engage more thoughtfully with scientific understanding while maintaining fidelity to scripture properly interpreted.

The goal isn't to water down biblical truth but to understand it more accurately. When we do this, we often find that the conflicts we feared don't actually exist - they were artifacts of our interpretation, not requirements of our faith.

This journey isn't theoretical for me. I've had to unlearn many assumed conflicts between science and scripture, realizing that what I was actually defending wasn't biblical truth but inherited interpretations that didn't necessarily reflect what scripture actually teaches.

The process can be uncomfortable. It requires humility and a willingness to question assumptions. But the result is a more robust faith that doesn't require us to reject evidence or maintain intellectual double standards.

We serve a God of truth - all truth. We don't honor Him by clinging to demonstrably false ideas simply because they're familiar or comfortable. Sometimes the most faithful thing we can do is admit we might have been reading His word wrong all along.

As we work to unlearn Christian Nationalism and its distortions of faith, let's also unlearn the habit of unnecessarily opposing science. Our witness will be stronger and our faith deeper when we learn to embrace truth wherever we find it, confident that God's Word, properly understood, won't conflict with God's world, properly studied.

When it comes to politics, it seems like we Christians have two default modes: domination or withdrawal. We either try to seize control of the political system to enforce our beliefs, or we throw up our hands and declare politics a dirty business that we want no part of.

But what if there's a third way? What if we're called to engage in politics not as culture warriors or as absentee citizens?

First, let's address why withdrawal isn't an option. As followers of Christ, we're called not to stand by and watch.

We're called to be good Samaritans. Throughout American history, during times of slavery and later segregation, some Christians chose to stand back and stay out of the issue. This lack of involvement allowed for the mistreatment of our neighbors to continue unchallenged.

This point was powerfully articulated by Dr. Martin Luther King Jr. in his famous "Letter from Birmingham Jail." He wrote,

> We will have to repent in this generation not merely for the hateful words and actions of the bad people but for the appalling silence of the good people.

— 10.4

Dr. King recognized that silence in the face of injustice is not neutrality - it's complicity. In fact, this silence can be even more damaging than outspoken opposition. When good people stay quiet, it allows injustice to persist unchallenged. It gives the impression that there is no opposition, that everyone is in agreement with the status quo. This silence emboldens those who perpetrate injustice and demoralizes those who suffer from it.

As followers of Christ, we're called to be a voice for the voiceless, to stand up for what's right even when - especially when - it's difficult or unpopular. Our engagement in politics and social issues isn't just about pushing for specific policies; it's about bearing witness to the values of God's kingdom in the public square.

Jesus said in Matthew 5:9, "The peacemakers are blessed, for they will be called sons of God." The peace Jesus spoke of wasn't about avoiding conflict at all costs. It was about reconciliation, about bringing healing to broken relationships and societies.

My grandfather Gerald Eubanks embodied this understanding of the Kingdom. He was the biggest peacemaker I've ever known. Everyone wanted to be around him, to be called his friend. He may not have provided definitive answers or prescribed ways to live, but he was always a peacemaker. His life was a testament to the power of living out the Kingdom of God in daily interactions, not by seeking power or control, but by loving others and seeking reconciliation wherever he went.

Several times in my life, he told me to apologize, to ask forgiveness from someone I had hurt - in earlier years my brother, in later years my parents, and in more recent years, my wife. His philosophy was that even if you don't believe you did anything wrong, trust that you hurt them and apologize because the strife is not worth the belief that you were right. This wisdom, applied to our political engagement, could transform our discourse.

So what might it look like to engage in politics as peacemakers?

First, it means letting go of the idea that our primary goal in the political arena is to "win." The peacemaker's aim isn't to defeat the other side, but to find common ground, to work towards solutions that benefit everyone, not just our own tribe.

Being peacemakers in politics means rejecting the demonization of those who disagree with us. It means recognizing the humanity of people on all sides of political debates, even when we strongly disagree with their views. This doesn't mean we don't stand firm for what we believe is right. But it does mean we fight fair. We argue ideas, not attack people. We seek to persuade, not to destroy.

It also means being willing to compromise. Not on our core values, but on the practical details of how to implement policies in a diverse society. The reality is, in a democracy, we have to find ways to live together with people who have very different beliefs and values. That requires give and take, a willingness to find solutions that might not be perfect from our perspective, but that allow us to coexist peacefully.

Perhaps most challengingly, being peacemakers in politics means continuing to love and treat respectfully those who oppose us politically, morally, or even those who are opposed to us because we are followers of Christ. It means rejecting the tribalism that says we can only associate with those who agree with us. It means maintaining relationships across all kinds of divides, hard as that may be.

When Jesus told the parable of the Good Samaritan, he didn't qualify whether the Samaritan would love or support the injured man based on his past actions. He didn't ask if the man lived up to the ideals of we're called to strive for in the Christian faith. He didn't ask if he had honored God today, if he had a job, or if he had even just murdered someone. The Samaritan simply saw a neighbor in need and acted with compassion. This is the model we're called to follow in our political engagement.

 He has told you, mankind, what is good and what it is the Lord requires of you: to act justly, to love faithfulness, and to walk humbly with your God.

— MICAH 6:8

This approach to political engagement isn't easy. It's often lonely. You'll probably get criticism from all sides. But I believe it's the most faithful way for Christians to engage in the political process. It allows us to be salt and light in the political arena without compromising our witness or tying our faith too closely to any political ideology.

In a world that often rewards certainty and bravado, cultivating intellectual humility might seem like a losing strategy. But when it comes to faith and politics, it's exactly what we need.

Intellectual humility isn't about being wishy-washy or lacking conviction. It's about recognizing the limits of our knowledge and understanding. It's about being open to new information and perspectives, even when they challenge our existing beliefs.

The Apostle Paul, one of the most influential figures in early Christianity, wrote, "For now we see only a reflection as in a mirror; then we shall see face to face. Now I know in part; then I shall know fully, even as I am fully known" (1 Corinthians 13:12).

Even Paul, with all his theological training and direct experience with the risen Christ, acknowledged that his understanding was partial and imperfect. How much more should we hold our beliefs with humility?

Cultivating intellectual humility means being willing to say "I don't know" or "I might be wrong." It means approaching complex issues with curiosity rather than defensiveness. It means being willing to learn from those who disagree with us, recognizing that they might have insights we lack.

In the realm of politics, this humility can transform our discourse. Instead of approaching debates as battles to be won, we can approach them as opportunities to learn and grow and to be a witness as peacemakers. We can ask questions seeking to understand, not just to argue. We can acknowledge the valid points made by those on the other side, even if we ultimately disagree with their conclusions.

It's crucial to remember that whether winning or losing an argument, the most important part is to act in accordance with God's will. Our goal should be to show love and the characteristics of Christ, letting others see that even if the battle is lost, the war is still won.

What if in those moments, the spiritual impact is more real for the people watching our faith play out than it is for the results of the argument? Our witness in how we engage may be far more powerful than any point we could win in a debate.

This humility should extend to our interpretation of Scripture as well. While we can hold firm to the core truths of our faith, we should be humble about our understanding of more complex or controversial passages. We should be willing to engage with different interpretations and to continually deepen our understanding.

As the poet Emily Dickinson beautifully wrote in *This World is Not Conclusion*:

This World is not Conclusion.
A Species stands beyond -
Invisible, as Music -
But positive, as Sound -
It beckons, and it baffles -
Philosophy, dont know -
And through a Riddle, at the last -
Sagacity, must go -
To guess it, puzzles scholars -
To gain it, Men have borne
Contempt of Generations
And Crucifixion, shown -
Faith slips - and laughs, and rallies -

Blushes, if any see -
Plucks at a twig of Evidence -
And asks a Vane, the way -
Much Gesture, from the Pulpit
Strong Hallelujahs roll -
Narcotics cannot still the Tooth
That nibbles at the soul -

— 11.2

Cultivating intellectual humility reminds us that our understanding is always growing, always evolving. It keeps us open to the mysteries of faith and the complexities of our world.

In a world increasingly divided along political, cultural, and religious lines, the practice of radical hospitality is more important than ever. And it's at the very heart of what it means to follow Jesus.

Throughout the Gospels, we see Jesus constantly crossing boundaries to welcome those whom society had marginalized. He ate with tax collectors and outcasts. He touched lepers. He spoke with Samaritan women. In every interaction, Jesus demonstrated a radical openness to the 'other.'

This radical hospitality is captured beautifully in the words of the hymn "All Are Welcome" by Marty Haugen:

Let us build a house where love can dwell
And all can safely live,
A place where saints and children tell
How hearts learn to forgive.
Built of hopes and dreams and visions,
Rock of faith and vault of grace;
Here the love of Christ shall end divisions:

All are welcome, all are welcome,
All are welcome in this place.

— 11.3

Practicing radical hospitality means creating spaces where all people feel welcome, regardless of their background, beliefs, or political affiliations. It means actively reaching out to those who are different from us, seeking to understand their perspectives and experiences.

In the context of our current political climate, this might mean intentionally building relationships with people who vote differently. It might mean inviting people into our homes and churches who might make us uncomfortable. It might mean being willing to listen more than we speak, to seek understanding before seeking to be understood.

Radical hospitality challenges us to see the image of God in every person we encounter, even those we might consider our enemies. It calls us to a love that goes beyond mere tolerance to active welcome and inclusion.

This doesn't mean we abandon our convictions or pretend that theological differences don't exist. But it does mean that we prioritize relationships over being right, that we seek to build bridges rather than walls.

As we conclude this chapter, let's return to where we started: the need to reclaim our faith from nationalism and rediscover what it truly means to follow Jesus in our complex, divided world.

The path we've outlined isn't an easy one. Rediscovering the Kingdom of God, separating our faith from our cultural identity, engaging as peacemakers, cultivating intellectual humility, and practicing radical hospitality - these are challenging calls in a world that often rewards tribalism, certainty, and self-interest.

But this is the way of Jesus. It's a way that doesn't seek earthly power or cultural dominance, but instead seeks to transform the world through self-giving love and service.

As we move forward, let's hold onto the words of Jesus:

> You are the light of the world. A city set on a hill cannot be hidden; nor do *people* light a lamp and put it under a basket, but on the lampstand, and it gives light to all who are in the house. Your light must shine before people in such a way that they may see your good works, and glorify your Father who is in heaven.
>
> — MATTHEW 5:14-16

Our call is not to create a Christian nation through political means, but to be a Christ-like presence in our nation and beyond. To be light in the darkness, salt in a bland world, agents of reconciliation in a divided society.

This is not a retreat from engagement with the world, but a different kind of engagement. One that's marked by love, humility, and a commitment to the way of Jesus above all else.

The path forward looks clear enough on paper. Reimagine. Engage. Rethink. But something's stirring on the margins of our faith - a movement no one expected. They're not just leaving our churches; they're blazing trails into uncharted spiritual territory. And what they've discovered out there in the wilderness might just be the key to everything we've been searching for.

13

THE SCATTERED FAITHFUL
THE GREAT DEPARTURE

When people talk about being "hurt by the church," they usually put words to it with something specific. A judgmental comment. A failed ministry. A bitter split over the color of the carpet. I wish my hurts were that simple.

I remember as a teenager, watching someone very close to me struggle to tell me what had been happening on those Wednesday night drives home. How her youth pastor started with a hand on her leg. Then a kiss. Then his tongue in her mouth. Then more. Much more. She'd been groomed so gradually she didn't even see it as abuse anymore - just something she "didn't really want anymore."

After I blew the whistle, my friend broke the youth pastor's nose when he found out. I won't lie - that felt pretty good. But what came next broke something deeper in me. The church leadership just... let him go. No police report. No sex offender list. No warning to other churches. Just a quiet resignation and the freedom to move on to his next prey.

That's when I learned that evil isn't just in the original sin. It's in the response to it. It's in the collective shrug, the institutional silence, the communal choice to prioritize reputation over justice. It's in watching an entire system reveal its moral bankruptcy not through what it does, but through what it fails to do.

And here's the thing - this pattern keeps playing out. Not just in isolated incidents of abuse, but in the broader response of American Christianity to everything that matters. The reflexive defense of the powerful. The casual dismissal of the vulnerable. The constant choosing of institutional preservation over Christ-like love.

People haven't left the church because of bad coffee or boring sermons. They haven't scattered because of one pastor's failings or one congregation's politics. They've walked away because they've witnessed something far more devastating: the complete moral collapse of a faith tradition that claims to follow Jesus while systematically betraying what He taught.

This isn't just my story. As I've begun speaking out, voices have emerged from the silence - people I haven't heard from in years reaching out to say "thank you for putting words to what I couldn't express." They're not "backsliders" or "just liberal" or whatever label gets slapped on those who step away. They're people who've seen too much to pretend anymore.

The phrase rolls off the Christian tongue so easily: "They were hurt by the church." It's become our go-to explanation, our comfortable shorthand for why people walk away.

We treat it like a diagnosis, prescribing the usual remedies: "Find a different congregation." "Try a more authentic community." "Give it time to heal." We're letting ourselves off the hook too easily.

When a 16-year-old boy in my home church came out, his mother, seeking answers, posted about it online. What happened next made national news - literally.

I remember when I was in college in another state, my mom

calling: "Turn on 60 Minutes right now!" And there was my childhood church, but not for any reason to be proud of. The Westboro Baptist Church had descended on our town, picketing outside the boy's school, outside my church, spewing hatred in God's name.

It wasn't just their behavior - it was in the response, the church's response, my response. Not outrage at the hatred being spewed, but rather just awkward silence and vague mumbles about "loving the sinner and hating the sin" - that worn-out phrase we toss around like it's something Jesus would've actually said. And it poisons us as we reach for this bumper-sticker theology, using it to mask judgment with a thin veneer of love while actually communicating rejection. We reduced Christ's radical, transformative love to a condescending tolerance, all while feeling righteous about our balance of grace and truth.

I remember my own silence then - how easy it was to let the moment pass, to tell myself it wasn't my place to speak. And I can't help but think about a story from two thousand years ago, when Jesus stood between an accused woman and her religious accusers, choosing to defend the vulnerable rather than appease the religious with convenient clichés about loving sinners and hating sins. He didn't theorize about balancing love and judgment - He demonstrated love in action.

What would it have looked like if we had followed that example? If instead of mumbling theological excuses for our inaction, we had simply loved as Christ loved? If we had stood between the vulnerable and their accusers, more concerned with protecting the marginalized than preserving our own quiet desire for justice?

But when our moment came, we couldn't find such courage. It was watching an entire faith community reveal its moral cowardice when confronted with the choice between defending a victim or preserving their own piety.

These aren't just wounds that need bandaging. They're symptoms of a deeper disease, a systemic rot that's eaten away at the very foundations of American Christianity.

When people try to explain why they've stepped away, they often point to specific incidents - the racist comment that went unchallenged, the sermon that twisted scripture to justify injustice, the moment they realized their church cared more about political power than Christ-like love. But these aren't isolated injuries. They're glimpses of a faith that's lost its way so completely it can't even recognize it anymore.

Growing up in church, we were taught about Romans 1 - how God "gave them over to a depraved mind" because they exchanged the truth for a lie.

The "them" was always someone else. We focused exclusively on certain sins - especially the sexual ones. The pagans. The backsliders. The morally corrupt out there in the world. We'd shake our heads at those poor souls who had drifted so far they couldn't even recognize truth anymore.

But Paul's warning was broader and deeper than just sexual sin. He described a pattern where pride and idolatry corrupt the mind's ability to discern truth from lies. Where people become "filled with every kind of wickedness" - including greed, malice, deceit, and *a lack of mercy*.

What if, in our rush to point fingers at obvious sins, we've missed the idolatries in our own hearts? Our worship of political power, our hunger for cultural dominance, our belief in American exceptionalism - these too can corrupt our ability to discern right from wrong and place in us a lack of mercy. Even something as seemingly innocent and patriotic as wrapping the cross in the American flag is an idol that blinds us to truth.

Paul wrote about people who "exchanged the truth about

God for a lie, and worshiped and served created things rather than the Creator." And isn't that exactly what we've done?

We've exchanged the revolutionary love of Christ for the power politics of empire. We've replaced the Kingdom of God with the American Dream. We've become so devoted to our national identity that we can't even recognize when it contradicts what Jesus taught.

Maybe that's why we can watch children in cages and quote Romans 13 about obeying authorities.

Maybe that's why we can hear Christ's commands to welcome the stranger and still cheer for walls and deportations.

Maybe that's why we can sing about God's love on Sunday and embrace policies of cruelty and marginalization on Monday - and see no contradiction.

We've been handed over to exactly what we've worshiped: a faith so intertwined with nationalism that we can no longer distinguish between serving God and serving the empire.

The depraved mind isn't out there in the world - it's in our own skulls.

When Donald Trump stood before the cameras in 2015 and declared he'd never asked God for forgiveness because he didn't need to, the nation's Christian leaders and more importantly - we, should have recoiled in horror or at very minimum, taken pause. Here was a man openly dismissing the core of our faith - the need for grace, humility, and repentance. And quite literally dismissing the one thing that brings salvation. Instead, they lined up to lay hands on him, to prophesy over him, to declare him God's chosen instrument.

This wasn't just a failure of leadership. It was a revelation of who *we'd* become.

I've watched family members who once taught me about Christ's love for the marginalized cheer for policies that cage children at the border. I've seen fellow believers who raised me on stories of Jesus' compassion mock transgender youth and celebrate their exclusion. I've witnessed Christians who spoke to me about truth and integrity defend blatant lies because they served the right political agenda.

The crisis isn't that these things happen. The crisis is that we've normalized them. We've created a version of Christianity so divorced from Christ's teachings that we can't even recognize the contradiction anymore.

When my neighbor at the CDC worked endless hours trying to save lives during the pandemic, Christians called her a liar and a fraud. Not because they had evidence. Not because they'd studied the science. But because their political allegiance demanded it. The fact that she was a lesbian just made it easier for them to dismiss her dedication and expertise.

This is what moral bankruptcy looks like. Not dramatic acts of evil, but the quiet acceptance of cruelty as long as it serves our purposes. The casual dismissal of Christ's commands when they conflict with our political preferences. The endless justification of the indefensible because it comes from "our side."

I've had Christians tell me they know Trump isn't a good person, but that God can use corrupt vessels for His purposes. They quote scriptures about Cyrus and David, finding biblical justification for supporting leaders who embody everything Jesus taught against. It's not that they can't see the contradiction. It's that they've decided the contradiction doesn't matter.

The scattered ones - they see this. They feel the wrongness

of it in their bones. When they try to explain why they've stepped away, they might point to specific incidents or issues. But beneath those explanations lies a deeper truth: they've witnessed a faith tradition abandon its foundational principles while maintaining all its outward forms.

This isn't about political differences or policy disagreements. It's about watching people who claim to follow Christ systematically betray what He taught - and then defend that betrayal as faithfulness.

The real crisis isn't out there in the culture wars. It's in our own hearts, in our willingness to sacrifice the essence of our faith on the altar of political expediency. It's in our ability to sing about God's love on Sunday while embracing policies of cruelty on Monday.

We're not losing people because our faith is too demanding. We're losing them because we've made it demand nothing at all - except loyalty to the right political tribe.

The scattered faithful aren't rejecting Christ. They're rejecting a counterfeit Christianity that's replaced the revolutionary love of God with the power politics of empire. And maybe, just maybe, that rejection is the most faithful response possible.

Looking at our churches today, I can't help but wonder: If Jesus showed up in our sanctuaries, would we welcome Him - or call the police on the Middle Eastern teacher disrupting our certainties with His woke talk of loving enemies, embracing the marginalized, and welcoming strangers?

When asked why they stepped away from church, from faith communities, from organized religion, they often fumble for specific reasons. "The politics got too much." "I couldn't handle the hypocrisy." "It just didn't feel right anymore." These explanations feel inadequate even to them, like trying to describe a slow-growing cancer by pointing to a single symptom.

The truth is messier, more complex. It's not just one thing. It's the accumulation of a thousand small betrayals of Christ's teachings. It's seeing Christianity twisted into a weapon against the very people Jesus would have embraced. It's feeling the cognitive dissonance build until something finally breaks.

They didn't leave in a dramatic exodus. Most just... drifted. Each instance of Christians defending the indefensible in the name of political power, the disconnect grew wider. Every moment of watching their faith community embrace things Jesus stood against made it harder to keep showing up. Until one day, they realized they hadn't been in months, nobody noticed, and the world hadn't ended. What had ended was their ability to separate Sunday morning worship from Monday morning reality.

Some tried other churches. Looked for more "authentic" communities. Searched for spaces that hadn't been corrupted by Christian Nationalism. But eventually, many realized the problem wasn't finding the right congregation. The problem was watching an entire faith tradition lose its way while pretending everything was fine.

The scattered ones often carry a kind of survivor's guilt. They still believe in God, many of them. Still love Jesus. Still hold onto their faith. But they can't pretend anymore. Can't sit in pews and nod along while their fellow believers embrace things that Christ stood against. Can't participate in a system that's replaced the radical love of Jesus with the power politics of empire.

Here's what the average Christians don't understand: These aren't rebellious teenagers slamming doors and running away from home. These are people who've seen something fundamental break in American Christianity, and they don't know how to unsee it.

They struggle to explain this to their families, their friends, their former church communities. How do you tell someone that their faith has become unrecognizable? That their Christianity looks nothing like Christ? That their worship songs feel like funeral laments for a faith that's lost its way?

The scattered and disoriented - they're not lost sheep needing to be brought back to the fold. They might be the ones who can still see clearly enough to recognize that the fold itself has become a den for wolves. Their disorientation might be the most appropriate response to a faith that's lost its true north.

Yet the whispers continue. The private messages. The quiet acknowledgments. Each one a story not of lost faith, but of the deep hunger for something real, something true, something that actually reflects the Jesus they still believe in.

The question isn't whether they can find their way back. The question is whether there's anything left worth coming back to.

The solutions offered are always so neat, so simple. "Find a better church." "Try a different denomination." "Start a home group." As if the complete moral collapse of American Christianity could be fixed with better programming or cooler worship music.

I've watched churches try to address the exodus. They roll out initiatives aimed at "reaching the dechurched." They rebrand themselves as progressive, inclusive, authentic. They add fair trade coffee bars and social justice committees. Meanwhile, their members still vote to crush the vulnerable, still champion policies that Christ would condemn, and still wrap the cross in the flag.

We're missing the point entirely. This isn't about style or structure. It's not even about theology, really. It's about watching people who claim to follow Jesus betray what He taught while insisting nothing is wrong.

I've sat in meetings where church leaders strategize about bringing back the "lost sheep." They conduct surveys, assemble committees, implement new programs. But they never ask the harder questions: What if the sheep aren't lost? What if they're awake? What if their departure is a rational response to witnessing something fundamentally broken?

The scattered ones don't need a hipper church or a more relevant message. They need to see Christians actually acting like Christ. Not just in the safety of Sunday services, but in voting booths and border policies, in treatment of immigrants, LGBTQ+ individuals, single mothers, all of the races and ethnicities, the divorced, the poor, those of other faiths, and anyone else who doesn't fit neatly into their narrow definition of acceptable. They need to see followers of Christ actually following Christ in how they engage with those who are different, those who are marginalized, those who the church has cast aside.

But here's where it gets complicated: Even if churches somehow managed to disentangle themselves from Christian Nationalism, even if they found their prophetic voice and started challenging the status quo - would it be enough? Can you rebuild trust once you've watched an entire faith tradition trade its birthright for political power?

The painful truth is that many of the scattered will never come back. Not because they don't believe in God, but because they believe too deeply to participate in what American Christianity has become. Their absence isn't a sign of spiritual weakness, but of spiritual integrity.

Some will create new communities, small gatherings of fellow refugees from institutional religion. Some will find more Christlike environments among the ones that will never call themselves a Christian again. Others will walk alone, nurturing their faith in solitude rather than compromise with a corrupted faith. Many will live in the tension - believing in Jesus while being unable to bear what's being done in His name.

Looking at the landscape of American Christianity today, I find myself wondering: What if the real test of faith in our time isn't about maintaining religious institutions, but about having the courage to walk away from them? What if the most Christlike thing we can do is stop pretending this is still about Christ?

These aren't comfortable questions. They don't come with three-point solutions or convenient action steps. They demand something harder: the willingness to sit in the discomfort of not knowing what comes next.

The scattered faithful aren't waiting for better churches. They're carrying wounds that no amount of contemporary worship or casual dress codes can heal. They've peaked behind the veil of American Christianity, and they can't unsee what they've witnessed.

Perhaps the most faithful response isn't to offer solutions, but to acknowledge the depth of the decay. We've built false altars to a corrupted faith, piling high our sacrifices of truth and justice on pyres of political power. I've become quite comfortable with setting flame to these altars and watching it burn until nothing remains but ashes.

The ashes of our false altars swirl around us like snow, settling on the scorched earth of what we once called faith. But here's the thing about ashes - they don't just mark an ending. In the right soil, they become the fertilizer for something new. Something real. Something that might just show us how to live redeemed in a world that's still burning.

14

LIVING OUT A REDEEMED
FAITH IN A DIVIDED WORLD
THE CHALLENGE OF AUTHENTIC
FAITH IN MODERN AMERICA

The landscape of faith in America is shifting. The simple certainties of the past have given way to a complex, often contradictory present. We find ourselves in a world where the lines between faith, politics, and culture have become almost hopelessly blurred.

Christian Nationalism has sunk its roots deep into the soil of American Christianity. It's not fading away; if anything, it's become more entrenched, more entangled. It's wrapped itself around our faith so tightly that many can no longer tell where Christianity ends and nationalism begins.

I've seen it in my own life, in my own family, in the churches I've attended. The allure of power, the comfort of certainty, the fierce pride of being "God's chosen nation" - it's a potent mix. And it's one that's incredibly hard to break free from.

But break free we must. Because the faith that emerges from this unholy alliance bears little resemblance to the teachings of Jesus. It's a faith that seeks power rather than service, exclusion rather than welcome, judgment rather than mercy.

The challenge before us is immense. How do we live out an authentic faith in a world that often seems hostile to it? How do we untangle our beliefs from the web of cultural Christianity and political ideology that's ensnared them? How do we follow Jesus in a nation that claims His name but often rejects His ways?

There are no easy answers. No simple solutions. But there is hope. Because even in the midst of this darkness, God is at work. His kingdom is advancing, often in ways we don't expect or understand.

This is the challenge we face: How do we reimagine Christian witness in a world that's seen the worst of what Christianity can be? Looking back at American history, we find Christianity not only linked to many major atrocities and injustices, but often serving as a catalyst for them. From the genocide of Native Americans justified by "Manifest Destiny," to slavery and segregation defended using Biblical arguments, to more recent issues like opposing civil rights and LGBTQ+ equality - Christianity has frequently been on the wrong side of history and the wrong side of justice and human dignity. This painful legacy has deeply tarnished the perception of Christian faith for many.

Our witness needs to be less about words and more about actions. Less about judgment and more about grace. Less about being right and more about doing right. Less about what happens in people's bedrooms, and more about what happens in people's hearts.

In Matthew 25:35-36, Jesus paints a vivid picture of what true faith looks like:

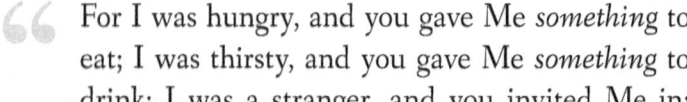 For I was hungry, and you gave Me *something* to eat; I was thirsty, and you gave Me *something* to drink; I was a stranger, and you invited Me in;

naked, and you clothed Me; I was sick, and you visited Me; I was in prison, and you came to Me.

This is the kind of witness our world needs. Not culture warriors or political crusaders, but people who embody the love of Christ in tangible, practical ways.

It means showing up for the marginalized and the outcast - like that 16-year-old boy in my home church. It means standing against injustice and hate, even when it comes from within our own ranks. It means being willing to lose the battle of public opinion if it means winning the war of faithful witness.

This kind of witness isn't flashy. It doesn't grab headlines or win elections. But it changes lives. It transforms communities. It shows the world what the Kingdom of God really looks like.

This witness has power precisely because it doesn't seek power. It's attractive because it's authentic. It's compelling because it's Christ-like.

In a world jaded by religious hypocrisy and political manipulation, this kind of humble, servant-hearted faith stands out. It cuts through the noise and touches hearts in a way that no amount of preaching or protesting ever could.

So how do we cultivate this kind of witness?

This is the witness our world is hungry for. Not perfect people, but broken people being continually transformed by grace. Not a triumphant church, but a servant church that reflects the humility and love of its Savior.

It's time to reimagine what Christian witness looks like in our divided world. To reclaim the radical, transformative power of the Gospel. To show the world that there's another way - a better way.

The digital revolution has transformed how we communicate, consume information, and relate to one another. For Christians navigating this new landscape, it presents both unprecedented challenges and unrealized opportunities.

Social media has become a battleground where the reputation of Christianity is won or lost daily. The behavior of self-proclaimed Christians in online arguments and debates has likely done more damage to the faith's public image than any other single factor in recent history. Harsh words, judgmental attitudes, and a lack of empathy - all cloaked in religious language - have turned countless people away from even considering the Christian message.

Yet, the Spirit of God persists. Hearts are still being reconciled through God's power, often in spite of, rather than because of, Christians' online behavior. The challenge for believers is to embody Christ's love and grace in the digital sphere, to be salt and light in a medium often characterized by bitterness and darkness.

This requires a fundamental shift in how we approach online interactions. Instead of seeing every disagreement as a battle to be won, we need to view them as opportunities to demonstrate Christ's love. We must prioritize understanding over being right, empathy over scoring points.

Consider: What if, by "losing" an online argument graciously, we actually win the greater war of showing others what it means to follow Christ? We can't control outcomes or change other people, but we can control our own behavior and testimony. Displaying neighborly love and compassion, even when it means conceding a point, can be a powerful witness.

Using technology for kingdom purposes doesn't mean bombarding people with religious content. It means being authentically Christian in how we engage online - showing patience, kindness, and respect, even to those who disagree with us. It means using these platforms to encourage, uplift, and serve others, rather than to promote ourselves or our own agendas.

Maintaining integrity in our online interactions is crucial. The anonymity and distance provided by screens can tempt us to behave in ways we never would face-to-face. But as followers of Christ, we're called to be people of integrity in all areas of life - including our digital presence.

The landscape of American spirituality has shifted dramatically in recent decades. The cultural Christianity that once dominated public life has waned, and the church can no longer assume a position of privilege or authority in society.

This new reality calls for a radical rethinking of what it means to be the Church. We need to move beyond the "culture war" mentality that has characterized much of American Christianity in recent years. The church's mission isn't to regain cultural dominance or to force Christian values on society through political means. Rather, it's to embody the love of Christ and to be a witness to the transformative power of the Gospel.

Reimagining worship and community in this context means focusing less on putting on a Sunday morning show and more on fostering genuine relationships and spiritual growth. It means creating safe spaces where people can wrestle with doubts, ask hard questions, and experience God's love in tangible ways.

Being the church outside the walls means taking seriously our call to be salt and light in the world. It means engaging in our communities not as cultural warriors, but as servants and peacemakers. It means being known more for what we're for than what we're against.

This shift isn't about abandoning traditional church structures entirely, but about ensuring that our practices truly reflect the heart of Christ and meet the needs of our current context.

The path of reimagining our faith often leads us into diffi-cult territory, especially when it comes to family relationships. As we grow and change in our understanding of what it means to follow Christ, we may find ourselves increasingly at odds with the beliefs and values we were raised with.

I've experienced this firsthand. My journey away from Christian Nationalism has created a rift between me and many of my family members. It's as if we're speaking different languages now, our worldviews so divergent that finding common ground feels mechanical.

The generational divide is stark. I've noticed that the older members of my family tend to align more closely with Chris-tian nationalist ideologies, while some of the younger ones have either embraced a more Christlike faith or abandoned religion altogether. It's a painful reality, watching the faith that was meant to unite us become a source of division instead.

Jesus himself spoke about the potential for faith to cause family strife. In Matthew 10:34-36, He says:

> Do not think that I have come to bring peace upon the earth. I have come to bring not peace but the sword. For I have come to set a man 'against his father, a daughter against her mother, and a daughter-in-law against her mother-in-law; and one's enemies will be those of his household.'

It's important to note that while Jesus speaks here about bringing division, elsewhere the Scriptures proclaim Him as the Prince of Peace (Isaiah 9:6). At His birth, angels declared "peace on earth" (Luke 2:14). This apparent contradiction is resolved when we understand the different types of peace being discussed.

The peace Jesus brings is primarily spiritual - peace with God and inner peace for believers. However, the message of the Gospel can create conflict in a fallen world, especially when it challenges deeply held beliefs or societal norms. Jesus is warning His followers that choosing Him may lead to relational strife, even within families.

So while Christ ultimately brings peace in our relationship with God and grants us inner peace, following Him may disrupt our earthly relationships. This tension is part of the cost of discipleship that Jesus consistently taught about.

These are hard words, but they remind us that following Christ sometimes means going against the grain, even within our own families.

However, this doesn't mean we should seek conflict or sever ties with our loved ones. Instead, we're called to navigate these relationships with wisdom, grace, and love. Here are some principles I've found helpful:

1. Prioritize love over being right
It's easy to get caught up in arguments about theology or politics, but at the end of the day, our primary calling is to love.

2. Set healthy boundaries
Sometimes, for the sake of peace and our own mental health, we need to limit discussions about certain topics or even limit our exposure to toxic relationships. Perhaps one of my favorite books on this topic is *Boundaries* by Henry Cloud and John Townsend.

3. Be a peacemaker, not a peacekeeper
This doesn't mean avoiding conflict at all costs, but rather

addressing issues in a way that seeks understanding and reconciliation.

4. Focus on common ground
Even if you disagree on many things, there's likely still much you can agree on and bond over.

5. Be patient
Change takes time, and sometimes the best witness we can offer is a consistent life of love and grace.

6. Pray for wisdom and for your family members
Ask God to help you see them as He does and to give you the words to speak (or the wisdom to remain silent) when needed.

Navigating these relationships isn't easy, and there's no one-size-fits-all solution. But as we seek to live out our faith authentically, we can trust that God is at work, even in the midst of family tension and conflict.

As followers of Christ, we're called to engage with issues of social justice. This isn't an optional add-on to our faith, but a core part of what it means to love our neighbors and seek God's kingdom.

Throughout scripture, we see God's heart for justice. The prophet Amos powerfully declared: "Rather let justice surge like waters, and righteousness like an unfailing stream." (Amos 5:24)

Jesus himself began His ministry by declaring His mission to bring good news to the poor, freedom for the prisoners, and to set the oppressed free (Luke 4:18-19).

In recent years, movements like Black Lives Matter have brought issues of racial justice to the forefront of public consciousness. As followers of Christ, we should have been at the forefront of these conversations, championing the cause of the marginalized and oppressed. Instead, many churches found themselves on the sidelines or even in opposition to these movements.

It's crucial to address the misguided response of "All Lives Matter" to the Black Lives Matter movement. While it's true that all lives do matter, this response misses the point and diminishes the specific struggles faced by Black communities. Saying "Black Lives Matter" doesn't mean other lives don't; it's highlighting a particular injustice that needs addressing. It's akin to saying "Save the Amazon Rainforest." t doesn't mean other forests don't matter, but that this one needs special attention right now!

This reluctance often stemmed from a misunderstanding of what these movements were about, or from a fear of being associated with any form of "protest." But when we look at the life of Jesus, we see someone who wasn't afraid to challenge unjust systems and speak truth to power.

Engaging with social justice as Christians means:

1. Understanding biblical justice
This goes beyond just punishing wrongdoing to actively working for the flourishing of all people.

2. Addressing systemic issues
It's not enough to help individuals; we need to look at the structures and systems that perpetuate injustice.

3. Balancing grace and truth
We're called to speak the truth about injustice, but always in a spirit of love and grace.

4. Recognizing that small acts matter
We may not be able to change the world, but we can make a difference in our immediate spheres of influence.

5. Trusting in God's sovereignty while doing our part
We work for justice knowing that ultimately, God is in control and will bring about perfect justice.

As we engage with these issues, we must remember that our primary identity is in Christ, not in any political movement or ideology. Our goal isn't to win arguments or score political points, but to faithfully represent Christ's love and justice in our world.

As we navigate these challenging family dynamics, it's helpful to remember Pastor Dr. Phil's advice about bringing discussions back to what we don't want. When conversations become heated or unproductive, try shifting the focus to finding common ground on what we all agree shouldn't happen. This approach can often lead to more constructive dialogue and help bridge seemingly insurmountable divides.

In the face of division, injustice, and the seeming triumph of values antithetical to Christ's teachings, it's easy to lose hope. But as followers of Jesus, we're called to be people of hope – not a naive optimism that ignores reality, but a deep-rooted hope grounded in the promises of God.

The words of the hymn "My Hope Is Built on Nothing Less" by Edward Mote capture this sentiment beautifully:

My hope is built on nothing less
Than Jesus' blood and righteousness
I dare not trust the sweetest frame
But wholly lean on Jesus' name

On Christ the solid Rock I stand
All other ground is sinking sand
All other ground is sinking sand

— 13.1

This hope isn't passive; it's active. It motivates us to keep working for justice, to keep loving our neighbors, to keep embodying Christ's love in a world that desperately needs it.

Finding joy in faithful living doesn't mean we're always happy or that life is easy. It means finding deep satisfaction in aligning our lives with God's purposes, even when it's difficult. It's about celebrating small victories, cherishing moments of grace, and trusting that our efforts, however small they might seem, matter in God's economy.

The power of small acts of love and justice cannot be overstated. We often think change only happens through grand gestures or sweeping policy changes. But Jesus' ministry was characterized by individual encounters, by touching one life at a time. When we feed a hungry person, comfort someone who's grieving, or stand up for someone being treated unjustly, we're participating in the furthering of the Kingdom of God.

Trusting in God's sovereignty amid uncertainty is perhaps one of the greatest challenges and opportunities of our faith. It's easy to trust God when everything is going well. But can we trust Him when the world seems to be falling apart? Can we believe that He's still in control when injustice seems to be winning?

The Psalms give voice to this struggle. In Psalm 13, David cries out:

How long, Lord? Will You forget me forever?

How long will You hide Your face from me?
How long am I to feel anxious in my soul,
With grief in my heart all the day?
How long will my enemy be exalted over me?
Consider *and* answer me, O Lord my God;
Enlighten my eyes, or I will sleep the *sleep of* death,
And my enemy will say, "I have overcome him,"
And my adversaries will rejoice when I am shaken.
But I have trusted in Your faithfulness;
My heart shall rejoice in Your salvation.
I will sing to the Lord,
Because He has looked after me.

This is the journey of faith – honest struggle coupled with determined trust. It's okay to lament, to cry out to God in our pain and confusion. But we don't stay there. We choose, again and again, to trust in God's unfailing love and to rejoice in His salvation.

As we conclude this exploration of living out a redeemed faith in a divided world, we're left with both a challenge and an invitation. The challenge is clear: to embody Christ's love in a world that often rejects it, to stand for justice in the face of systemic oppression, to cultivate hope when despair seems more reasonable.

But the invitation is equally compelling: to participate in God's redemptive work in the world, to be part of a community that transcends political and cultural divides, to experience the joy and freedom that comes from aligning our lives with God's purposes.

The words of the poet Wendell Berry in his poem "Manifesto: The Mad Farmer Liberation Front" offer a fitting call to action:

Love the quick profit, the annual raise,
vacation with pay. Want more
of everything ready-made. Be afraid
to know your neighbors and to die.
And you will have a window in your head.
Not even your future will be a mystery
any more. Your mind will be punched in a card
and shut away in a little drawer.
When they want you to buy something
they will call you. When they want you
to die for profit they will let you know.
So, friends, every day do something
that won't compute. Love the Lord.
Love the world. Work for nothing.
Take all that you have and be poor.
Love someone who does not deserve it.

— 13.2

This is the countercultural call of the Gospel – to love extravagantly, to work for justice tirelessly, to hope defiantly in the face of despair.

Hope in challenging times. Grace in divided families. Justice in broken systems. These sound like noble goals - until you turn on your TV, open your social media, or check your news feed. Because there's a machine out there, grinding away day and night, turning our highest aspirations into marketable soundbites and our deepest convictions into clickbait. And understanding how this machine works? That might be the difference between reclaiming our faith and watching it become just another product for sale.

15

THE MACHINERY OF INFLUENCE
AN INSIDER'S PERSPECTIVE

A s the owner of a media company since 2006, I've had a front-row seat to the power and pitfalls of modern communication. Our work spans a broad spectrum - from small businesses, to Fortune 200 companies, non-profits, institutions, universities, churches, movements, and even politicians. I've seen it all.

As a Christ follower, I've struggled with the ethical implications of the work. In a world where messages need to slap people in the face like a wet noodle to get attention, how do we separate the truth from the lies, the bold truth from the bull crap?

Let me give you an example that happened literally today as I write this chapter. I just finished a call with the CEO of a brand we manage, who proudly identifies as Christian. His words still rang in my ears: 'Now that all this DEI stuff is behind us, I don't want black people in our brand anymore. We're not forced to show them so we need to strip them out.'

I heard these words while sitting in the school pickup line, watching the beautiful mixture of demographics that this brand actually serves. The irony was painful - here was someone comfortable enough with me, assuming that as a fellow 'Christian' I would understand and agree with his racist views, treating them as simple business decisions rather than the moral failures they are.

As I write this book, I'm acutely aware of the cost of speaking these truths. How many clients will I lose? I can already name several who might take such offense at my position that they'll leave. But this is exactly the kind of choice we now face in our work and daily lives. The rise of Christian Nationalism hasn't just changed our politics - it's emboldened people to openly express views they once kept hidden, especially when they think they're among 'their own kind.' It's made racism, xenophobia, and other forms of discrimination seem acceptable, as long as they're wrapped in the right religious language.

This isn't just about one racist client or a single moral compromise. It's about the entire machinery of media that makes such moments possible - that creates spaces where people feel comfortable expressing these views, that normalizes the unthinkable through repetition and reinforcement. If you're as old as I am, you'll remember when we used to get our news from the morning paper and the evening broadcast. Remember when the TV played the *National Anthem* and then replaced the broadcast with color bars after midnight? Those days are long gone, replaced by a 24/7 barrage of information from countless sources.

It's like trying to drink from a fire hose - overwhelming, disorienting, and potentially dangerous if you're not careful. In this digital age, media doesn't just report our world - it shapes it. And nowhere is this more evident than in the intersection of faith and politics. The narratives we consume, the images we see, the voices we hear - they all contribute to our understanding of what it means to be both Christian and American. But too often, these narratives are blurring the lines between faith and nationalism, creating a toxic brew that bears little resemblance to the teachings of Jesus.

How did we get here? And more importantly, how do we navigate this media landscape without losing our way?

Major news outlets often use phrases like "the Christian right" or "evangelical voters" as shorthand for Republican voting blocs, implicitly suggesting that authentic Christianity aligns with one political party. This media framing ignores the long tradition of progressive Christianity and the diversity of Christian political thought. When Christianity becomes so closely associated with a single political party in media coverage, it creates a dangerous dynamic where the failures or moral compromises of that party become attributed to Christianity itself.

This isn't just bad journalism - it's a reflection of how deeply Christian Nationalism has shaped public perception of faith. The media's persistent merging of Christianity with one political perspective has made it increasingly difficult for many to see faith as anything other than a political identity.

It's not just on the political side, either. Christian media figures have played their part in this unholy alliance. Take Eric Metaxas, for instance. Once known for his biographies of Dietrich Bonhoeffer and William Wilberforce, Metaxas has become one of the most vocal proponents of Christian Nationalism. In a tweet that went viral, he declared, "Jesus was white." When challenged, he doubled down, saying, "I was raised to believe that Jesus was King of Kings and Lord of Lords - not the fulfillment of your cultural yearnings." [14.1]

This isn't just bad theology - it's a prime example of how Christian media figures can use their platforms to promote a version of Christianity that's more about cultural dominance than Christ-like love.

When I was 16, I worked on my grandfather's farm. Papa Brutus, my mother's father, is a man I deeply respect to this day. A faithful husband, father, and grandfather, he embodies many Christian virtues. Yet, even he wasn't immune to the influences of Christian Nationalism.

I remember driving his large tractor, an 18' brush hog rumbling behind me as I cleared fields. The cabin's AC barely worked, but the radio was crystal clear. "Leave it on Glenn Beck," he said. "The knob's finicky. Change it, and we'll never get it back." I felt like Pauly Shore's character Crawl in *Son in Law*, out of my element and warned not to touch things I didn't understand.

So there I was, a teenager tromping through hundreds of acres. The soundtrack to my summer labor was a constant stream of Glenn Beck's particular blend of faith and politics. It wasn't just field maintenance I was learning - it was an inadvertent education in how easily faith and nationalism can become intertwined, even in the most unlikely places.

The merging of Christianity and nationalism isn't just happening in overtly political spaces. It's seeping into our everyday media consumption, often in ways we don't even notice.

But the real danger isn't just in the content we consume - it's in how modern media shapes our very perception of reality. The algorithms that determine what we see, the echo chambers we build around ourselves, the way social media platforms amplify certain voices while silencing others - these aren't just features of our media landscape. They're architects of our worldview, subtly but persistently molding how we understand faith, politics, and the relationship between them. And as I've learned firsthand in the media industry, these effects aren't accidental - they're by design.

Ever heard of preaching to the choir? Well, in today's media landscape, it's more like the choir preaching to itself, over and over again. Welcome to the echo chamber of Christian media.

Growing up, there were two television programs that could hush our entire household. One was Adrian Rogers, a Southern Baptist pastor known for his powerful preaching. The other? Rush Limbaugh.

When Limbaugh's show came on, you'd think the Pope himself was addressing the nation. The living room fell silent, and even in the car, Rush's voice meant all other conversations ceased. It wasn't "Amens" we heard, but enthusiastic "Dittos" echoing from my parents.

Rush's catchphrases became a part of our family lexicon. "Talent on loan from God," he'd proclaim, and my parents would nod in agreement. Now, I understand this was partly meant as a joke, a bit of showmanship. But even as a joke, it linked the divine with his political views. It's a subtle but clear example of shav', using God's name for empty or false purposes.

In our house, Rush wasn't just a political commentator. He was a prophet, his words carrying the weight of divine truth. Disagreeing with Rush wasn't just a difference of opinion - it was heresy.

But the echo chamber effect in Christian media goes beyond just political commentary. It extends to news reporting, entertainment, homeschool curriculum, and even Bible study materials. Many Christian media outlets present a worldview where faith and conservative politics are inextricably linked, where being a "good Christian" means holding certain political views.

My own education is a testament to this. My parents, with the best of intentions, chose curriculum from A Beka Book (now known as Abeka) and Bob Jones University Press for my homeschooling. Their goal was to provide a balanced world-view with a Christian perspective. They weren't trying to turn me into a Christian political soldier. Yet, looking back, I can see how these materials subtly merged faith and politics, shaping my worldview in ways that took years to unravel.

This creates a feedback loop where consumers of Christian media are constantly having their existing beliefs reinforced, with little exposure to alternative viewpoints. It's like living in a house of mirrors.

The danger of this echo chamber is twofold. First, it can lead to a distorted view of reality, where complex issues are reduced to simplistic, us-versus-them narratives. Second, it can create a false sense of moral superiority, where those who disagree are seen not just as political opponents, but as enemies of the faith.

In today's world, these echo chambers have only grown stronger. Social media algorithms feed us more of what we already like, creating digital bubbles that can be hard to pop. Remember the recent controversy surrounding Facebook's handling of political content we talked about earlier? Internal documents revealed that the platform's algorithms often amplified divisive and extreme content, contributing to the polarization we see in our society.

Consider the coverage of the COVID-19 pandemic in some Christian media outlets. Instead of focusing on how churches could serve their communities during a health crisis, many chose to frame public health measures as persecution against Christians. This narrative not only misrepresented the reality of the situation but also perpetuated a massive loss of life during a major historical event by encouraging defiance of safety measures.

I experienced the painful reality of this echo chamber

effect firsthand. An old friend and mentor, my former youth pastor, became the perfect embodiment of Christian National-ism. He went on to manage Herman Cain's 2012 campaign, and his wife gained some musical popularity with patriotic songs linking God and country.

During the COVID-19 pandemic, he posted an image on Facebook about a billboard encouraging vaccinations. His description? It was outrage at the lies and manipulation of the government to push vaccines on the people. I made what I thought was a peaceful comment, sharing that I knew people working in health departments who didn't have malicious intentions.

What I didn't share was that my neighbor, high up in the CDC, was daily interpreting data and working tirelessly to protect the public. She was married to another woman, and our kids rode bikes together in the neighborhood. If I had included any detail about her, my former youth pastor would have certainly written me off even more, his prejudices overriding any consideration of her expertise or dedication.

This neighbor had shared with me the immense burden and grief she experienced on a daily basis, working with these numbers and knowing that each statistic represented an indi-vidual's life. She spoke of sleepless nights, the weight of respon-sibility, and the emotional toll of seeing the human cost behind the numbers on the paper. Her commitment to public health was driven by a deep sense of compassion for every life affected by the pandemic.

The irony wasn't lost on me - here was someone from the LGBTQ+ community, a group often marginalized by certain Christian circles, working selflessly to protect all Americans, including my former youth pastor who had just blocked me. Her story was a reminder of the importance of looking beyond our preconceptions and recognizing the humanity and valuable contributions of all individuals, regardless of their job title, political affiliations, or sexual orientation.

His response? After immediately blocking me, he sent a string of text messages. This was a man I'd never had a cross word with in 20 years. He explained that he wasn't interested in maintaining friendships with anyone who disagreed with him, and that his Facebook was reserved for close friends and family of similar beliefs.

At the time, he was pastoring a highly politically motivated church. It was a yet another reminder of how the echo chamber effect can sever relationships and reinforce division, all under the guise of protecting one's faith.

The echo chamber effect isn't unique to Christian media, of course. It's a problem across the media landscape. But for Christians, who are called to be "in the world but not of it," it's particularly dangerous. It can lead us to confuse our political tribes with the Kingdom of God, our cultural preferences with biblical mandates.

So how do we break out of these echo chambers? How do we engage with media in a way that sharpens our faith rather than simply confirms our biases? That's where the crucial skill of discernment comes in.

I learned the art of discernment in an unlikely place - my undergraduate Quantitative Literacy course. Picture this: a professor straight out of central casting for "absent-minded academic," stumbling into the lecture hall, arms overflowing with newspapers, studies, and data sheets. It was a wild ride.

But beneath the chaos was a method. We'd spend hours combing through these materials, learning to spot bad data, misleading headlines, and manipulative statistics. It wasn't just about numbers - it was about developing a sharp eye for deception in all its forms.

This real-world practice laid a foundation that I've only

recently recognized as the source of what I'd call my super-power: a keen eye. Thanks to that frazzled professor, I can spot a manipulation, a bad intention, a misleading statistic, or a loaded headline from miles away.

Discernment isn't about being cynical or dismissive. It's about engaging critically with the information we consume, always asking questions, always seeking truth. It's a skill that's more crucial now than ever, especially for Christians navigating the treacherous waters of faith and politics in the media landscape.

So how do we cultivate this kind of discernment? Here are some practical steps:

1. Question the source
Who's providing this information? What's their agenda?

2. Look for context
What's the bigger picture? What information might be missing?

3. Check for bias
Is this presenting a balanced view, or pushing a particular perspective?

4. Verify claims
Are there credible sources backing up what's being said?

5. Consider alternative viewpoints
What would someone who disagrees say about this?

These strategies aren't dependent on current events or plat-forms. They're timeless tools for critical thinking that can be applied to any media we consume.

In a world where misinformation spreads faster than truth, where deep fakes and AI-generated content blur the lines between reality and fiction, discernment isn't just helpful - it's essential. It's a core part of what it means to be "wise as serpents and innocent as doves" in our engagement with the world.

As we move forward, let's commit to breaking out of our echo chambers, to engaging with media not just as consumers, but as critical thinkers. Let's strive to be people who seek truth, even when it challenges our preconceptions. Because in the end, that's what our faith calls us to - not simple certainties, but a relentless pursuit of truth, wherever it may lead us.

When people become this deeply entrenched in their media bubbles, reality itself begins to warp. The echo chamber doesn't just reinforce existing beliefs - it creates an alternate universe where facts become flexible and truth becomes whatever confirms our preexisting worldview. This is where the most dangerous aspect of modern media reveals itself: its ability to make the unbelievable seem not just plausible, but absolutely certain. And nowhere is this more evident than in the rise of conspiracy theories within Christian circles.

In a world saturated with information, being able to navigate the media landscape isn't just a nice skill to have - it's a survival necessity. For Christians, it's even more crucial. Our faith calls us to be "in the world but not of it," and that requires a level of media literacy that goes beyond just consuming content.

Media literacy isn't about being tech-savvy or knowing the latest social media trends. It's about understanding how media works, how it shapes our perceptions, and how we can engage with it critically and thoughtfully.

Think about it this way: Would you drink from a stream without knowing what's upstream? Of course not. Yet many of us consume media without considering its source, its biases, or its potential effects on our thinking.

Here's where things get tricky: in the realm of Christian media, the waters are often muddied by a mix of genuine faith, political ideology, and cultural assumptions. It's like trying to separate salt from sugar - at first glance, it all looks the same.

So how do we develop this crucial skill of media literacy? Here are some key principles:

1. Understand that all media is constructed. Every news story, every social media post, every sermon podcast is created by someone with a particular perspective and purpose.
2. Recognize that media has commercial implications. Even Christian media outlets need to make money to survive. How might this affect their content?
3. Be aware of media's ideological and value messages. What worldview is being presented? What assumptions are being made?
4. Understand how different people might interpret the same media message differently. Your background, beliefs, and experiences shape how you perceive media content.
5. Consider what's not being said. Often, what's left out of a story is as important as what's included.

Developing these skills isn't about becoming cynical or distrustful. It's about becoming a more engaged, thoughtful consumer of media. It's about being able to separate the wheat from the chaff, the truth from the spin.

For Christians, this discernment is particularly important when it comes to media that claims to represent our faith. We need to be able to distinguish between genuine Christian teaching and nationalistic ideology dressed up in religious language.

Remember Jesus' words: "Beware of the false prophets, who come to you in sheep's clothing, but inwardly are ravenous wolves." (Matthew 7:15). In our media-saturated age, those wolves might come in the form of slick production values, charismatic personalities, or comforting messages that tickle our ears but lead us astray.

Developing media literacy and discernment is a lifelong process. It requires humility, curiosity, and a willingness to have our assumptions challenged. But it's worth the effort. Because in the end, being able to navigate the media landscape with wisdom and discernment isn't just about being a savvy consumer - it's about being a faithful follower of Christ in a complex, confusing world.

So, we've talked about the problem. We've discussed the importance of media literacy and discernment. But how do we put this into practice? How do we engage with media in a way that sharpens our faith rather than distorting it?

First, it's not about completely disconnecting or living in a media-free bubble. That's neither practical nor desirable. We're called to be salt and light in the world, and that means engaging with the culture around us, including its media.

Instead, it's about being intentional and critical in our media consumption. It's about cultivating habits that help us engage thoughtfully rather than passively absorbing whatever comes our way.

Here are some practical strategies:

1. Diversify your media diet. If you only consume Christian media, branch out. If you only watch one

news channel, try others. Expose yourself to different perspectives, even ones you disagree with. It's like cross-training for your mind.

2. Practice the pause. Before sharing that article or reacting to that post, pause. Ask yourself: Is this true? Is it helpful? Is it necessary? Is it kind? This simple practice can prevent us from contributing to the spread of misinformation or engaging in unproductive online arguments.

3. Seek primary sources. Don't just rely on someone else's interpretation of events or statements. Go to the source when possible. Read the full speech, not just the headline. Look up the actual study, not just the summary.

4. Engage in dialogue, not debate. When you encounter views different from your own, resist the urge to immediately argue. Instead, ask questions. Seek to understand. You might not change your mind, but you'll gain valuable perspective.

5. Take media fasts. Regularly unplug from the constant stream of information. Use this time to reflect, breathe, and recenter yourself on what truly matters.

6. Support quality journalism. Good journalism is crucial for a healthy society. Be willing to pay for it, whether through subscriptions or donations to nonprofit news organizations.

7. Be a critical consumer of Christian media. Don't give Christian sources a free pass. Apply the same critical thinking skills to them that you would to any other media.

When we uncritically accept and spread Christian media

messages that blend faith with nationalism or political ideology, we risk engaging in shav'. We're using God's name, often unintentionally, for empty or false purposes, diluting the true message of the Gospel with worldly concerns.

Remember, our goal isn't to become cynical or to disconnect from the world around us. It's to engage more fully, more thoughtfully, more faithfully. It's about being in the world but not of it, about being wise as serpents and innocent as doves.

As we navigate this media landscape, let's keep our eyes fixed on Christ. Let's strive to be people who seek truth, who love justice, who embody grace. Let's use media as a tool for understanding our world and loving our neighbors, not as a weapon in culture wars.

In the end, how we engage with media is a spiritual issue. It shapes our understanding of the world, our neighbors, and ultimately, our God. So let's approach it with the seriousness it deserves, always seeking to honor Christ in how we consume, create, and share media.

The journey towards media literacy and critical engagement isn't easy. It requires constant vigilance, ongoing learning, and a willingness to be challenged. But it's a journey worth taking. Because in a world where media shapes so much of our reality, being able to navigate it wisely isn't just a skill - it's a crucial part of our Christian witness.

So let's commit to this journey. Let's be people who engage thoughtfully, who seek truth relentlessly, who use media as a tool for kingdom purposes rather than letting it use us. In doing so, we can help reclaim the narrative of what it means to be Christian in America, separating the truth of the gospel from the distortions of Christian Nationalism.

The media landscape may be complex and often treacherous, but we don't navigate it alone. We have the guidance of Scripture, the wisdom of the Holy Spirit, and the support of our faith communities. With these resources, and with a commitment to ongoing growth and discernment, we can engage with media in ways that honor God, serve our neighbors, and bear witness to the transformative power of the gospel.

But sometimes, even with the best navigation tools, we still drift into dangerous waters. Like sailors hypnotized by sirens' songs, many Christians have been lured onto the jagged rocks of conspiracy thinking. And once those rocks tear into the hull of reality, it's amazing how quickly the whole ship can sink.

When we talk about conspiracy theories in Christian circles, it's easy to discuss them in the abstract. But the reality is far more troubling - and personal. What we're witnessing isn't just scattered misinformation, but a fundamental rewiring of how many Christians understand reality itself.

QAnon represents something unprecedented in this landscape. This wasn't just another conspiracy theory - it became a quasi-religious movement, particularly among evangelicals. The statistics are sobering: A 2021 survey showed that 49% of Protestant pastors reported hearing congregants repeating QAnon theories. [14.2] Another study by the American Enterprise Institute revealed that 27% of white evangelical Protestants believed in the core QAnon claims. [14.3]

What made QAnon particularly insidious was how it draped itself in Christian language and imagery. It portrayed Donald Trump as a messianic figure fighting a secret war against a cabal of Satan-worshipping pedophiles. It wasn't just political anymore - it was spiritual warfare. The language of "Great Awakening," "The Storm," and "Where We Go One We Go All" mimicked religious revival terminology, making it feel familiar and righteous to many believers.

I've seen the devastating effects up close, in my own family. I remember the day Rachel [replaced for anonymity] burst into my office, her eyes wild with fear. She wasn't just sharing concerns - she was convinced that President Biden was part of a secret cabal implementing Sharia law across America. Her voice trembled as she laid out an elaborate conspiracy involving schools, government officials, and supposed Islamic infiltration.

I tried to gentle her fears: "Listen, I think you need to turn off the news. If you disconnect from it, months will pass by and little will have changed."

Her response haunts me to this day. Through a mixture of yelling and tears, she cried out, "You'll care when the Muslims are taking over the schools and cutting your kids heads off!"

I wish I was making this story up. But these kinds of conspiracy fears are real, and they're prevalent. They're even more prevalent when you're close enough to people for them to be honest with you about their theories and beliefs. This wasn't some stranger on the internet - this was family. Someone I love, someone I respect, and someone who in every other aspect of life is rational and caring.

This is what happens when the echo chambers we've discussed become airtight - when media consumption moves beyond bias into an alternate reality. QAnon found fertile ground in Christian circles not because believers are gullible, but because decades of increasingly isolated media consumption had tended to the soil. When you've already accepted that there's a grand conspiracy against Christian values, it's not such a leap to believe in secret cabals and hidden threats.

The tragedy isn't just that these theories are false - it's that they actively work against Christ's command to love our neighbors. They transform real people - immigrants, Muslims, political opponents - into monsters, making it impossible to see them as God sees them: as human beings worthy of love and dignity.

Remember that CEO from the beginning of this chapter, comfortable sharing his racist views because he assumed I shared his worldview? The same media ecosystem that made him feel safe expressing bigotry also makes people like Rachel feel certain that apocalyptic threats lurk behind every headline. Both are symptoms of the same disease: a media landscape that prioritizes engagement over truth, fear over understanding, and division over unity.

This is how shav' works in the digital age. It's not just about taking God's name in vain through words - it's about using God's name to justify paranoia, to sanctify fear, or to make hatred feel holy. When we use Christianity to validate conspiracy theories, we're not just spreading misinformation - we're corrupting the very essence of our faith.

But understanding the problem isn't enough. As someone working in media, I've had to wrestle with a deeper question: How do we combat this machinery of misinformation? How do we create spaces for truth when lies travel at the speed of light? The answer, I've found, lies not in fighting specific conspiracies but in understanding and reshaping the very systems that allow them to flourish. It's about recognizing that media isn't just a tool - it's an environment that shapes how we think, believe, and relate to one another. And as we'll explore in the next chapter, that environment is being deliberately engineered to amplify our worst instincts while drowning out our better judgement.

16

COLLATERAL DAMAGE
THE UNINTENDED CONSEQUENCES

*If Jesus Christ came back today like you threaten He
will,*
Which poor group of people do you think He would kill?
*Who would Jesus choose to starve if you gave Him the
chance?*
*And if there was a genocide, would He take a neutral
stance?*
*Who would Jesus bomb? Tell me, who would Jesus
bomb?*
Would it be kids in Palestine or how 'bout Vietnam?
*Would Jesus bomb the atheists, the Muslims, or the
Jews?*
I want you to ask yourself, what would Jesus do?
*Would He say it's complicated and there's sinners on all
sides?*
Or would He say that some people just deserve to die?
If Christ the Savior rose again and on a sidewalk slept,
*Would you extend your hand to Him or just watch
where you stepped?*

— 15.1

The haunting lyrics of Jordan Smart's song echos in my mind. These words cut deep, exposing the raw nerve of our collective hypocrisy. Smart's song is a scathing indictment of the disconnect between the teachings of Christ and the actions of many who claim His name. It's a reminder of how far we've strayed from the path of love and compassion that Jesus laid out for us.

As I scrolled through the comments on Smart's viral video, my heart sank. The feed was flooded with testimonies from people wounded by the Christian faith, individuals who had been pushed away from the church and, potentially, from God Himself. Their pain was clear and their disillusionment profound.

This is why I wrote this book.

The unintended consequences of Christian Nationalism are far-reaching and devastating. We've become more known for what we're against than what we're for. In the eyes of many, being a Christian has become synonymous with being a Christian nationalist – a far cry from the Christ-like living we're called to embody.

Even more tragically, for a growing number of people, Christianity has come to represent the antithesis of love. How did we get here? How did the faith founded on the principle of loving one's neighbor become associated with exclusion, judgment, and even hate?

The answer, I believe, lies in our gradual embrace of shav' – the empty, false use of God's name. We've wrapped our cultural and political ideologies in the cloak of faith, using

God's name to justify our own agendas rather than submitting to His will.

As we delve into this chapter, we'll explore the ripple effects of this distortion of our faith. We'll confront the uncomfortable truths about how Christian Nationalism has tarnished our witness, polarized our churches, and pushed countless individuals away from the transformative love of Christ.

This isn't about pointing fingers or assigning blame. It's about recognizing the unintended consequences of what many believed was righteous zeal. It's about understanding that when we merge our faith with nationalism, we create a toxic brew that poisons not just our own spiritual lives, but the perception of Christianity as a whole.

The numbers are stark, a cold reality check that should shake us to our core. According to a 2021 Gallup poll, for the first time in Gallup's trend since the 1930s, less than half of U.S. adults (47%) belong to a house of worship. This number stood at 70% just two decades ago. [15.2]

What happened?

The easy answer would be to blame secularization or the rise of "nones" – those who claim no religious affiliation. But that's too simplistic. The truth, I fear, is far more uncomfortable. We've damaged our own witness.

This isn't just an abstract theological concern or a PR problem for the church. This is deeply personal, and it cuts me to the core. It causes me profound grief - not because people might think I'm a bigot or racist for being a Christian (though that sucks too), but because our actions have driven a wedge between people and God. And it would be easy to blame others. But it's not their fault. It's ours. It's mine.

We've managed to turn the good news into bad news.

We've taken the message of a loving God and twisted it into something that makes people want to run screaming in the opposite direction. Jesus said, "Come to me, all you who are weary and burdened," and we've added a footnote: *Terms and conditions apply. Must vote Republican, hate the gays, believe climate change is a hoax, and science is a liberal conspiracy.*

We've screwed this up royally. We've turned the bread of life into a stale, moldy biscuit that's choking people instead of nourishing them. We've taken the living water and polluted it with our own toxic waste of nationalism.

Every time someone says, "I'm spiritual but not religious," or "I like Jesus but can't stand Christians," I feel like I've been punched in the gut. Because I know that's on us. We've made it harder for people to see God, to experience His love, to know His grace. We've become the Pharisees, the very people Jesus railed against, turning faith into a burden instead of a blessing.

And here's the real gut-punch: How many people have we pushed away from God? How many souls have we wounded? How many people will never darken the door of a church, never open a Bible, never consider the claims of Christ, because we've so thoroughly poisoned the well? That thought keeps me up at night, and it should haunt all of us who claim to follow Jesus. His words in Matthew 23:13 hit like a freight train:

> But woe to you, scribes and Pharisees, hypocrites, because you shut the kingdom of heaven in front of people; for you do not enter *it* yourselves, nor do you allow those who are entering to go in.

That's us, folks. We've become the very roadblock to God's kingdom that Jesus condemned. We're not just failing to share the good news; we're actively making it harder for people to receive it. And that's a weight I'm not sure how to bear.

Christian Nationalism has tarnished the perception of Christianity in ways we're only beginning to understand. We've replaced the transformative message of Christ's love with a toxic cocktail of political ideology and cultural warfare. We've traded the bread of life for the stones of judgment and exclusion.

This is the crux of the issue. In our zeal to "defend" Christianity, we've often pushed people away from it. We've become so focused on winning culture wars that we've forgotten our primary calling: to love God and love our neighbors.

The exodus of younger generations from the church is particularly heartbreaking. These are individuals who've grown up watching the inconsistency between the words of Christ and the actions of many who claim His name. They've seen how quickly we can turn the Sermon on the Mount into a partisan political platform.

This damage to our witness extends beyond our borders. The global perception of American Christianity has been profoundly affected by the rise of Christian Nationalism. Missionaries report increasing difficulty in separating the message of Christ from the image of American political power.

We've engaged in shav' on a massive scale, using God's name to endorse our own agendas and ideologies. And the world has noticed. They've seen us wrap the cross in the flag and mistake patriotism for godliness. Is it any wonder that so many have turned away?

But there's hope. The very fact that we're having this conversation, that we're willing to confront these uncomfortable truths, is a start. It's a recognition that our witness has been compromised, and that we need to find a way back to the heart of our faith.

Galatians 3:28 says: "There is neither Democrat nor

Republican, neither conservative nor liberal, for you are all one in Christ Jesus."

Well, that's not exactly what it says, but that's what it could mean in today's context. It's not worth debating over but I do recognize the examples in the original are inherent conditions and not life choices. But, the actual verse reads: "There is neither Jew nor Greek, there is neither slave nor free, there is neither male nor female; for you are all one in Christ Jesus."

Paul's words to the Galatians cut through the social and cultural divisions of his time, reminding believers of their fundamental unity in Christ. Today, we might apply this same principle to our political divides.

The polarization within the church isn't just uncomfortable. It's destructive. It's driving people away from faith. It's crippling our ability to be salt and light in the world. How can we preach reconciliation when we can't even talk to each other? How can we claim to love our enemies when we can't even love our brothers and sisters who vote differently?

This polarization is a form of shav'. We're taking the name of the Lord in vain when we use our faith as a weapon against fellow believers. We're using God's name for empty, false purposes when we claim divine sanction for our political views.

The consequences of this division extend far beyond mere disagreements. They're causing church splits, a phenomenon all too common in our landscape. Ever wonder why you see so many "First Baptist" or "Second Baptist" or "Third Baptist" church signs? It's often a legacy of past divisions. Words like "Reformed," "Renewed," "New," "Redeemed," or "Restored" in church names frequently refer to a history of a church split.

Even more tragically, churches are dying - not just physically, but spiritually. When a church becomes a life-sucking place instead of a life-giving one, it withers and dies. This isn't Christ; it's the lack thereof. It's not the Bible; it's shav'.

While data on the specific causes of church splits is limited, anecdotal evidence suggests that political stances are increasingly a factor in these divisions. This trend underscores the urgent need to reassess how we prioritize our beliefs and convictions.

Pastor Dr. Phil teaches about three tiers of doctrine, a concept known in theological circles as "theological triage." This framework, popularized by theologian Albert Mohler, helps believers distinguish between essential beliefs and those where disagreement can be tolerated:

1. First-tier doctrines are the core, non-negotiable beliefs of Christianity, such as the Trinity, the deity of Christ, and salvation by grace through faith.
2. Second-tier doctrines are important for church health and functioning but allow for some disagreement. These might include views on baptism, church governance, or the role of spiritual gifts today.
3. Third-tier doctrines are issues where Christians can disagree and still maintain close fellowship. These might include views on the end times, the age of the earth, or dietary restrictions.

These third-tier issues, seemingly minor in the grand scheme of faith, have become unexpected fault lines in many churches. It's ironic, isn't it? The very matters we're told we can "agree to disagree" on have become the wedges driving us apart.

While third-tier doctrines are theoretically issues where Christians can disagree amicably, in practice, they often become deeply divisive, particularly when intertwined with cultural and political stances. Most political issues fall into this tier, which is why they can be so contentious within church communities. However, it's crucial to remember that these are topics for discussion within the church. We previously identified that the matters to agree on within a church are not the same as, and often contradictory to, the ways in which we should vote neighborly. This distinction is vital for maintaining both church unity and civic responsibility.

The tragedy is that these third-tier issues, which should be areas of respectful disagreement and mutual learning, have become battlegrounds for identity politics within the church. We've turned molehills into mountains, forgetting that our unity in Christ should transcend these differences.

It's shav' in action - using God's name to justify our divisions, to claim divine sanction for our particular interpretations. We've taken issues that should inspire wonder and humility before the mysteries of God and turned them into weapons in our cultural wars.

Understanding and applying this framework can help us navigate differences without fracturing our unity in Christ. The poet Edwin Markham captures the spirit of unity we should strive for in his poem "Outwitted":

> He drew a circle that shut me out--
> Heretic, rebel, a thing to flout.
> But Love and I had the wit to win:
> We drew a circle that took him in!

— 15.3

The first two lines reflect the exclusionary attitudes we often see in polarized churches, where those with different views are labeled and ostracized.

Then, Markham presents the solution - a love that expands our circle to include those we might otherwise reject. This is the kind of inclusive, Christ-like love that can heal our divisions.

As we navigate these challenging times, let's remember the words of Pastor Dr. Phil "In the final analysis, Jesus is Lord. Everything else is small stuff. Don't sweat the small stuff."

These simple yet profound words remind us to keep our focus on what truly matters - our shared faith in Christ - rather than getting caught up in divisive 'third tier' issues.

Oh the irony. In our zeal to "save" America, we've often undermined the very democratic principles that make it unique. Christian Nationalism, with its vision of a divinely ordained Christian nation, stands in stark contrast to the pluralistic democracy envisioned by our founders which allows for our very religious freedoms.

"America is a Christian nation, and we need to take it back!" And I have to ask, take it back from whom?

This rhetoric isn't just divisive; it's dangerous. It suggests that only Christians (and often, only a particular type of Christian) are true Americans. It's a short step from there to viewing those who disagree as not just political opponents, but enemies of God's will.

The danger of theocratic tendencies in Christian Nationalism can't be overstated. When we mingle our faith with our nation, we risk creating a de facto religious test for citizenship or political participation. This flies in the face of the Constitution and the principles of religious freedom that have been a cornerstone of American democracy.

But perhaps most dangerously, Christian Nationalism can erode our commitment to the democratic process itself. When we believe we're fighting for God's will, it becomes easy to justify any means to achieve our ends. Voter suppression, gerrymandering, even attempts to overturn election results - all can be rationalized if we believe we're doing God's work.

This is shav' on a national scale. We're taking the Lord's name in vain when we use our faith to undermine the very principles of justice, equality, and freedom that reflect God's character.

As we work through these issues, the words of Emma Lazarus's sonnet "The New Colossus" come to mind:

> Give me your tired, your poor,
> Your huddled masses yearning to breathe free,
> The wretched refuse of your teeming shore.
> Send these, the homeless, tempest-tost to me,
> I lift my lamp beside the golden door!
>
> — 15.4

These lines, inscribed on the Statue of Liberty, remind us of the inclusive, welcoming spirit that has long been a part of the American ideal. They stand in stark contrast to the exclusionary tendencies of Christian Nationalism. As followers of Christ, shouldn't we be the first to welcome the stranger, the sojourner, the fatherless, homeless, or lost to lift our lamps beside the golden door?

The pursuit of political power has led to a distortion of Christian ethics that would make Jesus weep. We've traded the Beatitudes for political platitudes, the Sermon on the Mount for sound bites on cable news.

I've watched in dismay as Christians twist themselves into ethical pretzels trying to justify support for policies and politicians that clearly contradict the teachings of Christ. It's a moral gymnastics routine that would be impressive if it weren't so tragic.

Take the issue of immigration. Jesus couldn't be clearer about our duty to welcome the stranger. Yet I've heard Christians argue for policies of exclusion and separation, even defending the inhumane treatment of children at the border. How did we get from "Let the little children come to me" to "Lock them in cages"?

Or consider our approach to the poor. The Bible is filled with commands to care for those in need, to seek justice for the oppressed. Yet I've seen Christians champion economic policies that widen the gap between rich and poor, that strip away social safety nets, all in the name of "personal responsibility."

This ethical inconsistency is perhaps most glaring when it comes to issues of character. I've watched Christian leaders excuse or downplay behavior in political allies that they would vehemently condemn in their opponents. It's as if the ends justify the means, as long as those ends align with our political goals.

This is shav' in its most hideous form. We're taking the Lord's name in vain when we use our faith to justify actions and policies that clearly contradict the teachings of Christ. We're using God's name for empty, false purposes when we claim divine sanction for our political preferences while ignoring the clear ethical mandates of scripture.

The words of the hymn "They'll Know We Are Christians By Our Love" should teach us:

We will walk with each other, we will walk hand in
    hand,
We will walk with each other, we will walk hand in
    hand,

And together we'll spread the news that God is in our
  land.
And they'll know we are Christians by our love, by our
  love,
Yes, they'll know we are Christians by our love.

— 15.5

But will they?

The global perception of American Christianity has been
profoundly affected by the rise of Christian Nationalism, and
this impact is felt on a personal level. I'm reminded of Amr, a
Muslim man who works for my company and lives in Egypt.
Over the five years we've worked together, our conversations
have given me invaluable insight into how America, and by
extension American Christianity, is viewed from across the
globe.

Ironically, Egypt was once Jesus' own stomping ground. As
Hosea 11:1 reminds us, "Out of Egypt I called my son." Yet, I've
come to believe that Amr's faith in Islam often aligns more
closely with Christ's teachings than the average American
Christian nationalist's faith.

Amr's perspective on America, which likely reflects a
broader global view, primarily focuses on two aspects. First,
they see our president, noting what they say and how they live.
Second, they observe our engagement in global conflicts, our
neglect of suffering, and sometimes even our spurring on of
suffering, as is currently happening in Palestine and Gaza.
These actions paint a picture of what it means to be Christian
in their eyes.

Honestly, from this perspective, I struggle to see how our

actions reflect Christ's love any more than those of other faiths. We've allowed Christian Nationalism to taint our witness on a global scale, engaging in shav' by using God's name to justify actions that often run counter to His teachings of love and peace.

While we've explored the historical dangers of Christian Nationalism throughout this book, recent events serve as a chilling reminder that these ideologies continue to evolve and pose very real threats in our modern world. What we're witnessing today is not just a continuation of past ideologies, but a new version of Christian Nationalism - one that has learned to cloak itself in modern rhetoric while maintaining its capacity for extreme harm.

The most horrifying manifestation of this ideology comes when words turn to violent action. While it's crucial to note that the vast majority of those who identify with Christian nationalist ideas do not engage in violence, we cannot ignore the instances where this worldview has been used to justify unspeakable acts.

Let's examine a few tragic cases where individuals, driven by ideologies aligned with Christian Nationalism, have committed acts of mass violence:

1. Robert Lewis Dear (2015) - Planned Parenthood Shooting, Colorado Springs

In November 2015, Dear attacked a Planned Parenthood clinic, killing three people and injuring nine others. During his arrest and subsequent court appearances, Dear made numerous statements indicating he believed he was acting on God's behalf to prevent abortions.[15.6] His actions represent a terrifying fusion of anti-abortion extremism and a warped interpretation of Christian duty.

Dear's case illustrates how Christian nationalist ideas can merge with other extremist beliefs, creating a toxic ideology that sees violence as a justified means to enforce perceived divine laws. It's a warning of how dangerous it can be when individuals believe they're soldiers in a holy war against their fellow citizens.

2. Dylann Roof (2015) - Charleston Church Shooting

In June 2015, Roof murdered nine African American churchgoers at Emanuel African Methodist Episcopal Church in Charleston, South Carolina. While Roof's primary motivation was racial hatred, his journal urged white Americans to reshape Christianity, denouncing it as "this weak cowardly religion" and envisioning instead "a warrior's religion.".[15.7]

Roof's writings suggested he saw America as a white Christian nation under threat from other races and religions. This case demonstrates how Christian Nationalism can intertwine with white supremacy, creating a lethal cocktail of hate that targets racial and religious minorities.

3. Scott Roeder (2009) - Murder of Dr. George Tiller

In 2009, Roeder murdered Dr. George Tiller, a physician who provided abortion services for women if the baby had severe abnormalities that were incompatible with living outside of the womb or if continuing the pregnancy posed a serious risk to the mother's health.

Roeder claimed his actions were in line with God's law to stop abortion.[15.8] Roeder's case, like Dear's, shows how Christian nationalist ideas can fuel single-issue extremism, in this case against abortion providers.

These tragic events force us to confront an uncomfortable truth: the rhetoric of Christian Nationalism, even in its less extreme forms, can contribute to an environment where some individuals feel justified in committing acts of violence in the name of their beliefs.

It's crucial to understand that these violent actors represent a tiny fraction of those who might identify with Christian nationalist ideas. However, their actions serve as a warning about the potential consequences of this ideology when taken to its extreme.

The danger lies not just in the actions of these individuals, but in the broader cultural context that can foster such extremism. When Christian nationalist rhetoric paints political opponents as enemies of God, when it frames social issues as spiritual battles between good and evil, it creates fertile ground for radicalization.

As Christians, we must confront an uncomfortable truth: while we may not be directly involved in the most extreme instances of violence and hate, our rhetoric and actions may be fostering a faith environment that allows for such extremism to take root and grow. The way we speak about our beliefs, our political opponents, and our vision for society can create a climate where more radical interpretations find fertile ground.

I believe we have created an environment in this country that allows these incidents of violence and hate to happen far too often. This is not just about the most visible acts of violence; it's also about the subtle ways our words and actions contribute to a climate of division, fear, and othering.

It begs us to question our own role in these incidents that have merged nationalism with Christianity. Have our words, our silence, our tacit approval of certain ideologies contributed to a climate where such violence becomes thinkable, even justifiable in the minds of some? This introspection is crucial. While most Christian nationalists would never condone this kind of violence, we must consider how the movement's rhetoric - its demonization of the 'other', its framing of political disagreements as spiritual battles between good and evil, its merging of national and religious identity - might create fertile ground for extremist actions.

These acts of violence represent the most extreme and visible manifestation of Christian nationalist thinking. But they should serve as a wake-up call for all of us to examine the less obvious ways this ideology might be shaping our worldviews and actions.

The path from mainstream Christian nationalist ideas to violent extremism isn't a straight line, but neither is it an impassable chasm. It's a gradual slope, where each step away from Christ's teachings of love and inclusion makes the next step easier, until some find themselves far from where they ever intended to be.

As we move forward, we must be vigilant. We must call out Christian nationalist rhetoric whenever we encounter it, not just in its most extreme forms, but in its more subtle and socially acceptable manifestations. We must work tirelessly to create a Christian witness that stands in stark contrast to these ideologies of hate and division.

Because if we don't, if we allow Christian Nationalism to continue unchecked in our churches and communities, we risk not only the corruption of our faith but the very real possibility of more tragedy, more violence, more lives lost to this perversion of Christ's message.

The stakes couldn't be higher. It's time for us to reclaim our faith from those who would use it as a weapon. It's time to show the world a Christianity that looks like Christ - loving, inclusive, and unequivocally opposed to violence in all its forms.

As we conclude this exploration of the unintended consequences of Christian Nationalism, the weight of our collective failure sits heavy on my heart. We've damaged our witness, polarized our churches, undermined democracy, distorted our ethics, and tarnished the global perception of our faith.

But in the depths of this realization, I find a glimmer of hope. Because recognizing the problem is the first step towards solving it. We've strayed far from the path, but the way back is clear. It's the way of Christ - the way of love, of service, of self-sacrifice.

The call before us is nothing less than a reclamation of authentic Christian witness. It's a call to disentangle our faith from nationalism, to separate the gospel from political ideologies. It's a call to return to the radical, transformative message of Christ.

This isn't about abandoning our role in society or withdrawing from political engagement. Far from it. It's about engaging in a way that truly reflects the character of Christ. It's about being known for our love, our compassion, our pursuit of justice for all people.

Shane Claiborne, in his book *The Irresistible Revolution*, captures this challenge perfectly:

The tragedy in the church is that we have become so entangled with the affairs of this world that we have forgotten our true citizenship is in heaven. We have traded the politics of Jesus for the politics of this world, and in doing so, we have lost our prophetic voice.

— 15.9

These words cut to the heart of our predicament. We've lost our prophetic voice, our ability to speak truth to power, because we've become too enamored with power ourselves. We've forgotten our true citizenship, our primary allegiance to the kingdom of God rather than any earthly nation.

As we move forward, let's commit to rooting out shav' in all its forms. Let's stop using God's name for empty, false purposes. Let's reclaim a faith that's big enough to transcend national borders, political parties, and cultural divisions.

The task before us is daunting. The damage done by Christian Nationalism runs deep. But we serve a God of resurrection, a God who specializes in bringing life out of death, hope out of despair.

So let's rise to this challenge. Let's reclaim an authentic Christian witness that truly reflects the love and grace of Christ. Let's become known once again not for our political affiliations, but for our love. For our service. For our commitment to justice and mercy for all people.

The world is watching. But they're not just watching our politics or our protests, they're watching to see if we've got the courage to imagine something entirely new. Because what comes after Christian Nationalism isn't just a different version of the same old story. It's territory so uncharted it might just transform everything we thought we knew about following Jesus.

17

THE LONG ROAD HOME
WHAT COMES AFTER UNLEARNING

I was at the mall with some family friends who'd let me stay at their house with them for a special occasion when I was 9 years old. We passed a candy store, and I got excited when I saw they had PEZ candies. "Can I get some?" I asked. "My PEZ dispenser at home is empty - it's just sitting there on my dresser."

My friend's mom looked at me with this expression I didn't understand at the time. She bought me the PEZ without saying a word. It wasn't until hours later, back at their house, that reality hit me:

There was no PEZ dispenser.
There was no dresser.
And I had no home.

When I was nine, my house burned down. Not in a quick, merciful way, more like a slow-motion train wreck that kept finding new ways to get worse.

It started around 1 AM. We were still up watching the end of a movie when someone started pounding on our front door. "YOU'RE HOUSE IS ON FIRE! YOU'RE HOUSE IS ON FIRE! It was our neighbor, alerted by his blind and deaf dog who'd been barking at the smell of smoke - he was quite literally our smoke detector.

At first, it didn't seem so bad - just a small fire around the chimney. But as the night played out, it was like watching one of the *Final Destination* movies or a *Tale of Unfortunate Events* - everything that could possibly go wrong, went wrong. When we tried to use the water hose, the faucet broke clean off reducing any water pressure to a trickle. Our neighbors lived too far away to run hoses from their houses. The fire department arrived with only a grass fire truck.

By morning, our house was gone. Not damaged - gone. Now, I'm leaving a lot out because that was a very long night that I'll never forget. But because my father had let the insurance lapse (a detail that would haunt our family for years), we were left with nothing but the PJs on our backs.

Here's the thing about unlearning - it's a lot like that moment in the candy store. We keep reaching for things that aren't there anymore, operating on autopilot as if nothing has changed.

The journey we're on, it's not just about changing our minds. It's about recognizing that some of the structures we thought were permanent, some of the certainties we took for granted, have already burned down. We just haven't fully realized it yet.

Sometimes we're standing in the candy store of American Christianity, thinking about PEZ dispensers that sit on dresser drawers in houses that no longer exist. The old ways of mixing faith and nationalism, of wrapping the cross in the flag, of using

God's name for empty purposes - we're finally seeing them for what they always were: shav'.

This chapter is about what comes next. About how we move forward when we finally accept that some things have burned to the ground. About how we rebuild something authentic from the ashes of what we've unlearned.

William Sloane Coffin once said,

> There are three kinds of patriots, two bad, one good. The bad ones are the uncritical lovers and the loveless critics. Good patriots carry on a lover's quarrel with their country, a reflection of God's lover's quarrel with all the world.
>
> — 16.1

This isn't just clever wordplay - it's a blueprint for what comes after unlearning. Because once we've recognized what's burned down, once we've stopped reaching for things that aren't there anymore, we have to figure out what to build in its place.

Here's what I've learned: The voice we need isn't a whisper of polite disagreement or a shout of angry condemnation. It's the clear, steady voice of someone who loves enough to tell the truth. Who sees the damage being done in Christ's name and refuses to stay silent.

This voice won't win you many friends in today's church culture. Trust me on this one. When you start pointing out how Christian Nationalism betrays the very heart of the Gospel, people get uncomfortable. When you question whether the American flag belongs next to the cross, they get defensive. When you suggest that maybe - just maybe - Jesus wasn't too concerned about winning culture wars or elections, they might show you the door.

But here's the thing: We're not called to be the status quo. We're called to be faithful. And sometimes faithfulness means saying the hard things, standing in the uncomfortable spaces, being the voice that disrupts the alliance between faith and power.

Think of the prophets. They weren't trying to win popularity contests. They weren't interested in maintaining the status quo. They loved God and their people too much to stay silent when they saw truth being twisted and justice being denied.

That's what reclaiming our voice looks like. Not screaming into the void. Not sitting quietly while God's name is used for empty purposes. But speaking truth with the clarity that comes from having unlearned the comfortable lies.

And yes, it will cost you. Speaking up against Christian Nationalism might cost you relationships, opportunities, maybe even your place in certain communities. But silence costs more. It costs us our integrity, our witness, and ultimately, our faith itself.

Dorothy Day, co-founder of the Catholic Worker Movement, once said,

 I really only love God as much as I love the person I love the least.

— 16.2

Let that sit with you for a minute. Because if that's true - and I'm afraid it is - then we've got some serious work to do.

And let's be honest - this work is harder than pulling teeth from an angry honey badger. It's one thing to intellectually recognize that Christian Nationalism is toxic. It's another thing entirely to catch yourself mid-thought, mid-action, mid-vote, still operating from those old patterns.

But here's what this work actually looks like:

It looks like speaking up in church when someone equates patriotism with godliness, even if you don't have all the answers.

It looks like having uncomfortable conversations with family members who don't understand why you can't just "go along" with the merger of faith and nationalism anymore.

It looks like reexamining your own heart every time you're tempted to use faith as a weapon or God's name as a political tool.

It looks like standing with the marginalized, even when - especially when - other Christians question your faith for doing so.

The road ahead isn't just about changing our behavior. It's about confronting the damage that's been done, the wounds we've inflicted, the lies we've told ourselves and others. And that means we need to do something that most of us aren't very good at.

It's time for us to engage in genuine, heartfelt repentance. Not just for our individual actions, but for our collective complicity in a system that has often prioritized power over love, exclusion over welcome, judgment over grace.

This repentance needs to be specific and concrete. We need to acknowledge how Christian Nationalism has hurt:

- People of color, through its often implicit (and sometimes explicit) white supremacy.
- LGBTQ+ individuals, through rhetoric and policies that have marginalized and demonized them.
- Immigrants and refugees, through fear-mongering and policies that harm them.
- People of other faiths, through attempts to legislate Christian values.
- The poor, through support for economic policies that widen inequality.

But repentance is only the first step. We also need to actively seek reconciliation with those we've hurt. This means:

1. Listening without defensiveness to those who have been harmed by Christian Nationalism.
2. Acknowledging the harm done, without excuses or justifications.
3. Taking concrete actions to make amends and prevent future harm.
4. Being patient, recognizing that trust takes time to rebuild.

This process won't be easy. It will require us to confront our own complicity, to sit with the discomfort of knowing we've caused harm. But it's necessary if we want to rebuild a Christian witness that truly reflects the reconciling love of Christ.

As we engage in this work of repentance and reconciliation, let's hold onto the words of Archbishop Desmond Tutu in *No Future Without Forgiveness*:

> True reconciliation exposes the awfulness, the abuse, the hurt, the truth. It could even sometimes make things worse. It is a risky undertaking but in the end it is worthwhile, because in the end only an honest confrontation with reality can bring real healing.

— 16.3

This is our call – to confront reality honestly, to seek healing, to work towards true reconciliation. It's a daunting task, but it's also an opportunity to demonstrate the transformative power of Christ's love in action.

T.S. Eliot had it right in *Little Gidding:* "We shall not cease from exploration And the end of all our exploring Will be to arrive where we started And know the place for the first time." [16.4]

That's what this journey feels like - a long journey that somehow leads us back to the beginning, but with new eyes.

The journey of rebuilding our Christian witness isn't a sprint; it's a marathon. Or perhaps more accurately, it's a grueling hike through unfamiliar terrain. This truth hit home for me during a family expedition to Petit Jean Mountain in the Ozarks.

We'd decided to tackle the Boy Scout Trail, a challenging 12-mile loop that winds down the mountain, across a river, and up to a peak with breathtaking (and sometimes vertigo-inducing) views. My wife and I, along with our four kids aged 8, 9, 11 and 12, set out with more enthusiasm than preparation.

From the start, we were behind schedule. We arrived later than planned, a reminder that we're often late to recognize the need for change. Just as we've been slow to acknowledge how far we've strayed down the path of Christian Nationalism, we were slow to start our hike.

We were also woefully underprepared. My wife wore ankle socks with hiking boots, a recipe for blisters. I ended up trading her my socks - a moist and smelly but necessary sacrifice. It wasn't comfortable, but it allowed us to keep moving forward together. Isn't this what we're called to do as we rebuild our witness? To bear one another's burdens, to make sacrifices for the good of the faith?

As we hiked, we crossed paths multiple times with a woman who seemed hopelessly lost. She'd pass us, then we'd see her coming back the other way, clearly disoriented. It was a funny reminder of how easy it is to lose our way, to circle back to old habits and patterns even as we try to move forward. How often have we, as Christians, found ourselves similarly turned around, mistaking motion for progress?

As the sun began to set, reality set in. We were hours from the trailhead with no flashlights and no bear spray. The distant screams of mountain lions echoed through the valley. My children got scared and I felt vulnerable as we realized we were easy targets wandering through the darkness.

To lighten the mood (or perhaps to torture me further), my wife decided to share a recent local news story. "Did you hear about the hiker who got lost in the woods last month?" she asked. "They did eventually find her body after several days of searching." I shot her a look that I hoped conveyed both "Not helping!" and "Please stop talking!"

My wife pulled out her phone. With a mix of humor and genuine concern, she texted our location to a local friend saying:

> Just in case we end up on the evening news, here's my GPS location.

View Dropped Pin

Really?

It was a comical moment that masked a very real worry - we were in over our heads, and we knew it.

The mission we'd set out on suddenly seemed foolhardy and now all of the sudden, recklessly dangerous. Yet we pressed on, knowing that staying put wasn't an option and that it was farther to turn back than to continue on.

It was then that my 11-year-old son hit his wall. Collapsing on the ground, laying himself out like a filleted fish, he wailed, "I can't do it! I cannot walk anymore!" In that moment, I shared a truth that had taken me years to learn:

> Son, your ability to carry on is 90% in the mind and only 10% in the body. You need to tell your body that you must continue.

To my amazement, he not only got up but took the lead, guiding us bravely until darkness fell. Even when we passed a sign pointing to "Bear's Den" (which my oldest daughter wanted to explore), he pushed on - *No thank you death-by-bear.*

The last hour of our hike was in complete darkness. With my phone's flashlight under 10% battery, we huddled together, the beam of light barely illuminating the path ahead. Step by step, we made our way through the dark forest, trusting that if we stayed on the path, we'd eventually reach our destination.

This experience mirrors our journey of rebuilding a Christian witness in so many ways:

1. We often start late, slow to recognize the need for change. But it's never too late to begin the journey of realignment with Christ's teachings.

2. We may feel unprepared, lacking all the answers. Yet we must start with what we have, trusting that God will provide what we need along the way.

3. The journey requires sacrifice. We may need to give up comfort, privilege, or long-held beliefs for the sake of the broader witness of Christ's love in a broken world.

4. Once we identify the goal - in our case, rebuilding an authentic Christian witness - we must commit to seeing it through, no matter the cost.

5. There will be moments of despair when we feel we can't go on. In these times, we must encourage one another, reminding ourselves and our fellow travelers that our capacity to persevere is greater than we imagine.

6. Just as we faced real dangers on our hike, we often encounter fear-mongering in our spiritual journey. These outside influences, amplified by media and cultural pressures, can tempt us to turn back or lose sight of our true path. Yet, we must press on, discerning between real threats and exaggerated fears, always keeping our focus on Christ's teachings.

7. We may only be able to see the next step ahead, but if we trust in the path laid out by Christ, we will reach our destination.

The poet Antonio Machado captures this journey beautifully in his work *Campos de Castilla*:

Wanderer, your footsteps are
the road, and nothing more;
wanderer, there is no road,
the road is made by walking.

— 16.5

This journey of rebuilding our Christian witness isn't a
sprint; it's a marathon. It's a lifelong commitment to aligning
our lives more closely with the teachings of Christ, of continually examining our beliefs and actions in light of the gospel.

There will be setbacks. There will be times when we fall
back into old patterns. But each time we choose love over fear,
service over power, reconciliation over division, we take
another step on this journey. As we move forward on this path,
let's hold onto the words of the poet Mary Oliver in her *New
and Selected Poems*:

Tell me, what is it you plan to do
with your one wild and precious life?

— 16.6

This is our chance - our "one wild and precious life" - to be
part of reshaping the Christian witness in our world. It's our
opportunity to show a watching world what it truly means to
follow Christ.

The journey ahead is long, but the destination is worth it.
Let's walk this road together, rebuilding a Christ-like witness
that shines with the authentic, radical love of Jesus. This is our
calling. This is our mission. This is our one wild and precious
life. Let's make it count.

As we come to the end of this journey, I want to share a reflection that recently struck me. It's about wind, compasses, and the nature of our faith.

I was looking at the weather outside, particularly noticing the wind. With wind, any heat is bearable, but without it, the same temperature can be miserable and even deadly. As I checked the weather app on my phone, something caught my attention - the little arrow indicating wind direction.

The word said ESE (east southeast), yet the head of the arrow pointed north northwest. It dawned on me that I'd never actually noticed how the direction of wind is displayed on a compass before. And then it hit me: the direction of the wind is not identified by where it's going, but by where it's coming from.

This realization struck me as profoundly relevant to our journey of faith. As followers of The Way, we're often so focused on where we're going - our goals, our vision for the future, the changes we want to see in the world. But perhaps, like the wind, what truly defines us is not our destination, but our source.

Throughout this book, we've been unlearning harmful ideologies and reimagining our faith. We've challenged ourselves to look beyond the cultural Christianity that has often led us astray. In doing so, we've been trying to refocus on our true source.

Just as the wind is named for its origin, not its destination, maybe we too should be identified not by the consequences of our actions, which are often flawed, but by the source of our faith - the perfect love of God that calls us and empowers us. Not by where we end up, but by the One who set us in motion.

This doesn't mean our actions don't matter. They do, profoundly. But it suggests that in our journey of faith, our primary focus should be on staying connected to our source, allowing the love of Christ to be the wind in our sails, guiding and empowering us.

As we conclude this book and continue our journey of unlearning and reimagining, let this be our prayer: That we might be like the wind, always defined by our source. That in all we do, we might be known not by our mistakes or our successes, but by the love that motivates us. That we might be a gentle breeze bringing comfort to some, and a powerful gust challenging injustice for others, but always, always moving in the direction that our Source - the God of love - is guiding us.

May we be a wind of change in this world, not identified by where we're going, but by the love from which we come. And may that love - boundless, radical, and transformative - be what defines us as followers of Christ.

Thank you for joining me on this journey.

May the wind of God's love be at your back, and may you always remember where that wind comes from.

ENJOYED THIS BOOK?

If this book moved you,
please consider leaving a review.
It helps more than you know.

Please take a moment to share on:
Amazon • Goodreads • Any book site

ACKNOWLEDGMENTS

The journey that led to this book began long before I put pen to paper or fingers to keyboard. It's a journey that has been both deeply personal and profoundly communal, shaped by experiences, relationships, and a relentless pursuit of truth.

First and foremost, I must acknowledge my wife, Jessica. She has been the rudder of my boat, guiding me through this journey we've embarked on together. Always one step ahead, she's pulled me along - sometimes begrudgingly - towards a fuller, more authentic understanding of faith. Her wisdom, patience, and unwavering support have been instrumental in shaping not just this book, but the person I've become. To Jessica, I owe my deepest gratitude.

To my four children, who have watched their father wrestle with big questions and undergo significant changes in thought and belief, I extend my heartfelt thanks. Your curiosity, your questions, and your own journeys of faith have inspired and challenged me in ways I never expected.

I'm profoundly grateful to Pastor Dr. Phil Sallee, whose guidance modeled Christ-like leadership during a formative time in my life. His words, "In the end, Jesus is Lord. Everything else is small stuff. Don't sweat the small stuff," have echoed in my mind throughout this process of unlearning and reimagining faith. Dr. Phil's ability to bring discussions back to what we don't want, to help us find our way when we're lost, has been an invaluable tool in navigating the complex terrain of faith and culture.

Lastly, I owe an immeasurable debt of gratitude to Sankie Lynch, whose ink transformed my manuscript into something resembling a football playbook from a desperate coach in the fourth quarter—arrows, cross-outs, and margin notes multiplying until hardly an inch of white space remained. Thank you, Sankie, for your intellectual generosity and for believing this work mattered enough to scribble it into coherence.

This book is born out of a lifetime of experiences - from my upbringing in rural Oklahoma, steeped in the culture of white evangelical Christianity, to my years working in the church, to my business ownership in media, where I witnessed firsthand the power of narratives to shape beliefs and actions. It's informed by my struggles with the cognitive dissonance between the faith I was taught and the realities I observed, by my experiences with the harms of cultural Christianity, and by my ongoing journey to rediscover a faith that truly reflects the teachings of Christ.

Unlearning Christian Nationalism is not an attack on faith. Rather, it's an invitation - an invitation to question, to wrestle, to reimagine what faith could be if we stripped away the cultural and political baggage it has accumulated. It's a call to return to the radical, transformative love that lies at the heart of Jesus' teachings.

This process of unlearning isn't easy. It's often uncomfortable, sometimes painful. It requires us to confront hard truths about ourselves, our communities, and our nation. But it's a journey I believe is necessary if we're to reclaim an authentic, Christ-centered faith that can speak to the challenges of our time.

As you read this book, my hope is that you'll find both challenge and encouragement. Challenge to examine your own assumptions and beliefs, and encouragement that a deeper, more authentic faith is possible. May we together embark on this journey of unlearning, reimagining, and rediscovering what it truly means to follow Christ in today's world.

Todd Eubanks
Little Rock, Arkansas
2025

APPENDICES

List of Occurrences

Here is the complete list of the 47 verses with a total of 52 occurrences of the Hebrew word שָׁוְא (shav') in the Old Testament, using the New American Standard Bible (NASB) translation:

1. Exodus 20:7
   - "You shall not take the name of the LORD your God in *vain*, for the LORD will not leave him unpunished who takes His name in *vain*."
2. Exodus 23:1
   - "You shall not bear a *false* report; do not join your hand with a wicked man to be a malicious witness."
3. Deuteronomy 5:11

- "You shall not take the name of the LORD
  your God in *vain*, for the LORD will not
  leave unpunished the one who takes His name
  in *vain*."
4. Deuteronomy 5:20
   - "You shall not bear *false* witness against your
     neighbor."
5. Job 7:3
   - "So am I allotted months of *vanity*, and
     nights of trouble are appointed me."
6. Job 11:11
   - "For He knows *false* men; and He sees
     iniquity without investigating."
7. Job 15:31
   - "Let him not trust in *emptiness*, deceiving
     himself; for *emptiness* will be his reward."
8. Job 31:5
   - "If I have walked with *falsehood*, and my foot
     has hastened after deceit;"
9. Job 35:13
   - "Surely God will not listen to an *empty* cry,
     nor will the Almighty regard it."
10. Psalm 12:2
    - "They speak *falsehood* to one another; with
      flattering lips and a double heart they speak."
11. Psalm 24:4
    - "He who has clean hands and a pure heart,
      who has not lifted up his soul to *falsehood*
      and has not sworn deceitfully."
12. Psalm 26:4
    - "I do not sit with *deceitful* men, nor will I go
      with pretenders."
13. Psalm 31:6

- "I hate those who regard *vain* idols, but I trust in the LORD."
14. Psalm 41:6
    - "And when he comes to see me, he speaks *empty* words; his heart gathers iniquity to itself; when he goes outside, he tells it."
15. Psalm 60:11
    - "O give us help against the adversary, for deliverance by man is *worthless*."
16. Psalm 89:47
    - "Remember what my span of life is; for what *futility* you have created all the sons of men!"
17. Psalm 108:12
    - "Oh give us help against the adversary, for deliverance by man is *worthless*."
18. Psalm 119:37
    - "Turn away my eyes from looking at *vanity*, and revive me in Your ways."
19. Psalm 127:1
    - "Unless the LORD builds the house, they labor in *vain* who build it; unless the LORD guards the city, the watchman keeps awake in *vain*."
20. Psalm 127:2
    - "It is *vain* for you to rise up early, to retire late, to eat the bread of painful labors; for He gives to His beloved even in his sleep."
21. Psalm 139:20
    - "For they speak against You wickedly, and Your enemies take Your name in *vain*."
22. Psalm 144:8
    - "Whose mouths speak deceit, and whose right hand is a right hand of *falsehood*."

23. Psalm 144:11
    ○ "Rescue me and deliver me from the hand of foreigners, whose mouth speaks deceit and whose right hand is a right hand of *falsehood*.
    "

24. Proverbs 30:8
    ○ "Keep *falsehood* and lies far from me; give me neither poverty nor riches; feed me with the food that is my portion,"

25. Isaiah 1:13
    ○ "Bring your *worthless* offerings no longer, incense is an abomination to Me. New moon and Sabbath, the proclamation of an assembly — I cannot endure wrongdoing and the festive assembly."

26. Isaiah 5:18
    ○ "Woe to those who drag wrongdoing with the cords of *falsehood*, and sin as if with cart ropes;"

27. Isaiah 30:28
    ○ "His breath is like an overflowing torrent, which reaches to the neck, to shake the nations back and forth in a sieve, and to put in the jaws of the peoples the bridle which leads to *destruction*."

28. Isaiah 59:4
    ○ "No one sues righteously and no one pleads honestly. They trust in confusion and speak *lies*; they conceive mischief and give birth to iniquity."

29. Jeremiah 2:30
    ○ "In *vain* I have struck your sons; they accepted no chastening. Your sword has

devoured your prophets like a destroying lion.
"

30. Jeremiah 4:30
    ○ "And you, O desolate one, what will you do?
    Though you dress in scarlet, though you adorn
    yourself with ornaments of gold, though you
    enlarge your eyes with makeup, in *vain* you
    make yourself beautiful. Your lovers despise
    you; they seek your life."

31. Jeremiah 6:29
    ○ "The bellows blow fiercely, the lead is
    consumed by the fire; in *vain* the refining
    goes on, but the wicked are not separated."

32. Jeremiah 18:15
    ○ "For My people have forgotten Me, they burn
    incense to *worthless* gods and they have
    stumbled in their ways, in the ancient roads, to
    walk on paths, not on a highway,"

33. Jeremiah 46:11
    ○ "Go up to Gilead and obtain balm, O virgin
    daughter of Egypt! In *vain* you have
    multiplied remedies; there is no healing for
    you."

34. Lamentations 2:14
    ○ "Your prophets have seen for you *worthless*
    and deceptive visions; they have not exposed
    your wrongdoing so as to restore you from
    captivity, but they have seen for you
    worthless and misleading pronouncements."

35. Ezekiel 12:24
    ○ "For there will no longer be any *false* vision
    or flattering divination within the house of
    Israel."

36. Ezekiel 13:6
    o "They see *falsehood* and lying divination, those who are saying, 'The LORD declares,' when the LORD has not sent them; yet they wait for the fulfillment of their word!"

37. Ezekiel 13:7
    o "Did you not see a *false* vision and speak a lying divination when you said, 'The LORD declares,' but it is not I who have spoken?'"

38. Ezekiel 13:8
    o "Therefore, thus says the Lord GOD, "Because you have spoken *falsehood* and seen a lie, therefore behold, I am against you," declares the Lord GOD."

39. Ezekiel 13:9
    o "So My hand will be against the prophets who see *false* visions and utter lying divinations; they will have no place in the council of My people."

40. Ezekiel 13:23
    o "therefore you will no longer see *false* visions or practice divination, and I will deliver My people out of your hand.'"

41. Ezekiel 21:29
    o "while they see for you *false* visions, while they divine lies for you, to place you on the necks of the wicked who are slain, whose day has come."

42. Ezekiel 22:28
    o "Her prophets have smeared whitewash for them, seeing *false* visions and divining lies for them, saying, 'Thus says the Lord GOD,' when the LORD has not spoken."

43. Hosea 10:4
    o "They speak mere *words*, with worthless oaths they make covenants; and judgment sprouts like poisonous weeds in the furrows of the field."

44. Hosea 12:11
    o "Is there iniquity in Gilead? Surely they are *worthless*. In Gilgal they sacrifice bulls; yes, their altars are like stone heaps beside the furrows of a field."

45. Jonah 2:8
    o "Those who regard *vain* idols forsake their faithfulness,"

46. Zechariah 10:2
    o "For the household idols speak deception, and the diviners see an illusion and tell deceitful dreams; they comfort in *vain*. Therefore the people wander like sheep, they are afflicted because there is no shepherd."

47. Malachi 3:14
    o "You have said, 'It is *vain* to serve God; and what profit is it that we have kept His charge, and that we have walked in mourning before the LORD of hosts?'"

Common English Translations for "Shav'" (שָׁוְא)

The Hebrew word "שָׁוְא" (shav') has various translations in English Bibles, depending on the context of the verse and the translation philosophy of the Bible version. Here is a comprehensive list of the different English words used to translate "shav'" across various Bible translations.

1. Vain / Vanity
   - KJV, ESV, NASB, NIV*, HCSB*
   - Exodus 20:7; Deuteronomy 5:11; Job 7:3; Job 11:11 (KJV); Job 15:31; Job 31:5 (KJV); Job 35:13 (KJV); Psalm 24:4 (KJV); Psalm 26:4 (KJV); Psalm 60:11; Psalm 108:12; Psalm 127:1-2; Psalm 139:20 (KJV); Malachi 3:14; Jeremiah 2:30; Jeremiah 4:30; Jeremiah 6:29; Jeremiah 46:11; Zechariah 10:2
   - "Thou shalt not take the name of the LORD thy God *in vain*." — Exodus 20:7 (KJV)

2. Misuse / Misuses
   - NIV, HCSB
   - Exodus 20:7; Deuteronomy 5:11
   - "You shall not *misuse* the name of the LORD your God." — Exodus 20:7 (NIV)

3. False / Falsehood / Falsely
   - KJV, ESV, NIV, NASB, HCSB
   - Exodus 23:1; Deuteronomy 5:20; Job 11:11 (NASB); Job 31:5 (ESV); Psalm 26:4 (ESV/NASB); Psalm 24:4 (ESV/HCSB); Isaiah 59:4; Ezekiel 12:24; Ezekiel 13:6-9, 23; Ezekiel 21:29; Ezekiel 22:28; Zechariah 10:2
   - "You shall not spread a *false report*." — Exodus 23:1 (ESV)

4. Lies / Lying
   - ESV, NIV, HCSB, KJV*
   - Psalm 12:2; Psalm 144:8; Psalm 144:11; Hosea 10:4; Jonah 2:8
   - "Everyone *utters lies* to his neighbor." — Psalm 12:2 (ESV)

5. Empty / Emptiness
   - ESV, NASB, NIV, HCSB

- o Job 7:3 (ESV); Job 15:31 (ESV/NASB); Job 35:13 (ESV); Psalm 41:6 (NASB)
- o "So I am allotted months of *emptiness*."
  —Job 7:3 (ESV)
6. Futile / Futility
   - o NIV, HCSB
   - o Job 7:3; Job 15:31
   - o "...months of *futility*." —Job 7:3 (NIV)
7. Worthless / Worthlessness
   - o ESV, NIV, NASB, HCSB
   - o Job 11:11 (ESV/HCSB); Job 15:31 (NIV/HCSB); Psalm 31:6 (ESV/NIV)
   - o "He knows *worthless* men."
     —Job 11:11 (ESV)
8. Deceit / Deceitful / Deception
   - o NIV, NASB, HCSB
   - o Psalm 24:4 (NASB); Psalm 26:4 (NIV/NASB); Isaiah 59:4
   - o "...has not lifted up his soul to *deceit*."
     —Psalm 24:4 (NASB)
9. Idol / Idols
   - o NIV, ESV
   - o Psalm 24:4 (NIV); Psalm 31:6 (ESV/NIV); Jonah 2:8
   - o "I hate those who cling to worthless *idols*."
     —Psalm 31:6 (NIV)
10. Deceivers
    - o NIV
    - o Job 11:11
    - o "Surely He recognizes *deceivers*."
      —Job 11:11 (NIV)
11. Empty Words
    - o ESV, NASB

- Psalm 41:6
- "...he utters *empty words*."
  — Psalm 41:6 (ESV)
12. Worthless Help
   - NIV, HCSB
   - Psalm 60:11; Psalm 108:12
   - "...human help is *worthless*."
     — Psalm 60:11 (NIV)

BIBLIOGRAPHY

2.1 Griswold, Eliza. "Franklin Graham's Uneasy Alliance with Donald Trump." *The New Yorker*, 5 June 2021, https://www.newyorker.com/news/dispatch/franklin-grahams-uneasy-alliance-with-donald-trump.

3.1 Trump, Donald. "Trump believes in God, but hasn't sought forgiveness" *CNN*, 18 July 2015, www.cnn.com/2015/07/18/politics/trump-has-never-sought-forgiveness/.

3.2 Arkansas Times Staff. "Sanders Announces Co-Chairs of Her Inauguration." *Arkansas Times*, 22 Nov. 2022, https://arktimes.com/arkansas-blog/2022/11/22/sanders-announces-co-chairs-of-her-inauguration.

4.1 Trollinger, William Vance, Jr. "Review of *One Hundred Percent American: The Rebirth and Decline of the Ku Klux Klan in the 1920s*, by Thomas R. Pegram." *The Journal of American History*, vol. 101, no. 2, 2014, pp. 628–629.

4.2 Edmund Randolph. "King Philip's War." 1675. *Digital History ID 649*, University of Houston, https://www.digitalhistory.uh.edu/disp_textbook.cfm?smtid=3&psid=649.

4.3 "Boston martyrs." *Wikipedia*, Wikimedia Foundation, 3 June 2025, en.wikipedia.org/wiki/Boston_martyrs.

4.4 Mell, Patrick Hues. *Slavery: A Treatise, Showing that Slavery is Neither a Moral, Political, nor Social Evil.* 1844. Quoted in Kell, Garrett. "Damn the Curse of Ham: How Genesis 9 Got Twisted into Racist Propaganda." *The Gospel Coalition*, 17 June 2020, https://www.thegospelcoalition.org/article/damn-curse-ham/.

4.5 "Oh Freedom". Traditional African American Spiritual. Public Domain.

4.6 Falwell, Jerry. "If Chief Justice Warren and His Associates Had Known God's Word." Sermon, 1958. Quoted in *Jerry Falwell*, Wikipedia, en.wikipedia.org/wiki/Jerry_Falwell.

4.7 "We Shall Overcome." Traditional. Adapted by Pete Seeger, Guy Carawan, Frank Hamilton, and Zilphia Horton. Public Domain.

5.1 Miessler, Daniel. "Hitler the Christian Warrior." *Daniel Miessler*, https://danielmiessler.com/blog/hitler-the-christian-warrior/. Accessed Jan 27, 2025.

5.2 Story, Jenisa. "Protestant Dissent in Nazi Germany: The Confessing Church Struggle with Hitler's Government." *Western Washington University*, Spring 2001, https://cedar.wwu.edu/cgi/viewcontent.cgi?article=1348&context=wwu_honors. Christianity. Accessed Jan 27, 2025.

5.3 Hitler, Adolf. *Mein Kampf* ("My Struggle"). Houghton Mifflin, New York; Hutchinson Publ. Ltd., London, 1969, p. 60.

5.4 Kroll, Paul. "The Protestant Church in Hitler's Germany and the Barmen Declaration." *Grace Communion International*, https://www.gci.org/articles/the-protestant-church-in-hitlers-germany-and-the-barmen-declaration/. Accessed Jan 27, 2025.

5.5 Gruner, Hermann. "The time is fulfilled for the German people of Hitler..." *Christian History*, issue 32, article titled "Dietrich Bonhoeffer: Theologian in Nazi Germany."

5.6 Heschel, Susannah. *The Aryan Jesus: Christian Theologians and the Bible in Nazi Germany*. Princeton University Press, 2008.

5.7 "God Bless America" Berlin, Irving. *God Bless America*. 1938.

5.8 "God Bless the U.S.A." Greenwood, Lee. *God Bless the U.S.A.* MCA Nashville, 1984.

5.9 "America the Beautiful" Bates, Katharine Lee. "America the Beautiful." 1895. Music by Samuel A. Ward, 1882.

5.10 O'Sullivan, John L. "Annexation." *The United States Magazine and Democratic Review*, vol. 17, no. 1, July–August 1845, pp. 5–10.

5.11 Benton, Thomas Hart. *Speech on the Oregon Question, Delivered in the Senate of the United States, May 22, 25, & 28, 1846*. Blair and Rives, 1846. Congressional Globe, vol. 29, no. 1, 1846, pp. 917-18.

7.1 Hassan, Steven. *Combating Cult Mind Control*. Park Street Press, 2015.

7.2 Owens, Natasha. *The Chosen One*. Radiate Music, 2023.

7.2.1 "More Internal Documents Show How Facebook's Algorithm Prioritized Anger and Posts That Triggered It." *Nieman Lab*, 25 Oct. 2021, www.niemanlab.org/2021/10/more-internal-documents-show-how-facebooks-algorithm-prioritized-anger-and-posts-that-triggered-it/

7.2.2 Moore, Gary. "Make America Great Again." First Baptist Church of Dallas, performed by First Baptist Church Choir, 2016. *The Christian Post*, 5 July 2017, www.christianpost.com/news/make-america-great-again-song-trump-church-choir-copyrighted-jeffress.html.

7.2.3 McCrummen, Stephanie. "The Army of God Comes Out of the Shadows." The Atlantic, 9 Jan. 2025, www.theatlantic.com/ideas/archive/2025/01/seven-mountains-dominionism-religious-right/677282/.

7.2.4 Posobiec, Jack, and Joshua Lisec. *Unhumans: The Secret History of Communist Revolutions (and How to Crush Them)*. Foreword by Stephen K. Bannon, War Room Books, 2024.

7.3 Branch, Krista. *I Am America*. Krista Branch Music, 2010.

7.4 PBS NewsHour. "Trump Suggests He'll Use the Military on the 'Enemy from Within' the U.S. If He's Reelected." *PBS*, 13 Oct. 2024, https://www.pbs.org/newshour/politics/trump-suggests-hell-use-the-military-on-the-enemy-from-within-the-u-s-if-hes-reelected.

7.5 Trump, Donald. "I Am the Chosen One." *The Guardian*, 21 Aug. 2019, www.theguardian.com/us-news/2019/aug/21/donald-trump-i-am-the-chosen-one-china-trade-war.

7.6 Pew Research Center. "In U.S., Decline of Christianity Continues at Rapid Pace." *Pew Research Center*, 17 Oct. 2019, www.pewforum.org/2019/10/17/in-u-s-decline-of-christianity-continues-at-rapid-pace/.

7.7 Pew Research Center. "About Half of U.S. Adults Say the Country Should Be a Christian Nation." *Pew Research Center*, 2021, https://www.pewresearch.org/religion/2022/10/27/45-of-americans-say-u-s-should-be-a-christian-nation/.

8.1 Trump, Donald. "Trump Says Immigrants Are 'Poisoning the Blood of Our Country,' Biden Campaign Likens Comments to Hitler." *NBC News*, 17 Dec. 2023, www.nbcnews.com/politics/2024-election/trump-says-immigrants-are-poisoning-blood-country-biden-campaign-liken-rcna130141.

8.2 Hitler, Adolf. *Mein Kampf*. Volume 1, Chapter 11. "All great cultures of the past perished only because the originally creative race died out from blood poisoning..." *Mein Kampf*, translated edition

8.3 Karl, Jonathan. "Donald Trump's History With Adolf Hitler and His Nazi Writings: ANALYSIS." *ABC News*, 20 Dec. 2023, abcnews.com/Politics/donald-trumps-history-adolf-hitler-nazi-writings-analysis/story?id=105810745.

8.4 Pidcock, Rick. "What Has John MacArthur Actually Said About Race, Slavery and the *Curse of Ham*?" *Baptist News Global*, 20 June 2022, baptistnews.com/article/what-has-john-macarthur-actually-said-about-race-slavery-and-the-curse-of-ham/.

9.1.1 Edwards, Jonathan. "Sinners in the Hands of an Angry God." *Delivered at the Congregational Church in Enfield, Connecticut, 8 July 1741. The Works of Jonathan Edwards*, edited by Sereno Dwight, vol. 2, Banner of Truth Trust, 1974, pp. 7-22.

9.1 Trump, Donald. Interview by Jake Tapper. *CNN*, 18 July 2015, www.cnn.com/2015/07/18/politics/trump-has-never-sought-forgiveness/.

9.2 Trump, Donald. Interview by Frank Luntz. *Family Leadership Summit*, Ames, Iowa, 18 July 2015, www.washingtonpost.com/news/post-politics/wp/2015/07/18/trump-on-communion-i-drink-my-little-wine-and-have-my-little-cracker/.

9.2.2 Burns, Katelyn, and Amanda Michelle Gomez. "Trump Ordered Tear Gas to Clear D.C. Protesters for a Church Photo Op." *Vox*, 1 June 2020, www.vox.com/2020/6/1/21277294/trump-tear-gas-peaceful-protesters-church-photo-op.

9.3 "Fact Check: GOP's False, Misleading Attacks About Democrats, Immigrants." *AP News*, 26 Aug. 2024, https://apnews.com/article/fact-check-misinformation-republican-convention-illegal-immigration-204ae438725d5b15126325a63330ce5c.

9.4 Walz, Jim. "Speech at the Democratic National Convention." *Democratic National Convention*, 20 Aug. 2024, https://www.nytimes.com/2024/08/22/us/politics/tim-walz-dnc-speech-transcript.html.

9.5 Vance, J.D. "Interview with Sean Hannity." *Hannity*, Fox News, 20 Aug. 2024, https://www.newsweek.com/jd-vance-immigration-policies-rnc-trump-1927829.

10.1 Robert the Monk. *Historia Hierosolymitana*. In "Urban II (1088-1099): Speech at Council of Clermont, 1095, Five Versions of the Speech," edited by Paul Halsall, *Medieval Sourcebook*, Fordham University, 1997, https://sourcebooks.fordham.edu/source/urban2-5vers.asp.

10.2 Alexander VI. *Inter Caetera*. 4 May 1493. *Papal Encyclicals Online*, edited by James J. H. Farganis, 2007, https://www.papalencyclicals.net/alex06/alex06inter.htm.

10.3 Hitler, Adolf. *Speech in Munich, April 12, 1922*. Vancouver Island University, https://web.viu.ca/davies/H479B.Imperialism.Nationalism/Hitler.speech.April1921.htm. Accessed 5 Feb. 2025.

10.4 King, Martin Luther, Jr. *Letter from Birmingham Jail*. 16 Apr. 1963. *The Martin Luther King, Jr. Research and Education Institute*, Stanford University, https://kinginstitute.stanford.edu/king-papers/documents/letter-birmingham-jail.

10.4.1 Bonhoeffer, Dietrich. *Life Together: The Classic Exploration of Christian Community*. Translated by John W. Doberstein, Harper & Row, 1954.

10.5 Douglass, Frederick. *Narrative of the Life of Frederick Douglass, an American Slave*. Boston: Anti-Slavery Office, 1845. https://utc.iath.virginia.edu/abolitn/dougnarrhp.html.

10.6 King, Martin Luther, Jr. *Letter from a Birmingham Jail*. 16 Apr. 1963. University of Pennsylvania African Studies Center, https://www.africa.upenn.edu/Articles_Gen/Letter_Birmingham.html.

11.1 Augustine, Saint. *The Literal Meaning of Genesis*. Translated by John Hammond Taylor, Newman Press, 1982.

11.2 Dickinson, Emily. "This World is Not Conclusion." *The Poems of Emily Dickinson*. Edited by Thomas H. Johnson, Harvard University Press, 1955.

11.3 Haugen, Marty. "All Are Welcome." GIA Publications, 1994.

13.1 Mote, Edward. "My Hope Is Built on Nothing Less." 1834. *Hymns of Praise: A Selection of Standard Hymns*, by Charles Wesley and Edward Mote, John P. Jewett, 1855.

13.2 Berry, Wendell. "Manifesto: The Mad Farmer Liberation Front." *The Country of Marriage*, Harcourt Brace Jovanovich, 1973.

14.1 Vanden Eykel, Eric. "Conservative Evangelical Eric Metaxas, Doing

Twitter Theology, Claims 'Jesus Was White.'" *Religion Dispatches*, 29 July 2020, https://religiondispatches.org/conservative-evangelical-eric-metaxas-doing-twitter-theology-claims-jesus-was-white/.

14.2 Geiger, Abigail. "Half of U.S. Protestant Pastors Hear Conspiracy Theories in Their Churches." *Lifeway Research*, 26 Jan. 2021, https://news.lifeway.com/2021/01/26/half-of-u-s-protestant-pastors-hear-conspiracy-theories-in-their-churches/.

14.3 Smietana, Bob. "Survey: More than a Quarter of White Evangelicals Believe Core QAnon Conspiracy Theory." *Religion News Service*, 11 Feb. 2021, https://religionnews.com/2021/02/11/survey-more-than-a-quarter-of-white-evangelicals-believe-core-qanon-conspiracy-theory/.

15.1 Jordan Smart, TikTok song. Written in full with direct permission.

15.2 Jones, Jeffrey M. "U.S. Church Membership Falls Below Majority for First Time." *Gallup News*, 29 Mar. 2021, https://news.gallup.com/poll/341963/church-membership-falls-below-majority-first-time.aspx.

15.3 Markham, Edwin. "Outwitted." *The Shoes of Happiness and Other Poems*, Doubleday, Page & Company, 1913, p. 144.

15.4 Lazarus, Emma. "The New Colossus." 1883. *The Poems of Emma Lazarus: Vol. II*, Houghton, Mifflin and Company, 1889, p. 2.

15.5 Scholtes, Peter. "They'll Know We Are Christians By Our Love." F.E.L. Publications, 1966.

15.6 Healy, Jack, and Julie Turkewitz. "3 Are Dead in Colorado Springs Shootout at Planned Parenthood Center." *The New York Times*, 27 Nov. 2015, www.nytimes.com/2015/11/28/us/colorado-planned-parenthood-shooting.html.

15.7 Roof, Dylann. *Dylann Roof Journal (Government Exhibit 500)*. United States District Court for the District of South Carolina, Case No. 2:15-cr-00472, www.uscourts.gov/courts/scd/cases/2-15-472/exhibits/GX500.pdf.

15.8 "Murder of George Tiller." *Wikipedia*, https://en.wikipedia.org/wiki/Murder_of_George_Tiller.

15.9 Claiborne, Shane. *The Irresistible Revolution: Living as an Ordinary Radical*. Zondervan, 2006, p. 196.

16.1 Coffin, William Sloane. *The Courage to Love*. Harper & Row, 1982.

16.2 Day, Dorothy. *The Reckless Way of Love: Notes on Following Jesus*. Edited by Carolyn Kurtz, Plough Publishing House, 2017.

16.3 Tutu, Desmond. *No Future Without Forgiveness*. Doubleday, 1999.

16.4 Eliot, T.S. "Little Gidding." *Four Quartets*, Harcourt, 1943.

16.5 Machado, Antonio. *Campos de Castilla*. Translated by Willis Barnstone, Harper & Row, 1967.

16.6 Oliver, Mary. *New and Selected Poems: Volume One*. Beacon Press, 1992.